Ken Evans. e Joanna Hewitt Taylor

Learning from Bosnia

The Abrahamic Dialogues Series
David B. Burrell, series editor

EDITORIAL BOARD
Ibrahim Abu-Rabi', Hartford Seminary
Susannah Heschel, Dartmouth College
Donald J. Moore, S.J., Fordham University

James L. Heft, ed., *Beyond Violence: Religious Sources of Social Transformation in Judaism, Christianity, and Islam.*

Learning from Bosnia
Approaching Tradition

Rusmir Mahmutćehajić

*Translated by Saba Risaluddin
and Francis R. Jones*

Fordham University Press
New York 2005

Copyright © 2005 Fordham University Press

All rights reserved. No part of this publication may be reproduced, stored in a retrieval system, or transmitted in any form or by any means—electronic, mechanical, photocopy, recording, or any other—except for brief quotations in printed reviews, without the prior permission of the publisher.

The Abrahamic Dialogues Series, No. 2
ISSN 1548–4130

Library of Congress Cataloging-in-Publication Data

Mahmutćehajić, Rusmir, 1948–
  [Bosanski odgovor. English]
  Learning from Bosnia : approaching tradition / Rusmir Mahmutćehajić ; translated by Saba Risaluddin and Francis R. Jones. — 1st ed.
    p. cm.
  Includes bibliographical references and index.
  ISBN 0-8232-2453-8 (hardcover)
  1. Bosnia and Hercegovina—Ethnic relations. 2. Bosnia and Hercegovina—Religion. 3. Pluralism (Social sciences)—Bosnia and Hercegovina. I. Title. II. Series.
  DR1673.M33813 2005   2005006634

Printed in the United States of America
07 06 05   5 4 3 2 1
First edition

In the Name of God, the Merciful, the Most Merciful

(How often must I tell you that you know
Nothing about me—
Nothing about my arrow and bow
Nothing about my sword and shield
That you have no idea how sharp is my steel
That you know nothing about my poor

Body or
The bright flame
That burns
Inside)

I'm waiting for you
Because I know you
You'll come back one day

(This you've vowed
By chalice and cross and blade of sword
Drunk with chants of damnation and incense smoke)

So,
Come on then

I've long grown used to your ravages
As if to the throes
Of a disease from far away

As to the icy waters swept savagely along
By this night river of darkness that grows
Ever more swift
And strong.

Mak Dizdar, *Message*

Contents

Author's Note   ix
Foreword   *Adam B. Seligman*   xi
Preface   xxiii

Prologue   1
Introduction: The Achievement of Bosnia   5
1   The Forms of Expression of a Single Truth   17
2   Submissiveness, Emotion, and Knowledge   27
3   The Apprenticeship of Submission and Freedom   37
4   The Lower Horizons of Freedom   48
5   Pride and Humility   58
6   The Dispute over Names   67
7   The Word Held in Common   76
8   Wealth in Poverty   85
9   Other Gods but Him   94
10   Two Histories   104
11   The Ideology of Nation   114
12   The Chasm of the Future   125
Epilogue   135

Notes   141
Bibliography   157
Other Works by Rusmir Mahmutćehajić   163
Index   165

Author's Note

Although excerpts from an earlier version of this English translation appeared in *Sophia: The Journal of Traditional Studies* 8, no. 2 (Winter 2002): 49–82 under the title *A Bosnian Response: Tradition and Modernity*, the entire English text of *Bosanski odgovor: O modernosti i tradiciji* (Zagreb: Durieux, 2001) is published here for the first time.

Foreword Adam B. Seligman

To a great extent, the twentieth century can be said to both begin and end in Sarajevo. The murder of Archduke Franz Ferdinand on June 28, 1914, and the outbreak of the First World War brought an end to the complacent belief in material progress and ameliatory politics that had characterized nineteenth-century European civilization. Heir to Cartesian method and positivist science, the nineteenth century—more than any other period—assumed that rational thought, empirical investigations and a presuppositionless universality would provide sufficient bases for the correct organization of the social world. The First World War shattered these assumptions.

What followed—communism, fascism, Nazism, the anticolonial and national struggles of the twentieth century—were all forms of what Eric Voegelin termed "modern gnosticism," that is, movements organized around a divinized people, an elite or class who would usher in the *Endzeit*. Through correct knowledge of the true telos of history, modern mass Gnostic movements sought to realize salvation through their own actions in history. But, as Voegelin warns: "Self-salvation through knowledge has its own magic and this magic is not harmless. . . . The attempt at world destruction will not destroy the world, but will only increase the disorder in society."[1] Though the destruction unleashed by these secular messianic movements was incalculable, many people continued to believe in their emancipatory potential. As the final act of the horrific dramas of the twentieth century, performed in the midst of a largely silent Europe, the genocidal war against Bosnia put an end to these beliefs.

An end, it was also a beginning. The mass murder and ethnic cleansing of Europe's major indigenous Moslem population, carried out in full view of the world, was to herald our contemporary reality of intransigent religious identities, the "clash of civilizations," and an increasing inarticulateness of all attempts at dialogue between different peoples, religions, and worldviews. In today's world, when the citizens of Lodi in North Italy pour pig urine on a site designated for a mosque, when synagogues are bombed in Paris as in Istanbul, when religion continues to provide the source of conflictual identities from the Sudan to the Gujarat in India and from Bosnia to Britain, it is clear that we need to seriously rethink our understanding of the importance of the terms of identity, solidarity, and our relations to one another in our different societies.[2]

For, rather than opening ourselves up to dialogue, we are closing ourselves off from the other. Our present condition is marked, not so much by a "clash of civilizations," or even by the now oft-remarked "clash within civilizations," as by a "clash of civilization," in the sense of an organizing center of values, goals, and structuring premises. But civilization can only exist when it is open to its margins, to its limits and boundaries. When it turns in on itself and abandons its margins, it abandons itself. "Civility," for Samuel Johnson, meant "politeness, the rule of decency and freedom from barbarity." "To civilize" was "to reclaim from savageness and brutality." In many respects, our own civilization seems beset by an increase in savageness and brutality. The barbarians may, indeed, be at the gates—but only insofar as the gates are closed.

To remain open to the other, and thus to our own margins, is a tremendously difficult enterprise. It involves recognizing our own extremely limited apprehension of truth. It involves our admission that transcendent truth is, in its very transcendence, inaccessible to us. What must ensue from this realization is nothing less than a constitutive modesty in our epistemological premises. Truth can only develop in conversation, in dialogue, that is, through engagement with what is beyond ourselves, beyond our boundaries. What we reclaim from savageness and barbarism is, finally, nothing less than ourselves.

The transcendent nature of the "One Truth," the consequent plurality of truths accessible to humankind, and the tolerance of difference that must ensue were the subjects of a crucial set of lectures given by Karl Jaspers in the University of Groningen in 1935:

> Since it is impossible for man to have Transcendence in time as a knowable object, identical for everybody like something in the world, every mode of One Truth as absolute in the world can in fact only be historical: unconditional for this Existenz, but, precisely for this reason, not universally valid. For, since it is not impossible but only psychologically infinitely difficult, for a man to act according to his own truth, realizing at the same time the truth of others which is not truth for him, holding fast to the relativity and particularity of all universally valid truths—since it is not impossible, he must not shirk this highest demand for truthfulness which is only apparently incompatible with that of others.[3]

In arguing for the ontological necessity of difference that arises from the contingent, mutable, and immanent nature of our own understandings, Jaspers is demanding a stoicism in the face of uncertainty; he is calling on us to recognize the particular nature of our own truth claims, and not to retreat into an easy relativism. He is in fact calling for a tolerance predicated on a belief, not in relativist, but in transcendent, truths. Hence:

> The plurality of truths is untrue at the moment when they are seen externally as many, as determinable standpoints; for every standpoint can also absorb him who thinks it. They become even more untrue when they become mutually indifferent and simply rest alongside one another. What will not and what can not become the same, nevertheless, become related through Transcendence which touches the One, which, even if our gods be different, discovers the God, which requires of us not to relapse into the distraction of warring multiplicities related only by indifference or the struggle over room to exist. There is the sophistry of easy tolerance which wishes to be valid, but not to be really touched. On the other hand, there is the truth of tolerance which listens and gives and enters into the unpredictable process of communication by which force is restrained; in such a process, man reaches from his roots to the heights possible for him.[4]

Tolerance of difference, of the other who is different, is here based neither on indifference nor on relativism—but rather on principled engagement with the other, on a process of dialogue and communication that is, itself, structured by the very recognition of the transcendent nature of truth. Tolerance is thus not the solution to all contradictions. It does not make a fractured universe whole. But it does preserve the integrity of self, of the other, and of their interaction. For without it, we are left with the eradication of difference that inheres in all attempts at overcoming multiplicity and plurality, and which is but a succumbing to narcissism, whether collective or individual. In face of our human condition, mature discipline is the best we can do if we are to avoid doing ill. This is perhaps not far from an idea of civility, of proper behavior, and not far, perhaps, from the Confucian virtue of *li*, a propriety that, in uniting the ethical with the legal, sets reasonable limits to the satisfaction of desires. Echoes of the same virtue can be found in the Islamic *hilm* and in the Jewish *anva* (both of which mean "humility"). Thus dialogue can go well beyond the confines of secular political theories to embrace many different conversations, languages, social assumptions, religious civilizations, and, finally, many different concrete others.

And it is here, very much within the civilizational assumptions of Western monotheism—but in an as yet relatively unexplored vein (at least unexplored to most scholars in the European and North Atlantic traditions) that we encounter the thought of Mahmutćehajić. Rusmir Mahmutćehajić was born in Stolac, Herzegovina, in 1948 to a family whose roots in the region go back to the sixteenth century. Inheritor and beneficiary to a tradition of guardianship of Bosnia's unique cultural heritage (as attested to in a number of sultanic *berats*, or charters), his family was on the Partisan side of the war of 1941–45. Mahmutćehajić received his higher degrees in electrical engineering and assumed university positions at both the University of Sarajevo and, as Dean of the Faculty of Electrical Engineering, at the University of Osijek in Croatia at different periods in the 1980s. In this period he published a number of internationally significant papers in pure physics and mathematics. However, his close friendship and political work with Alija Izetbegovic (future founder of the Party of Democratic Action, the SDA, and president of Bosnia-Herzegovina) brought him to the attention of the Tito government and its repressive apparatus. After the fall of communism and from 1991 to 1992, he was the Deputy Prime Minister of the Government of the Republic of Bosnia and Herzegovina, and from 1992 to 1994 the Energy Minister in the same government. In this period, he exercised the duties of the President of the Social Affairs Committee of Bosnia and Herzegovina and Vice-President of the Committee for the Referendum on State Independence of Bosnia and Herzegovina. It must be noted that Mahmutćehajić was instrumental in establishing the core of what became the Bosnian Army which succeeded in stymieing the attempts of the Serb forces to capture Sarajevo. In August 1992, "he almost single-handedly engaged in the strategic war against the Serbian forces that were strangling the Bosnian capital ... promoted and organized the manufacture of weaponry, frustrating at the same time the Serbian military industry."[5] Then, as an act of opposition to the prevailing political defeatism that acceded to the Dayton agreement, he resigned from all political positions and started his continuing work on the interpretation and rearticulation of the political, social, and economic position of Bosnia in the world, of which the book is one important artifact. It is, like so many of his writings, an exercise in translation and in dialogue which calls on readers first and foremost to put their preconceptions aside, to listen, to read carefully and deeply—and in silence.

Drawing on his experience of the war and of the extremely fragile and fractious peace that followed, Mahmutćehajić gives us an understanding of human life and meaning that contrasts the agenda of modernity—whether that of scientism as an ideology or of the nation-state as locus of identity—with the truths of tradition. "The modern enterprise," he reminds us at the beginning of the present volume, "views the human individual as an answerable question, reducing the individual to the quantifiable and finite world of space and time. Any connection between the individual and what is both infinitely distant and infinitely close is blocked by this absolutization of the finite, thus barring the individual self from openness and receptivity to the infinite. We have set ourselves the task of mastering the world, and everything that testifies to the self, the world, and God is viewed in terms of that task. In our urge to absolutize the finite, we have placed the human individual at the center of the world, and allow nothing to exist beyond the duality of the individual versus the material world."

In response to this modernist reading, Mahmutćehajić recalls for us the truths of tradition, a tradition that takes transcendence and transcendent truth seriously and so reopens a way, at once old and new, to recognition, dialogue, understanding, and thus also to a tolerance predicated on principles quite different from that of the autonomous individual of modern conceptions. Speaking a language almost identical to that of Jaspers, Mahmutćehajić recalls a Bosnian reality of Roman Catholic, Eastern Orthodox, Muslim, and Jewish identities, where each provided a way, a truth of tradition that, even though "each [had] its own exclusive sacred doctrine . . . did not mean that the human redemption they guaranteed applied only to some while excluding others. The adoption of one sacred doctrine and its corresponding sacred Way was exclusive only for the individual choosing it. [Even so,] this did not deny the right of the Other to adhere to a different doctrine and follow a different path, with an equal potential for redemption. . . . In other words, the rightness and completeness of a tradition (*din, traditio, religio*) includes its own particular language, symbols, and meanings; yet redemption—the Unicity of the Divine, of which all diverse languages, symbols, and meanings speak—lies behind it."

This is precisely the lesson of Karl Jaspers. Not simply a truth of philosophy, however, it has been, at different times, in different places a truth of life as well. And as we all know, it was precisely this truth, this reality that was the target of the aggression against Bosnia. The purposeful destruction of mosques (some 1,200 mosques were destroyed in the 1992–95 war), of the National Library in Sarajevo, of any and every monument to intercommunal life and multiethnic purposefulness was an avowed aim of those who set out to impose a rigid separation of peoples, identities and religions within a territory that had been a model of intercommunal, interethnic, and interreligious habitus. The success of this aggression, recognized to no small extent in the peace agreement signed at Dayton, which effectively separated different areas as well as the different religious communities of Bosnia and Herzegovina can be measured in the very growth and continual spread of fundamentalist religions among diverse sections of the populace.

Toward these, Mahmutćehajić is unrelenting and scathing in his critique: "They equate the truth, which is nonindividual and supraindividual, with its interpretation, which is invariably personal and conditional. It is here that the basic contradiction between fundamentalism and true tradition lies. There is no tradition that permits the individual or group, solely on the basis of its own assertion, to proclaim its own knowledge to be infallible and absolute."

Like Jaspers in his time, Mahmutćehajić in ours is arguing against both the absolutizers and the relativizers. Painfully aware of the dangers of the first and the weakness of the second, he too like Jaspers expounds a humanity (and humility) of the way, of the path, of the tradition as the only possible mode of existence that can preserve our mutuality, and thus our true individuality.

This is a voice we have heard before—although one we have failed, time and again, to hearken to. It is the voice of Jaspers and of Niebuhr. It is the voice of Martin Buber and of Emmanuel Levinas. It is the voice that calls on us to see God in our responsibilities before the other. It is the voice that admits of the infinite plentitude of the I-Thou, and of the obligations it entails. When Mahmutćehajić tells us, "In the traditional outlook, the self is open to the Infinite, which sets and maintains the forbidden, or the sacred. From this derives a duty toward the Other that is unconditional and nonnegotiable," he is speaking in the language of Buber and of Levinas. This is the language of ethics before ontology, of "the deep inclusion in the world before the countenance of God" and of the "commanded action" that he who "steps before the countenance" is responsible for.[6]

This is also the language of self-restraint, of the reining in of desire and of the responsibility that desire entails. It is a language we are familiar with from the Jewish German philosopher Hermann Cohen, who, in the early decades of the twentieth century, argued the centrality of monotheism to that process by which the stranger was turned into the "fellowman": "Humanity is already so rooted in the stranger, that the slave, as stranger, can be admonished to the bond of gratitude."[7]

Gratitude demands restraint, however, a restraint that, at the end of the day, must rest on a form of humility in the face of transcendence. This, no doubt, was what early-twentieth-century English social thinker and historian R. H. Tawney, at home in both the Socialist movement and the Anglican Church, meant when he wrote:

> What is wrong with the modern world is that having ceased to believe in the greatness of God, and therefore the infinite smallness (or greatness—the same thing!) of *man*, it had to invent or emphasize distinctions between *men*. It does not say, "I have said, 'Ye are gods'!" Nor does it say, "All flesh is grass." It can neither rise to the heights nor descend to the depths (these meet in a spiritual exaltation which may be called either optimism or pessimism). What it does say is that *some* men are gods, and that some flesh is grass, and that the former should live on the latter (combined with pâté de fois gras and champagne), and this is false. For what elevates or depresses, what makes man regarded from one

point of view as an angel and from another an ape, is not something peculiar to individuals, but characteristic of the species, something which cannot distinguish between men, precisely because it is inherent in man.[8]

Without restraint, there is no dialogue; without silence, there is no language; and without tolerance, there is no communal life. Common to all is a reining in of desire, an ability to suffer desire frustrated, rather than a continual calibration of desire quantified. From Bernard de Mandeville, David Hume, Adam Smith, and from all of modernist politics and social thought, we learn the capacity to bear frustrated desire as a compromise of interest realization (desire delayed). A calculus of delayed gratification is, however, altogether different from the bearing or suffering—the carrying (*nasa*)—of unrealized desire that is at the core of tolerance and of its connection to transcendence.

To turn to the transcendent dimension is thus to turn our attention from *fear* of the other to *awe* of the Wholly Other and to realize that the problem of Desire is the religious problem par excellence. For it is religion that recognizes desire, recognizes, that is, the problem of Being out of which Desire springs. Problematizing existence, transcendent religion drives the self to encounter Being and so discover Desire as opposed to simple lust.

It is thus in and through transcendence that Being is problematized, and the consciousness of that nothingness from which Desire springs made possible. In a sense, religion not only recognizes Desire, but also generalizes it (in different ways in different civilizations). It is therefore only in and through particular religions that a true tolerance and engagement with the other can be sought, a tolerance that is neither indifference nor relativism nor the tolerance of a balance of power between mutually absolute masters, indeed, a tolerance predicated, not on the dynamic of Desire and its recognition, but on the always particular work of restraint in the face of Desire. It is in this context that the mutually *politique* balance of power within a society of masters is shown to be not a tolerance predicated on the dynamics of desire and its recognition but one of interaction eviscerated of desire and characterized only by lust (and its pleasures). Tolerance becomes an almost personal virtue or attribute, an indicator of purely personal pluralism or worldliness in matters of taste, art, cuisine, sexual mores, religion, or olfactory stimulants.

Where Desire resides, there resides fear also. Fear of the other can, however, be transformed into awe of the Wholly Other, *das ganz An-*

dere, which was the generalization of Desire achieved by axial or transcendent religions. As Mahmutćehajić argues, the absolutist rule of reason ignores both, and attempts to define Desire away. But the ghosts of reason always return: Desire is not to be denied or defined away. What *is* defined away, however, is the dynamic of tolerance, of restraint and endurance—of the work of the slave, of the dialogue of suffering. A position of tolerance can only emerge from the crucible of recognition. It can only be expressed in the face of Desire. It is expressed primarily in the work of translating Desire, rather than in imposing recognition.

And this work can only exist, can only begin (indeed, can only make sense), in a world where the problematic nature of Being is recognized—by definition, in the face of transcendence. And as Mahmutćehajić following in the tradition of Jaspers, Voegelin, Buber, Cohen, Levinas, and others reminds us, this is the language of tradition from which, and only from which, a true dialogue may be effected.

To quote Hermann Cohen again, on the very origins of ethics:

> The correlation of man and God is in the first place that of man, as fellowman to God. And religion proves its own significance first of all in this correlation of the fellowman to God, in which, indeed, man as fellowman becomes a problem and is engendered through this problem. The share of religion in reason is the share of religion in morality, and no problem of morality takes precedence over this problem of the fellowman. The possibility of ethics is tied to this problem.[9]

The problem of the "fellowman" is the problem of tolerance. Here, then, is a basis for human validation, mutuality, respect, and tolerance very different from the one we have come to expect in the modern world: ethical action predicated, not on any set of "ontological" rights the human subject may have, but rather on the very constitutive conditions of human existence in the world. Such a basis, Mahmutćehajić hastens to remind us, exists among all the monotheistic, axial religions in whose image of a Creator God the human was formed. Whether we look to Qur'anic injunctions against coercion in matters of religion, or to biblical decrees on justice for the stranger, or yet to the Sermon on the Mount—all give expression to a shared and fundamental truth of human existence as correlative to God and Being. It is precisely this shared traditional appreciation of the problem of existence that makes translation, mutuality, and dialogue possible.

Such dialogue is premised on the existential or epistemological humility that the very encounter with the transcendent generates. The Tawney quotation presented above touches on parts of this, as does the Jewish idea of humility (*anva*) that is central to all monotheistic traditions. A similar Islamic concept, that of *hilm,* provides a similar repertoire, combining the qualities of "moderation, forbearance and leniency with self-mastery and dignity." According to the great Islamic scholar Ignaz Goldzhier, *hilm* joins moral integrity with mildness of manners and is juxtaposed to the *jahiliyya,* that pre-Islamic period of Arab tribal warfare where emotions governed actions and where "haughtiness, arrogance and insolence" ruled, rather than the humble submission of Islam. Toshihiko Izutsu's study of *jahiliyya* and of *hilm* provides us with a good sense of how central these terms are to the inner phenomenology of Islam, how the "haughtiness" of the *jahiliyya* contrasts with the forbearance of the *halim* in defining the idea of Islamic behavior. In the transvaluation of values wrought by Muhammad on Arab society, forgiveness and leniency were considered *halim*—attributes of the Patriarch Abraham and, ultimately, of God—and the value of tribal vengeance was replaced with that of forgiveness. Existential modesty and humility, no less than epistemic doubt, exist within religious traditions as principles of tolerance rooted in the very ways we face the other. Here, too, we encounter Buber's dialogue of mutual relation as formulated within a different religious tradition.

The centrality of these concepts to Islam and the exquisite articulation of them in the present volume are matters of no small significance (Mahmutćehajić devotes an entire chapter to the idea of humility). For, even though most of us, as Western, English-speaking readers, are familiar with arguments of similar import from within the twentieth-century philosophical tradition—whether in the universalist or Christian articulations of Jaspers, Voegelin, or Niebuhr or in the very particular Jewish discourse of Hermann Cohen, Martin Buber, or Emmanuel Levinas—few of us have heard them voiced in the Islamic idiom. There are, of course, many works of traditional Islamic philosophy, religion, and political thought—and many excellent studies of them—now available in English. There are, as well, rapidly expanding libraries of Islamic apologetics, also in English, works by scholars great and small arguing the essential compatibility of Islamic thought with the assumptions of Western democratic theory and practice. Indeed, the English-language works of Islamic modernizers are legion—however questionable their political and social effects might be.

What we have not had, at least not until publication of the present translated volume, is a traditional Islamic discourse that addresses the perennial problems of existence—in their contemporary guises—with a message fully formed from within this tradition. Here, in English, Mahmutćehajić gives us just such a discourse. Not an apologetic, not a defense of Islam in the face of the horde of its current detractors, nor a presentation of Islam for more sympathetic non-Muslim readers, *Learning from Bosnia* is rather an engagement with the most pressing political and ethical issues of our time—from deep within the tradition of the Prophet Muhammad.

The rethinking of our constitutive modern secular and liberal assumptions of self and society is, itself, not a new project.[10] In a certain sense, it can be said to have been an aspect of the modern project since its inception. Until now, however, such rethinking has not incorporated the voice of Islam. Tradition, as variously understood in the West, has been taken up almost exclusively by Christian critics such as Hans Gadamer and by a handful of Jewish interlocutors. The voice of Islam and of tradition as represented by Muslim thinkers has been muted and ignored—and the reality of well over a billion inhabitants of our planet effectively denied.

This then is the context of Mahmutćehajić's stunning achievement, which, again I stress, is neither polemic nor apologetic. Here is a calm, considered, and highly articulated engagement with the existential challenge of our time from within a grammar and a structure—what Eric Voegelin would have termed the "order"—of Islam. Of course it will be argued that there is no one Islam, no one vision of what is a world-historical civilization. And that no doubt is correct. There is no more one Islam than there is one Christendom or one Judaism. Yet that does not prevent us from discussing Judaism or Christianity as civilizational units despite the specificity of their historical experience. And this historical specificity is no less central to Mahmutćehajić's program. For he presents us the universal vision of Islam as it was interpreted in the very specific reality of a small but critical corner of Europe, that is of the indigenous European Muslim community of Bosnia and Herzegovina. This was a land defined by boundaries. It was the boundary between Eastern and Western Christendom. It was on the boundary of Christianity and Islam. It was the boundary of the Austro-Hungari⸺ Empire, as it was the boundary of the Ottoman Empire. The rea.

Bosnia was a reality of boundary-work. Its successes and failures were the successes and failures of work on the boundaries. Margins were everything. Dialogue, and mutual engagement of the different truth communities, made up the core dynamic of its history.

As many now know, these margins were precisely the target of the Serbian and Croatian assaults, and the reality of postwar Bosnia is one where exclusive and modernist ethnonational, religiously articulated identities are replacing the margins of traditional communities with hard and fast borders—between sections of Bosnia's different religions and communities as well as within people's own individual consciousness. The nature of religion in Bosnia could not help but change in the wake of the war, and the changing face of Islam in contemporary Bosnia is one example of the failure (understandable, but failure nonetheless) to maintain marginal identities in the face of a nationalist ideology of impermeable boundaries. It is clear that Mahmutćehajić believes that this changing nature of religious communities in modern Bosnia, where religion becomes but a form of romantic sentimentality in the service of different ethnonationalisms, is a horrific and dangerous development. Its results, he would warn us, will be more devastating for the historical reality of Muslims in Europe and elsewhere than the Serbian and Croatian aggression against his country carried out less than a decade ago. The destruction of traditional ways of knowing and of being, he would warn us, is carried out not only under the assault of tanks or even of global capital markets but also in the transformation of tradition into ideology—which is happening every day, not only in Bosnia and not only in Islam, but within the churches, synagogues, temples, and mosques the world over.

The call to take tradition seriously is perhaps the most important lesson we can take away from our engagement with Mahmutćehajić's thought. The Bosnian reality as it was experienced before the war ("neither Serbian nor Croatian nor Muslim, but rather as inclusively Serbian and Croatian and Muslim") is a social reality as well as an ideational truth that we have to learn to abide by if we are not to enter into that chasm of barbarism that seems to open before us. This is the truth expressed in the words of Karl Jaspers as quoted earlier. It is a truth of plurality that cannot exist but in reference to transcendence. It is Mahmutćehajić's powerful claim that this moral reality and the truth of its existence can, furthermore, not be appreciated outside of particular traditions. The language of his tradition just happens to be Islam. He challenges us to find our own.

Preface

Available in the original Bosnian, and soon in French and Italian as well, the entire text of *Bosanski odgovor: O modernosti i tradiciji* appears here in English for the first time. An earlier version of the present translation (see "Author's Note") has inspired a variety of comments from readers and translators. A question frequently asked of that version is, why "a Bosnian response" when the book contains relatively few references to the political, cultural, and social situation of Bosnia?

When a writer's efforts are transformed into a book that is sent out to readers, some of them known and many of them not, the writer needs to listen carefully to their comments, for only then can that writer better understand and interpret the writer's self and the world. When a reader opens and starts reading this book, knowing perhaps less about the writer who has sent it and more about the Bosnia of the title, the reader's own preconceptions, combined with the observation that the book's title seems not to match its content, might prompt the question just raised. It is a question the book does in fact attempt to answer; and though the answer might not be the expected one, this can only benefit the reader. Indeed, because a little knowledge is all too often a dangerous thing, the very purpose of writing this book is to disconfirm the reader's expectations. In failing to find the expected answer, the reader is returned to the question, which in turn makes the reader more receptive to the actual answer—to how the destiny of Bosnia can serve both as a paradigm and as an antiparadigm for the human condition. Though the adjective *Bosnian* can be read as a paradigm for the pluriformity of human attitudes toward the world and God, this is not and cannot be its only or its final reading. The Bosnian tradition of accepting the inevitability of, and thus the right to, differing Christologies among people who speak the same language and share the same history can also find itself reduced to the antiparadigms of confessionalism, ethnicism, and ultimately nationalism.

The descent into nationalism excludes the possibility of and the right to diversity. Differences become implacably reduced to territories with clearly defined boundaries, within which everything that is other and different must either cease to be or become subordinate to the majority. Power and quantity pass judgment on weakness and frailty, which means that power and quantity become the arbiters of beauty and clemency. Authority is vested in whatever is greater in number and superior in power. Multiformities of ritual, heritage, and temple (synagogue, church, and mosque) are replaced by a single, homogeneous entity, which instigates and upholds violence. In this process, the sanctity of the human individual, of the temple, and of nature itself becomes lost.

Each individual is part of the world as a whole, but is also its image. As all that is dispersed through the world is gathered together in the individual human being, the human individual must also encompass the original purity of nature. This original purity is no one's, because it belongs to no single, specific individual; but as it belongs to the Creator, it is also everyone's. The temple is the point where all things that are dispersed through the world, all the Creator's manifestations, are brought back together by humankind. The temple is a place of human openness toward the Absolute, for in it the exteriority of the world is focused and concentrated through the interiority of humankind. Hence the temple belongs to no one but the Creator, which also makes it the property of each individual.

Nowadays, it is difficult for many to understand why the original purity of nature and the authenticity of the temple should be preserved, and in this very difficulty we recognize and see corroborated the tension between the modern and the traditional. Both extremes, modernity and tradition, are premised on a crucial question: what is reality and what is its opposite? At either extreme, the question may be ignored, or it may be asked so forthrightly that only one answer is possible: that, by "translating" what lies beyond, one should accept all that is alien and unknown. Another possibility is that reality, in all its multiplicity, may be distorted by the presence of the observer at its center. The question, however, tends to be answered only in extremis, when danger reveals the true worth of life and demands the revelation of a wisdom based on first principles.

The events that befell Bosnia at the turn of the millennium—its people slaughtered and expelled, assaulted and humiliated, its villages and towns ravaged—were not merely a Bosnian issue. No individual or nation, no region or state remained unaffected by them, though their involvement took different forms. It was human individuality as a whole that suffered. To list and describe these various experiences would be an endless task, and however deep one may penetrate, their essence may well remain elusive. This is why this book attempts, on a more general level, to differentiate between the modern and the traditional worldview, allowing "a Bosnian response" to take shape along their intersection.

The modern enterprise views the human individual as an answerable question, reducing the individual to the quantifiable and finite world of space and time. Any connection between the individual and what is both infinitely distant and infinitely close is blocked by this absolutization of the finite, thus barring the individual self from openness and receptivity to the infinite. We have set ourselves the task of mastering the world, and everything that testifies to the self, the world, and God is viewed in terms of that task. In our urge to absolutize the finite, we have placed the human individual at the center of the world, and allow nothing to exist beyond the duality of the individual versus the material world.

Even the traditional worldview has been subordinated to the modern enterprise. Its true content has been suppressed until it survives only in small groups, or in a few isolated individuals that are marginalized from the political and cultural mainstream. An intellect-driven approach toward the world, with its focus on asking *why*, is misunderstood and hence has little if any influence on the political order. Evidence of this is to be seen in the loss of all awareness that *nature* and *the temple* are crucial manifestations of the Sacred. If they survive at all, it is as mere subimages within the modern model of knowledge. In this mindset, the human individual is no longer the sum and whole of all creation, is no longer that which is wholly open to the Creator. People can neither comprehend the world's diverse phenomena nor accept them as the limitless expressions of the utterance that is also concentrated in the human individual. Instead of living in and with this diversity, modernity's egocentrism subjugates and wreaks havoc on it, for this egocentrism cannot access its transcendental unity. The human body is seen not as an extension of Intellect or Spirit, but as self-sufficient—and whatever remains within its isolated finiteness is directed toward the domination of the outer world.

The consequences of this are to be seen everywhere—in politics, culture, and economics. What humankind is doing to itself and the world is merely the reflection of ignorance masquerading as knowledge. We labor under the illusion that we have no unattainable infinity ahead of us as our ultimate goal, a goal in which humility and modesty would become the most powerful affirmations of our achievements. Hence examining the Bosnian experience is beneficial in that it draws attention to the difference between those two worldviews, as contrasted to the extreme by the misfortunes of this country and people. If the drama that is the world as a whole is not reflected in each individual human being, neither the individual nor the world can be endowed with dignity and sanctity. Then the path that leads to God can be followed neither through the individual nor through the world. The path may be direct, as it seems to many people in the modern world. It involves the destruction of Reality as manifest in creation. In this worldview, the human self is not to be improved, nor are the prophets and the revealed scriptures a wellspring of knowledge, nor is human perfection the thoroughfare that leads to the Creator. The outcome is an insensitivity to the suffering that inevitably accompanies not only the destruction of the natural world and the temples, but also humanity's desperate attempt to escape pain and death. All this is a reflection of how the modern individual is left without a sense of openness to the supreme—that which lends our mystery a purpose.

In describing modernity and tradition as an opposition, one may seem to be reducing the inexhaustible abundance of worldly phenomena to a seductive but simplistic duality. There are many traditions and many modernities, both in name and in content. This does not, however, rule out the possibility of distinguishing between the two worldviews. It is possible to determine the essential common content of all modernities that sets them apart from all traditions, and vice versa. And if one weighs up the differences and similarities on the basis of these core features, one can come to a knowledge of oneself in the one question that remains unanswerable.

Modernity and tradition, however, share a common feature: neither accepts the existing social order. Both see the prevailing order as imperfect, and any social order as changeable. In modern political ideologies, the fraught process of changing the social order is reduced to the human level, to humankind's potential for reaching perfection by a human path. In faith-based traditions, change is linked to the appearance and cessation of revelation. Prophecy and revelation bring about a break with a prevailing social order in which connections with Reality have become denatured or forgotten, and thus lost. Prophecy and revelation aim to reestablish the link between humankind and society on the one hand, and Reality on the other. When the revelation itself ceases, the link is passed from person to person as a system of knowledge, belief, and conduct. No single recipient can be its sole owner or final interpreter: what has been passed on becomes part of history, and is interpreted in terms of human virtue—of which modesty and generosity are the key components.

Every individual, like every society, acknowledges and bears witness both to its own imperfection and to its potential for turning toward the Absolute. In bringing ourselves to focus on the Absolute, we are also striving to survive. According to tradition, no one may claim the right to perfection as attested to by its prophets. But no one lacks the potential to draw closer to this perfection by associating oneself with it. By following "the finest example," we draw closer to the Absolute, to Unity. As individuals, we are open to the Absolute, but the very fact of our existence also makes us dependent on it. And openness to the absolute means that no conclusion we may reach can be final: perfection can be attained only by concluding that no conclusion can be reached. In every tradition, this manifests itself in a variety of epistemological disciplines, such as theology, cosmology, and spiritual psychology. How far political processes that justify themselves via such disciplines should be seen as well grounded depends on the stance of these disciplines. Because no answer and even no question about the human individual, society, the world, and God can be final and irrevocable, whenever theology, cosmology, and spiritual psychology close themselves off from the Absolute and become reduced to mere quantity, the political order associated with them manifests itself as a grotesquerie in which individual and collective degeneration, perversion, and violence become inevitable.

This book does not intend to address all these questions and answers; indeed, it focuses on just a few aspects of this impossibly large task. But even if "a Bosnian response" is only sketched out, it is hoped that this might generate questions that are human in the full sense of that indefinable adjective. This is something that all readers need—both those who speak Bosnian and those who receive the message in translation, by crossing boundaries of language and culture. And translation is possible only because humankind is one, notwithstanding the infinite multiplicity of manifestations and experiences that it may encompass. This "Bosnian response" does not deal with the countless details of society, politics, culture, or economy; rather, it brings together the principles that manifest themselves as nonplace and nontime in the place and time known as "Bosnia." This seems to be a way of acknowledging human dignity in its three essential components—the spiritual, the corporeal, and the social. All three facets of humanity are as much in jeopardy in Bosnia as elsewhere in the world. The prologue, introduction, twelve chapters, and epilogue that constitute this book were written and arranged so as to provide an outline of the elements of traditional intellectuality that differ from the habitual cosmological, anthropological, and psychological perspectives of modernity. Those two outlooks intermingle in them intentionally—to complement the usual representations of the exoteric content of the Bosnian issue with an insight into the nature of the self and the truncated nature of its prevailing interpretations.

I wish to express my gratitude to the translators, Saba Risaluddin and Francis R. Jones, and to Abdulah Šarčević, Mile Babić, Keith Doubt, Šaćir Filandra, and Adam B. Seligman, who read the book and whose oral and written comments have helped to clarify some of its obscurities. Excerpts from an earlier version of the English translation have been published in the journal *Sophia*, which made them available to a larger number of English readers worldwide. Professor Paul Ballanfat has translated the book into French from the earlier English translation, and he, too, made some valuable observations on the text; Diletta Bovino has translated it into Italian. Some valuable comments and suggestions for possible improvements to the text have resulted from contacts with these translators, reviewers, and readers. In expressing my thanks to both translators and readers, I want to assure them their observations and suggestions will be included, with due acknowledgment, in texts still to be written. In addition, certain additions and clarifications have been made after considering the observations of readers thus far and in the hope of reaching many more.

Sarajevo, September 5, 2003

PROLOGUE

Every ideology offers the promise of an end to killing. And yet the killing continues to this day—and it is unreasonable to hope that there will be none in the future. Both the promise that it will end and the likelihood that the promise will not be honored accompany the ritualization of violence and killings. After the Holocaust, every understanding of the world, humankind, and God that has been proffered and developed within the enterprise of modernity as a whole should have been subjected to critical reexamination. Nothing should have been spared scrutiny through the lens of different perspectives and different values. What happened in Bosnia was merely yet another testimony to the fact that neither the promises nor the killings have come to an end. But no thorough reexamination of the major worldviews and proclamations of the modern European age has been undertaken, nor is there any prospect that it will be. In the accounts of the Truth belonging to the Semitic tradition, the world began with Eden, and in Eden there was the serpent. The question is whether it will end with nothing but the serpent, a serpent that will have devoured the entire world, snatching at the very last bird.

Perhaps the notion of the perfectibility of the human self[1] and the understanding, derived from this notion, of achieving a shift from the old suffering to a new concord, is a perpetual spur to violence and killing. If the only credible sciences are those that regard the quantifiable world as the sole world, human perfection is denied. The human individual then becomes a factor that changes both itself and the world, but with the premise that its self, too, is definable and therefore quantifiable. It consciously sacrifices its perfectibility for the sake of the uncertain promises of science, and reduces everything to manifestations without a Reality that transcends them and without the openness of the self as the channel and release for all its contingencies, its conditionalities. Are both the world and the human individual really present as a nonperfectibility that they can themselves eliminate by persistent change and shifts in thought? Is there in the individual an inspired, imbued, uncreated, and uncreatable center in relation to which it is always perfect?

These questions, which touch on crucial understandings of the self and authority, and of the self-regarding insularity of being, would appear to be capable of leading to a more informed insight into the disregard of God, the world, and humankind and, concomitantly, the shift of focus toward outlooks in which evil and good, suffering and concord would be discerned as other than a manifestation of ever-increasing tribulations. For is not every movement mere chaos unless it derives from, is guided by, and bears witness to Peace? Are not all the signs in the outer world and the inner world of the self, the macrocosm and the microcosm, meaningless if they do not praise the Silence? As Ananda K. Coomaraswamy says: "Our experience of 'life' is evolutionary: *what* evolves? Evolution is reincarnation, the death of one and the rebirth of another in momentary continuity: *who* reincarnates? Metaphysics prescinds from the animistic proposition of Descartes, *Cogito ergo sum*, to say, *Cogito ergo EST*; and to the question, *Quid est*? answers that this is an improper question, because its subject is not a what amongst others but the whatness of them all and of all that they are not."[2]

This is an essay in which the shifts and reversals, exertions and easing of tension in addressing the unanswered questions of the Bosnian destiny are tested in the hope of discovering the ignorance, the nonknowledge that calls for confirmation in knowledge. The current state of the world is inevitably reflected in every occurrence of the day. Some reflections, however, are sharper and more composed. The prevailing preoccupation with knowledge without an awareness of the Ineffable, with motion without focus on Peace, and with plurality uncorroborated by Unicity, makes the individual ever feebler and ever more distanced from the Truth, the Way, and Virtue, the essence of the perennial wisdom in all the profusion of its language and meaning. For this reason, the Bosnian experience is a universal experience. It does not offer any new knowledge, for upheavals and slaughter are everywhere. But perhaps it might inspire a critically inquiring attitude toward our own unknowing, the acceptance of which might bring us closer to an answer.

It should be pointed out that the term "Manichaean or any other sort of heretic" is the equivalent of the term "the Other" in the discourse of today. This abjuration was the result of the will and demands of external, non-Bosnian authorities, and what was publicly foresworn was the authentic will and way of life of the Bosnian people. Their land, both before and after this event, had been and would be the home of different religions and rituals—Roman Catholicism, Eastern Orthodoxy, Islam, and Judaism; the unity of these different sacred teachings and ways represents the principle of its continuity.

In the year 1463, toward the end of the Bosnian kingdom, when the country was riven with discord among the elements of this unity, a meeting took place between the friar Anđeo Zvizdović, the custodian of the community of Bosnian Franciscan monks, and the Sultan Mehmed al-Fatih, the head of the Ottoman Empire, which had expanded that same year to include parts of Bosnia. The meeting produced a letter of covenant in which these two leaders acknowledged one another on the basis of the sanctity of their paths to God:

> Let no man hinder or obstruct either the above-mentioned [Christians] or their churches. Let them live in my dominion. And for those who have fled, let them be free and secure; let them return and live without fear in the lands of my dominion within their monasteries.[3]

These selected examples from Bosnian history are an indication of the general tendency of Bosnians to secure their right to different sacred paths. Such attempts were always connected with the presence and power of outside actors. This was to be reflected in the country's changing legal status, while its sum total continued to be constituted by religious diversity as its essential feature. Throughout most of its history, in nearly every Bosnian town, Christians—both Roman Catholic and Eastern Orthodox—Muslims, and Jews have lived side by side. Indeed, the typical panorama of a Bosnian town is defined by its churches, mosques, and synagogues—a focus of diverse discourses on the one truth that is apprehended emotionally rather than intellectually. Moreover, this Bosnian totality has survived in spite of frequent external actions directed against it.

From these diverse religious languages, then, a pattern of tolerance necessarily emerged. These differences were maintained over long periods, their origins to be found neither in apathy nor in the contemporary

INTRODUCTION
THE ACHIEVEMENT OF BOSNI[A]

It is difficult to find any book on contemporary issues published in [the] last decade of the second Christian millennium that does not also [deal] with Bosnia and Herzegovina.¹ Unfortunately, this is not the resu[lt of] any interest in the distinctive nature of Bosnia and its history, alth[ough] there has long existed sufficient justification for that. Addressing [Bos]nia has been prompted, rather, by the war that devastated this co[untry] as the world looked on, its contemplation of events recast into a [sense] of shame. Yet, despite the many books written about the war, an[d read] and interpreted according to various ideological matrixes, b[oth the] country and the war against it remain, for the most part, misund[erstood].

Bosnia is the only European country that throughout its his[tory has] been entirely based upon a unity of religious differences, the [dif]ferences that are central to the peace and stability of the wor[ld in the] coming millennium. This tendency can be illustrated with th[ese para]digmatic accounts from the history of Bosnia.

In the year 1203, in the presence of their head of state[, Ban] Kulin, and before the papal chaplain and ambassador, Johan[nes de Ca]samaris, Bosnia's religious leaders were encouraged to renc[unce] elements of their Christian faith and rituals that did not con[form to] regulations of the Roman Church. In doing so, they were [also to] change their attitude toward the Other, as the followin[g quote] makes plain: "and no one of whom we would be certain [is a] Manichaean or any other sort of heretic shall we accept t[o live with] us."²

right of "choice" (based, in this case, on the notion of the autonomous self and the sufficiency of reason for any judgment on good and evil). Rather, the origins must lie in the roots themselves of religious singularities. This Bosnian orientation toward tolerance over the centuries can be delineated in the intuitive and tacit acknowledgment of the Other, the different, and the acceptance that our ignorance of Others calls for a discourse directed toward them, which presupposes both a willingness to hear them and the acknowledgment of their right to reply. Only in listening to the Other can we see how our knowledge resonates in the self of the Other, who, it is assumed, does not know what we are saying. The historical course of tolerance can also be portrayed as a transformation of the stranger into one's neighbor or kin through speech and listening, in a process of continual translation from one sacred language into another. In the case of the Bosnian Muslims, this is indicated by their attested interest in the Holy Scriptures of the Christians. They acquired these scriptures, read them, and compared them with the Qur'an.[4] They believed that familiarity with the Other served to confirm their conviction that their own choice was a valid one.[5] As a result, the entire Bosnian heritage—definable as Christian, Jewish, and Muslim—was part of a general heritage that did not deny diversity, but was the basis for a continuous debate in the quest for concord and the transformation of enemy into friend and stranger into neighbor.[6] There is an explicit doctrinal explanation for this in the commandment not to revile that which is sacred to the Other. Because God is sacred, this attribute of His may be transmitted to the world and its phenomena. This means that as regards its first principle, every sacredness is of God and with God. It may be interpreted in such a way as to mean *association* with and *attributing* to God; but this does not entail any contradiction between it and its original, authentic meaning. Just as understanding and interpretation are human attributes, so, too, are error, depravity, and culpability. Instead of passing judgment with rebuke or invective, it is wiser to acknowledge one's own ignorance in the face of the unacceptable is expected. And such acknowledgment is a prerequisite for transcending the boundaries between the known that is in the self and the unknown outside it. Reviling the sacred is also unacceptable from the perspective of the tradition of the One God: "Abuse not those to whom they pray, apart from God, or they will abuse God in revenge without knowledge."[7]

Differences can always be discerned in regard to the Other and the Other's tradition: differences that are, for the Other, incontestable and sacred, but utterly incomprehensible to another tradition. This must not lead to the conclusion that one should deny these differences utterly, for this would mean contesting the possibility of debate in the quest for a harmony of opposites and according to oneself, as contingent self, the position of absolute and final arbiter. Yet every human self, regardless of how far it has sunk into oblivion, is capable of discourse on the Truth and its attainment. Although in Bosnia's past this has been sensed rather than explicitly stated as an understanding of unity in diversity, there are examples of an explicit and energetic call for tolerance and dialogue. In this instance, two examples of the attitude toward the Other are instructive. In the seventeenth century, Muhammed Hevaji Uskufi expresses his opposition to intolerance and hatred based on appeal to religious differences, and in a prayer to God calls for the enhancement of unity in diversity:

> As Thou didst of a single lineage create [mankind], so in Thy mercy constitute [us] in brotherhood, not by faith from the east and the west, [but] from all sides, and unite [us] on the way [as] kin and friend. Merciful God, we pray unto Thee, we prostrate ourselves to Thee now, set the sinners among us on the right path, that they may not go astray, that they may have faith and wisdom, Amen.[8]

Abdulvehab Ilhamija, a spiritual teacher who lived and wrote at the turn of the eighteenth century, makes it clear that the refutation or reviling of other sacred traditions is a form of apostasy from one's own: "To denigrate, revile, or dishonor those persons and that which they hold sacred which from the religious perspective truly merit respect is to deny [God]."[9]

And in the midst of the antifascist struggle in 1943, the Bosnian people responded to the bloodshed and destruction by declaring the resurrection of their country, by declaring their country, which they saw as neither Serbian nor Croatian nor Muslim, but rather as inclusively Serbian *and* Croatian *and* Muslim, to be the free land of Bosnia and Herzegovina, a land united in brotherhood, where the full equality of all of its citizens—Serbs, Muslims, and Croats—would be secured.[10]

Although the different religious communities were assembled together in a single country that always formed part of some great empire, its God was the same as the God of others. The ego of the stronger community thereby found expansion and affirmation in its own nation, not in its link with Eternity. This was the worst of sins. The sacrosanct nature of the weaker community was a principled constraint on all quantitative supremacy. Whenever that supremacy was adopted as a principle, the possibility of Bosnia, as of any other unity in diversity, was in jeopardy. Bosnia then seemed to belong to the more powerful and more numerous, in disregard of the principled right of those who were in a minority. The modern notions of homogeneous nation-states thus undermined and dismantled the Bosnian unity into a relationship of quantity and power. In the nineteenth and twentieth centuries, Bosnia appeared to many to be a barely comprehensible exception. Bosnia's Muslims were fundamentally other despite being part of every European identity. They were incomprehensible and uncertain in the prevailing notions of the self just as were the Jews of Europe. It was only with modern crises that Bosnia was transformed into the paradigm of the world as a whole and became a crucially important case for understanding the truth of the self as its alter ego.

Thus the recent war against Bosnia and Herzegovina is merely part of this historical sequence. It was a war waged as a preagreed and coordinated action by its neighbors and their allies, along with the involvement of internal elements of destructive intent, for the purpose of annihilating its unity in diversity. It was brought to an end by the Dayton Peace Accords, imposed by the United States of America and its allies. Included in this negotiation process were the major instigators of the war, foremost of which were Serbia and Croatia; and as a result of Dayton, the partition created by the war was legitimized as the new reality. The country was thus brought to a crossroads from which it could proceed to one of two equally probable scenarios: total disintegration or reunification. Whichever the outcome, the free market, privatization, and the introduction of capitalism have been accepted as inevitable. Communist Bosnia was destroyed by the war; what is left of the country needs to be transformed into a democratic and capitalist country. However, there are many arguments in support of the assertion that the free market alone, especially if promoted by aggressive Western investors looking for quick profit, offers only crumbs of genuine assistance for the civil institutions and democracy it claims to be supporting.

Civil society is crucial to the renewal and survival of Bosnia. Establishing such a society, in all its complexity, directly challenges the mutually exclusive ethnonational programs that exploit both liberal and traditional arguments to continue carving up Bosnian society along ethnic and religious lines. Under current conditions, the external powers forcibly maintaining Bosnia in existence cannot attain their goal of providing the missing confidence if two essential and symbiotic factors for building and strengthening confidence are not recognized: the call that springs from tradition and the inescapable need to build an internally consistent civil society. This cannot happen, however, without a critical reexamination of all the self-engendering interpretations of Bosnian society. And just as neither air nor water conform to the borders imposed by the partition of the Bosnian state and the rifts in Bosnian society, so too these interpretations cannot remain without an unremitting consideration of the wider political and human context. No long-term attempt to establish a social order and a lasting structure for social interaction can be viable, therefore, except on the basis of the development of stable relationships of trust among members of society. Trust is not simply a matter of accountable behavior on the part of all the actors in the social system. For the most part, such behavior can be explained and predicted by means of social rules, in which confidence is based on a set of underlying norms. Trust, however, also encompasses those forms of behavior of the Other that cannot be fully described or presented.[14] This is the awareness of the freedom of the Other, that without trust may engender either violence or ignorance.

The traditional society of Bosnia remained viable for century after century. The cohesion of its religious communities was manifest in a confidence that arose more from the sense of each person's connection with God than from an understanding of the arguments for social harmony. In the modern society of Bosnia, internal tensions are rising, differences are becoming ever more incomprehensible by the Other, and the need for demarcation, for isolation within distinct, homogeneous territories is becoming more and more marked. The individual self as the source of morality, notwithstanding all ideological proclamations and expectations, has failed to replace the inexplicable power of the old confidence. Hatred is becoming ever more a part of life, as differences can no longer be translated, no longer be read in terms of each other's particularity, nor can they be translated into any single form of the new secular ideologies that have grown out of the Enlightenment model. The panorama of Bosnian towns, where the vertical of the minaret and the bell tower soared above all the buildings, shaped through the centuries by the diverse traditions and by those who adhered to them as the symbol of God's magnitude in knowledge and justice and the human virtues of clemency (*hilm*) and humility, has turned into a set of lifeless, somber forms in which some "obscure" and "irrational" history has long since come to an end. The diversities of Judaism, Christianity, and Islam, as long as they were still a living reality, shed light on the remembrance of and prayer to God, which are possible solely as a free human act. But when the remembrance of God dwindles and is lost, when prayer is transmuted into the coercion of repetition, then those diverse histories, rites, and arts become dominated by a sense of otherness, which is a spur to fear; and the inviolability of otherness that sustains that fear is turned into hatred.

In Ivo Andrić's famous words:

> Yes, Bosnia is a country of hatred. That is Bosnia. And by a curious contrast, which in fact is not so curious, and might be readily explained by careful analysis, it is also true to say that there are few countries with such firm belief, exalted strength of character, so much tenderness and loving passion, such depth of feeling, of loyalty and of unshakeable devotion, or with such a thirst for justice. In the impenetrable depths beneath all this, though, there lie concealed burning hatreds, entire hurricanes of fettered, repressed hatreds that are ripening as they await their hour. The relationship between your loves and your hatred is like the ratio between your high mountains and the invisible geological strata, a thousand times larger and weightier, that underlie them. You are thus condemned to live on deep layers of explosive that are ignited from time to time by the very sparks of those loves of yours, of your ardent and fierce emotions. Perhaps your greatest misfortune is precisely that you do not suspect just how much hatred there is in your loves and passions, traditions and pieties.[15]

In Andrić's story, Maks Levenfeld, a Sarajevo Jew, concludes these reflections on hatred as the obverse of love with this picture:

> Anyone who lies awake at night in Sarajevo can hear the voices of the Sarajevo night. The clock on the Catholic cathedral strikes the hour with ponderous confidence: 2 A.M. More than a minute elapses (seventy-five seconds, to be exact—I counted) before the Orthodox church clock, albeit with a weaker but piercing chime,

also announces its own 2 A.M. A moment later the clock-tower by the Bey's mosque strikes the hour in a hoarse, faraway voice, but it strikes eleven, that ghostly Turkish hour, by the strange reckoning of distant, alien parts of the world. The Jews have no clock to strike their hour, so God alone knows what time it is for them, whether by the Sephardi reckoning or the Ashkenazi. So at night, too, while everyone is asleep, difference keeps vigil in the counting of the desolate small hours, dividing these sleeping people who, when awake, rejoice and mourn, feast and fast to the march of four different and antagonistic calendars, sending all their wishes and prayers to one heaven in four different ecclesiastical languages. And this difference, at times visible and overt, at times invisible and insidious, is always similar and often wholly identical to hatred.[16]

The narrator of this tale announces, as it begins, "I'm an atheist, you know." It is worth reiterating that this fictional reflection takes place shortly after World War I. Never in the past three centuries has there been a greater concentration of expectation and euphoria than in the ideological promises of that period: that the world would be set free from its murderous past and that a new era would dawn full of "programmed hopes." But what meaning can there be, what meaning for that narrator of hatred, in Bosnia's sacral diversity? What hope is there for Bosnia if amnesia must prevail over the remembrance of Absolute Plenitude?

The second Christian millennium ended with the Bosnian tragedy as its most potent symbol, in which the country and its people endured the most brutal forms of slaughter, destruction, and degradation. The source of this suffering was not eliminated by the people's cries for help, nor did it run dry when the guns fell silent. To look on indifferently, to fail to speak out against these horrors is equivalent to consenting to evil disguised as retaliation—a disguise that is a denial of justice, and will be doomed, sooner or later, to oblivion. Faced with such suffering and trauma in Bosnia, the only response is to rediscover an understanding of human existence and survival under such circumstances. As the ravaged, fractured state testifies, the language, meanings, and symbols of the Bosnian totality and of all its individual elements are in many respects mutually untranslatable. Furthermore, this renders them incomprehensible to outsiders, whose fears metamorphose into hatreds.

New light must be shed, new interpretations are needed of this society, but these must derive from the openness of individuals and cut across all differences. It will be impossible to liberate this society from its present state of disruption without the revival and dissemination, on the part of its members, of knowledge of themselves and the world. To emerge from the current confrontation and suffering, we need to return to an individual interiority that is potent enough once again to illuminate and interpret society in all its complexity, without allowing any single element to become isolated in a false sense of self-sufficiency, or to be taken for granted. The rebuilding of Bosnia depends on continually striving to know who we were and what we have become, where we have come from and where we are now, whither we are hastening and what we are ridding ourselves of. None of these questions has a final or sufficient response. To be human means to be involved in the interpretation of every question and every answer. The countless multitude of interpretations does not refute the Unicity of the Truth. No quest, no response can attain it. But this does not mean that it is not crucial to the entire multiplicity of human options. Individual, social and global circumstances are susceptible to change, and thus the languages, meanings and symbols through which people, their communities, and the world as a whole and its Creator are interrelated. Bosnia, too, needs reinterpreting. This means that a different light should be shed on the prevailing meanings, languages, and symbols. Traditional intellectuality offers just such a possibility. Though it is hard to predict the changes based on that possibility, it is extremely simple to assert that, unless we accept that we are open to the supraindividual and nonindividual truth, there can be no redemptive interpretation.

1. The Forms of Expression of a Single Truth

Two contrary social tendencies have characterized Bosnia throughout its history. In one of them, religious differences are reconciled through coexistence based on confidence within the framework of different sacred paths. In the other, those differences are in confrontation with one another. These two essential tendencies were in earlier centuries interwoven with the religious affiliation of the people of Bosnia. The arguments for diversity were justifiable on the basis of individual sacred traditions. A breach of trust and responsibility toward others represented *grehota*,[1] a violation of God's commandments, which imbue every being and every phenomenon. This sense of the sacredness of the Other and the Other's right to be different permeated the whole of Bosnian society. It was on this basis that society was defined as "us" for all of its members, even though, within that sense, there were clearly defined affiliations to individual religious communities—Roman Catholic, Eastern Orthodox, Muslim, and Jewish. Although these affiliations were comprehensive, with each having its own, exclusive sacred doctrine and sacred Way, this did not mean that the human redemption they guaranteed applied only to some while excluding others. The adoption of one sacred doctrine and its corresponding sacred Way was exclusive only for the individual choosing it. And although one person could not embrace two sacred teachings or two paths, this did not deny the right of the Other to adhere to a different doctrine and follow a different path, with an equal potential for redemption.

But just as redemption, which is interpreted by all sacred teachings and toward which all sacred ways lead, is possible only in the Absolute, so, too, every exclusiveness is, in its ultimate meaning, at the same time a universal inclusiveness. In other words, the rightness and completeness of a tradition (*din, traditio, religio*) includes its own particular language, symbols, and meanings; yet redemption—the Unicity of the Divine, of which all the diverse languages, symbols, and meanings speak—lies behind it. To take an analogy from the Bosnian landscape, one can reach the summit of Visočica Mountain, whose name means literally "exalted in humility," by three well-marked, beaten paths that meet on the mountain peak, which is known as "Džamija," a place of meeting, of coming together, a place of prostration, of attaining sublimity through humility.[2] In the Bosnian Sufi tradition, these three paths or ways leading to Unicity correspond to the diverse sacred doctrines and ways to God.[3] Tensions between people manifest themselves in their present reality, and can be said to be the expression of an untrammeled present the consequences of which are conflicting and irreconcilable interpretations of both past and future. Trapped by the present, the human individual thus loses its awareness of the Reality that defines it. In the sacred map of Bosnia, which sketches in every path, past and future alike, the Visočica summit is evidence of the first principle as the essential condition for mastery over the present. Without a human awareness and remembrance of the presence and proximity of the first principle, the human individual becomes oblivious to or distorts its primal human nature. Tradition, by contrast, offers knowledge and existence in which both these potentials are implicit. The offer is accompanied by an absolute orientation toward the original and ultimate human perfection in regard to the Truth.

Thus all the diverse forms of that one and only tradition (henceforth "the tradition") which is always behind Truth's individual and different forms in space and time make possible its "translation" or transmission—and the need to hear the Other regardless of what constitutes the Other's Otherness. The word of the tradition is that very plenitude of diversity and plurality, which reveal from hour to hour and everywhere the one, same, and ever-immutable Truth. From such a concept of "us" stemmed the intermeshing and intermingling of people of different sacred traditions throughout Bosnia.[4] Historically speaking, there were no ethnically or religiously homogeneous parts of Bosnia. Every child in this country grew up in an environment that included the call to prayer from the minarets of the mosques and the ringing of church bells from church steeples; children had to establish their own identity in the clearly visible plurality of holy rituals. The demand for recognition of these different features on the basis of confidence presupposed a uniform response to the Other in all the Other's manifestations. This Bosnian "we" can be illustrated through the logic of "neither Serbian nor Croatian nor Muslim, but *both* Serbian *and* Croatian *and* Muslim." This means that "we" as society, history, and territory in their entirety can survive only by denying that any individual has an exclusive right to the entirety, only by confirming that the society as a whole belongs to each individual member of its unity of differences. The survival of this pattern can be observed throughout Bosnia both geographically and historically over the past one thousand years, but so can the roots of bloodshed and destruction in the failure to understand this pattern—or in its deliberate betrayal. Although, in some peripheral areas, this paradigm has already long since been destroyed, history confirms that changes in this fundamental state have been the consequence of external designs against Bosnia and of actions taken as a result of these designs.[5]

Indeed, Bosnian society has been marked throughout its history by an effort to establish, in various ways, modalities to resolve the tensions between the transcendental and the mundane orders. In this effort, what is held in common and what is individual, what is shared and what is distinct have influenced the development of various structures and institutions. This historical process is persuasively described in the words of Shmuel N. Eisenstadt:

> Organizationally the crucial aspect is, of course, the existence of some type of organized church which attempts to monopolize at least the religious sphere and usually also the relations of this sphere to the political powers. But of no lesser importance is the doctrinal aspect—the organization of doctrine, that is, the very stress of the structuring of clear, cognitive, and symbolic boundaries of doctrine.[6]

Inasmuch as the entire history of Bosnia is connected with the discussion of Christology and its shaping into a multitude of different expressions, it is fair to acknowledge not only the important organizational differences between religious communities, but also their doctrinal consensus regarding the *sacredness* of the human individual regardless of the individual's choice of holy doctrine and sacred path. Accepting every individual in principle as representative of the totality of humanity breaches the boundaries of organizational and doctrinal differences: "and whosoever gives life to a soul, shall be as if he had given life to mankind altogether."[7] This truth, which forms the basis of every social system, is also expressed in the words of Emile Durkheim: "Since each of us incarnates something of humanity, each individual consciousness contains something divine and thus finds itself marked with a character which renders it sacred and inviolable to others."[8] Therein lies all individualism, and that is what makes it doctrinally necessary.

Bosnia's premodern multifaceted character was maintained as the stabilizing force of a society permeated with a sense of the supremacy of the transcendental over the mundane. The position of the individual in each of the sacred traditions present in Bosnia presents an image of the transcendental order. Redemption, according to these doctrines, means bridging the tensions between the transcendental and the mundane. Without this premodern link with sacrality, it is not possible to explain the survival of the multireligious and multiethnic society of Bosnia through history. Of course, this should be viewed in the light of the fact that the medieval Bosnian kings accepted the Bosnian Church as a religious organization acting outside the authority of the prevailing church structures; and that the Ottoman Empire, finding a basis for tolerance within Islam, recognized religious and ethnic diversity as the true, sacred nature of the world. In addition, Austro-Hungary for the first time in European history recognized the rights of Bosnian Muslims as equal citizens of a Christian empire.[9]

The much desired and precipitated disintegration of the Ottoman Empire, and then of the Austro-Hungarian Empire, was prompted by increasingly stronger nationalist programs that were a priori defined as based on the right to liberation from "foreign rule." These programs incorporated the rise of nationalist elites (i.e., pressure groups committed to the nationalist cause, whose members potentially formed the ruling cadre of the emergent monoethnic nation-state), the development of nationalist ideologies, and the establishment of nationalist organizations. These three essential elements of the nationalist program were per se rational, intellectual enterprises conceived in the inner circles of the nationalist elite, but their purpose was that of building the nation-state as an expression of the will of the "people." Such programs excluded every element of social heritage that was unconnected with the majority ethnic group as organized through the nationalist program. Accordingly, the role of ideology was to persuade, encourage, and reinforce the belief on the part of these individuals that they were actors in the program of creating a nation-state. This was an entirely rational undertaking—indeed, one that expressed the very nature of modern rationalism[10]—but was in complete contradiction with the universal concept of *grehota*, of right and wrong, that holds together the religious differences within one and the same society. The essential distinction between two views of the self is recognizable in this contradiction. In the first, the self is a closed system, with reason the basis of its self-sufficiency. In the second, the self is open to the Transcendent and cannot be reduced solely to its rational component. The program of the nation-state is not compatible with the pattern "not neither-nor but both-and" that functions within the sphere of religious universality. Such a universality cannot survive within the reductionism characteristic of nation-state programs.

It can be said of the Bosnian diversity, as lived prior and contrary to modernism, that it was a matter of feeling rather than of thought. When, however, it became the subject of thought and disenchantment, this unity in diversity was compelled to disintegrate into its component parts, with the loss of unity. What is more, these component parts began striving to overpower, repress, and obliterate one another. Even where there was potential for a positive interpretation of this diversity, the interpretations being offered remained on the flimsy, fragile margins of society, as properties of an intellectual or doctrinal elite, almost wholly powerless in the face of the popular mainstream for which knowledge was more in the flesh than in the brain. And when out of those intellectualized feelings, Bosnian multiculturalism managed to forge a rational framework for itself based on the precepts of modern ideology, it was left without its transcendental unity, and thus without a principled basis for tolerance between the different languages, symbols, and meanings of religious plurality.

Moreover, the need and potential for a comprehensive interpretation of religious diversity has now become, perhaps for the first time, a global issue. The exoteric diversity of religions—Hinduism, Buddhism, the Chinese traditional religions, Judaism, Christianity, and Islam—is both evident and incontrovertible in today's world. But existence itself has levels that correspond to different levels of knowledge. The fact that religions differ exoterically does not, and cannot, deny their esoteric unicity. The fact of their having been revealed, and their link with the supreme principle, means simply and solely that unicity is confirmed by multiplicity.

No understanding of that stance is possible, however, without clearly distinguishing between the traditional and the modern outlook on Being. In every tradition, Being has many levels, which are at one and the same time linked with and distinct from unicity. Modernity reduces that totality of being to the quantifiable world. From this perspective, in the Marxist narrative the order of being is represented as a natural process, complete in itself. Nature is in a state of development or evolution, a process of which humankind is one of the "products," "directly a creature of nature."[11] As such, humankind is both a part of nature and in opposition to it, taking part in nature's development and orienting it with its work, which in its highest degree—technology and industry—is based on the natural sciences. In thus shaping nature, humankind, through its work, approaches plenitude of being; in this model, nature, humankind, and history are utterly disassociated from Transcendence. At its basis is a leveling of nature, in the sense both of what is in opposition to humankind and of what is its *essence*. That this is an unsustainable hypothesis can be readily confirmed by reference to the first human individual, which could not have produced itself, although this issue must remain taboo if the edifice is to be preserved: the denial and prohibition of this issue is the *myth* on which the entire model rests. Thus the Marxist model entails a revolt against Transcendence. Although differently defined, this brittle postulate, any critical examination of which is taboo, can also be found in the speculations of Hegel, Nietzsche, and Heidegger, as key interpreters of humankind and the world within the framework of modernity.[12] The self so viewed is subject to two interdictions: one human, deriving from philosophical speculation, and one Divine, set wholly outside Eternity and Infinity. To accept the first interdiction entails the exclusion of the second, and this in turn leads to the reduction of the self into a closed system that is adopted as the measure of all else.[13] If, however, the second interdiction is accepted, then, with Eternity and Infinity as its measure, the self discovers its primal openness. Paradoxically, however, its individuality will falsely appear identical to Eternity or Infinity, or in other words, to God, whenever the Divine ceases to be its central, focal point. From the first approach there derives the adoption of society as the determinant of human destiny, or as god. Openness to Transcendence, but without the central position of the interdiction, turns the individual into God. But when this openness has the interdiction at its heart, the diverse forms of the tradition are seen as deriving from the unicity of the Logos, and all their different languages, symbols, and meanings remain translatable through this center.

Without this center, the human enterprise in the material world also seems to be without limits. The result of the aspiration for that inner openness to be transmuted into outer limitlessness—building "a city and a tower, whose top may reach unto heaven"[14]—is to "confound their language,"[15] the language of diverse nations. Out of its experience of disease and death, evil and injustice, fear and hatred, humankind defies the order of being, denying and rejecting any sequence rooted in transcendence and, in return, proffering itself, from itself alone. Languages, symbols, and meanings become tied solely to the quantifiable world, and humankind alone is their source and measure, alone their arbiter. Even if they are translatable, they are no longer evidence of unicity.

The perspective of the tradition is wholly contrary to this outlook. Here languages are translatable through an external interdiction, which bears witness to heteronomous authority: "And of His signs is the creation of the heavens and earth and the variety of your tongues and hues. Surely in that are signs for all living beings."[16]

This traditional anthropology stands in contrast to that of the world and the human self as a closed system. It both demands and gives a response to the question of the diversity and unity of religions, for diversity of religions has an utterly different meaning in the traditional perspective from the one it bears in the mental world of modernity.

Theological speculation is inevitably a view from the contingent onto the absolute. Without a worldly revelation as an external framework for a specific religion, it cannot become a true tradition. Resolving the issue of diversity thus involves valorizing the language of the revelation to which the observer is linked: in that, differences can never have principled validity, although their redemptive role may be acknowledged. An external approach of objective detachment, by contrast, disregards or repudiates the essence of religion, and reduces it to certain forms of its manifestation—social reality, the class struggle, its ontogenetic development. But this is just one way of seeing things; as such, it is incomplete. Several common forms, or to put it better, the diverse "rootednesses" of religion in the self, are indeed identifiable: the moral imperative, the sense of utter dependence, the silence of the sacred, and the distinction between the sacred and the profane. It is clear, however, that this concerns the human side of the relationship between humankind and God, and the issue of the *origin* of human knowledge about the phenomena remains unresolved. Attempts to deduce from every religion the golden rule that determines the good and beautiful in human relations in the world do not resolve the quandary, for humankind attains freedom in relation to God, to Whom beauty and good are but modes of manifestation. Thus the shared essence of religion remains undiscovered in every one of these "objective" approaches.

Although the sense of this transcendental unity of religions, manifest in exemplars of the sacred and the good, can be discerned throughout the history of Bosnia, the ideologies of the modern era have swamped that fragile traditional reality with their volition for external power. In the modern worldview, the human individual is centered in knowledge, which is regarded as being located only in its self. Everything external to this is not knowledge. This is contrary to the traditional image in which only God is omniscient, and in which this omniscience manifests itself in the world in dualities. The resolution of this modern contradiction thus calls for a clearer insight into this lost outlook on traditional knowledge, in which what makes the human individual is its ability to hear and receive the Word through which the Mystery manifests Itself, which connects the individual with the first principle at every present moment: "To God belongs the Unseen in the heavens and in the earth. And the matter of the Hour is as a twinkling of the eye, or nearer."[17]

The seat of intellect, in the traditional teachings, is the "eye of the heart," the uncreated center of humanness: here lie being, knowledge, and bliss in oneness and sameness.[18] They are such for all eternity and at every present moment. The separation of the heavens and the earth, which were originally a single whole,[19] sets in motion their course through space and time. The unicity of being is affirmed by the plurality of phenomena; the plenitude of knowledge scatters into a plethora of signs; and bliss is the sense of unity in every being and every sign because, in being and knowledge, this reveals the primal and ever immanent sacred unicity. Is not the somewhat melancholic sensing of purpose as the depth of humanity evidence of this? Because neither the beginning nor the end of the eternal *now* is exhausted in any creation or manifestation—nor in any of their individual elements—the descent of revelation from the Word toward the world of appearances becomes, in the human individual, an ascent from the cosmos, or the signs in the external world, toward interiority, an ascent from the signs in the self toward the truth. The entirety of doctrine is sent down in that eternal now to the heart, where the known, the knower, and knowledge are one. This descent is a single axis that inseparably joins the unplumbable depths and the infinite heights. It is ever one, whole, notwithstanding its discernment in space and time: "Truly it is the revelation of the Lord of all Being, brought down by the Faithful Spirit upon thy heart."[20] These Divine words point to this:

> My slave ceaseth not to draw near unto Me with devotions of his free will until I love him, and when I love him I am the hearing with which he heareth and the sight with which he seeth and the hand with which he graspeth and the foot on which he walketh.[21]

The course of time is a history of forgetting. Drawing near, which is the result of willing submission, as the first station of resistance to forgetting, leads to loving, or love. That which is loved becomes known. And the knower wants nothing other than the bliss of fulfillment in and with the Known. Thus the human intellect becomes endowed with knowledge both inner and outer, and human consciousness is continually graced with the ability to contemplate a Reality that is wholly other, and yet is none other than the very core of the self, the Self of the self. That spirit is of a higher degree than matter, and that knowledge of the Real is the same as the Real Itself, and is adumbrated by a sense of consciousness as a state of being that is higher than the material. The tradition comprises the wise utterances that link knowledge with the First Intellect and Cause of all that is sacred. But the Sublime Intellect, that is to God as a ray is to the sun, is scattered through the fragmentations and rejections of every phenomenon. Human reason is merely one of the forms of that fractured and rejected manifestation of the Intellect. In its origins its light is Divine. But taking any of its reflected modes as an elemental principle, so reducing Being to just one of its levels, is described in the tradition as a satanic[22] focus upon oneself as an element with its own light, regardless of that Self's presence in every self, that is, as taking a god other than God. Knowledge becomes thereby closed, to the exclusion of the Known. According to the tradition, the worlds and the selves hold within themselves, like the whiteness of a sheet of paper, all the multitude of signs that speak of the Truth. Knowledge that arises from the worlds flows into the signs from the Intellect, from God. But from that same source come the news and the messengers into the midst of humanity, by which the Divine speech takes on human language.

If this is so, human language can never exhaust all that unicity incessantly bestows upon it as its center. The question of human suffering and misery has no response unless it is associated with that which language cannot exhaust. Will, faith, and sanctity are the components of being. No expressible relationship between them exhausts being. If we are able to rule our will and submit through it to whatever it may mean, this demands a response of love. But love transcends will and is not fulfilled by any image to which knowledge leads. Love leads humanity to being by that which is known and to cognition by that which is loved. As long as the two differ, the self is in a state of tension. This drama cannot be resolved without the full meaning of enduring all that is inseparable from human aspiration to survival and happiness. This aspiration is not to be reduced to mere feeling: it directs us toward faith as the simultaneity of love and knowledge the union of which attains Beauty or Sanctity. But neither does this resolve the human predicament, if it is comparable with anything. The supreme human potential is limitlessness, of whose entire and inexhaustible revelation all phenomena may be merely the signs.

2. Submissiveness, Emotion, and Knowledge

If the perennial orientation toward Beauty and Sanctity, as the expression of the human aspiration to survival and happiness, is translated into modern terms, it is inseparable from the idea of nation as the consciousness of social affiliation. With this consciousness, individual aspiration, expressed in a specific language, simply means that the Divine Unicity is reduced to being in and with the nation. Alterity, particularly the alterity with which such a nation is in direct contact, must then be experienced, understood and interpreted as lesser and weaker in principle, in consequence of its being separated from the true God. To see how that perennial loss of contact with Transcendence and the consequent understanding of "one's own nation" as a higher value are expressed through the Bosnian experience, we must focus on how the modern anti-Bosnian ventures have been articulated.

The programs of both Serbian and Croatian nation-states were established over the last two centuries and developed within the framework of two multinational empires—the Ottoman and the Austro-Hungarian. The question of demarcation and separation from the Other became central to both programs, the first of which is fundamentally connected with Eastern Orthodox and the second with Roman Catholic Christianity. Both of them attempt to demarcate and separate people on this basis, and both find in Bosnia elements of the population that can be claimed for inclusion in their presumed ethnoreligious entities. For its part, Bosnia's population is mixed—it is formed not only of members of these two ethnic groups but also includes a Muslim population.

This mixed structure existed in premodern times as a society marked by the consciousness of interrelatedness, friendship, and confidence, bases for tolerance that, as we have seen, are grounded in the individual sacred traditions. They operate within and from the interiority, exclusivity, and completeness of each individual sacred tradition, but find justification for the existence of the Other and the different in the Unicity of God, Who manifests Himself in these different forms of the tradition.

These very elements of social cohesion were identified by the proponents of the respective ethnonational programs as essential obstacles to the attainment of their set goals. Mixed societies based on friendship, confidence, and trust stand in the way of the demarcation of ethnoreligious territories. In this context, the call for liberation from imperial rule became associated with the struggle for ethnonational recognition, in which, in line with the differentiation and antagonism between the traditional and the modern worldview, there is a denial, directly or indirectly, of the human individual's awareness of itself and the world as the manifestation of the Divine Word. In this mental world, reason acquires a different role, by which the diverse potentials of human existence are seen solely as erroneous beliefs to be surmounted in the course of "historical development."

In this struggle, the elemental "Other" becomes those who are closest to the adopted ethnoreligious identity, those who are only slightly different. If religious traditions, however, remain true to the openness of the human individual to eternity and infinity, they will resist the reduction of difference to an ideologized ethnonational program, whose aim is demarcation, a redrawing of borders. In an authentic traditional outlook, denial and exclusion of the Other are impossible without simultaneously relinquishing the openness of the self to the Absolute. Any revolt against others who define their relationship with God in a different way is at the same time a revolt against God. The fact that human salvation from disease and death lies beyond the quantifiable world demands speech and commandments from humankind that bear witness to its openness to Infinity and Eternity. To regard or treat life in an irresponsible manner is *grehota*, which extends to both the Beginning and the End. Whenever there is the desire to remake God into "Our God," with the concomitant denial that He is also the God of the Other, of all others, God is Himself repudiated, and turned into an idol. This idol then demands the exclusion of everyone in the secular order, of which the false god itself is the measure, who does not accept this equation and interpretation of the truth; this is what happens whenever religion is co-opted as a means in a national ideology. Then the testimony of tolerance is repudiated: "Dispute not with the People of the Book save in the fairer manner, except for those of them that do wrong; and say, 'We believe in what has been sent down to us, and what has been sent down to you; our God and your God is One, and to Him we have surrendered.'"[1]

Then evil and injustice cease to be the sole criterion of demarcation between people. "Our God," who is not the same as "their god," becomes the arbiter of these distinctions, and the self and society alike seal themselves off, while imposing their interpretation of themselves as the whole and exclusive truth.

Conversely, friendship toward and confidence in these "Others" become fundamental obstacles to demarcation and separation, and their repulsion and annihilation an integral part of the program. But understanding such processes of bloodshed and destruction resides in the deepest layers of the self, those which can remain unshaken even after the boundaries of a social system are negated and the underlying rules of social unity broken. This is the point of encounter between understanding and belief. The two levels of the self, that of reason and that of faith, become distorted in the service of a particular ethnoreligious program.[2] The predominance of "disengaged reason" is the fundamental element of modernity, and the reason why the ebbing strength and apparent unsustainability of the Bosnian unity in diversity is linked to the spread of modern ideologies in the complex region of southeastern Europe. And here the modern concepts of tolerance enter the social scene, while at the same time the principled tolerance that derives from the very essence of the sacred traditions is repressed. With the exclusion of the presence of transcendence, or the vertical that passes through all the worlds, humanity is reduced to a closed social and ideological system, and its nature can manifest itself in disassociation from the sense of *grehota*. The remaking of the world to achieve an ideologically determined objective then becomes an end to which even the self must be subjugated, and the notion of the future becomes more important than the human individual as its source.

If we are torn between our rational potential, as superior, and our inner impulses, as inferior, sin and error lose all meaning; along with every other phenomenon, we lose our aura of sanctity and become "located" between rational calculation and the feeling that arises from the subrational component of the self. No desire can cross the boundaries of that isolation, for this would mean that the desire in question would be subject to extinction at the point whence the reasons for error spring. The feeling of sin testifies to and fosters the simultaneous bond between the self and the world or the outer horizons as horizontal presence and the Self as principle, which sends its signs down to those horizons, eternally remaining connected with them. Further, this is a matter of the world and the self.

The world contains forms; the human self contains desires. Every tradition is in its own way an expression of the oneness in which all the forms in the world exist, and to which different human desires lead. These four crucial elements—the world, forms, the self, and desires—determine three essential aspects of human nature: the submissive, the emotional, and the intellectual. Although the truth is one, these aspects are expressed in various ways in humankind. Each individual tradition, as well as respect for humankind, can be said to contain the one truth that underlies the different traditions. When the substance of different traditions is subjected to a systematic examination, there are difficulties in explaining the differences, but these are primarily linguistic. The doctrine of every tradition is flexible enough to reconcile different manifestations of the truth, though it is left to the holy and the wise to see the single reality that lies behind the variously structured differences, and even when they find the truth behind those differences, they may relate it in different ways.

Religions differ in both their exoteric and esoteric aspect. Transcending this state of difference demands a confirmation of the conditionality of each form and each expression. In this way, truth becomes disassociated from individual forms and languages, so as to be expressible through each of them. Truth is constantly present, but the human self can be absent, as when it forgets Unicity. The presence of truth in the self does not depend on language or form. Both absence and presence may have various names, but truth itself does not depend on that. Although there is no conceivable doctrine capable of embracing all this diversity; a doctrine that does not presuppose the inexhaustible potential of expressing what is its very essence cannot be called a "tradition" in the full sense of the term.

At the center toward which all traditions lead is the Absolute Light. Language as differentiation is conditioned by that center, but the center is not conditioned by language. In other words, notwithstanding the great variety of individual traditions, two essential aspects remain: the doctrine and the way. Human nature has three planes: will, love, and knowledge, each of which can take two complementary expressions: detachment and action, stillness and zeal, differentiation and unification. Connected through doctrine and the way, these expressions form two sides of the same being, that is, the degrees or stations of wisdom, which are will-love-knowledge or fear-love-knowledge.

Despite the great abundance of possible modes of expression, which are unique in form although they always remain connected with one and the same Reality, they can be classified in a manner that permits their plurality to confirm the unity of the perennial teachings. Nevertheless, because the exclusivity of any individual tradition does not require insight into the forms through which the doctrine of another is expressed, limitations in interpreting different forms of tradition often result in their being perceived as "flawed" or "erroneous." This obscures the truth that Unicity can be manifested and confirmed only through multiplicity. Comparative analyses of different expressions of the supraindividual and nonindividual truth, which is not dependent on either time or language, are therefore needed in order to banish the existing all-prevailing confusion over the contingent nature of traditions engendered by the plurality of possible expressions.[3]

Faith and intelligence can be understood on two different levels. As certainty emerging from beyond the state of being, faith transcends intelligence. On the other hand, the discernment from which intelligence starts in order to reach Unicity transcends faith. Taking one or the other of these views is an emotional choice, from which much confusion arises. From this it also follows that it is possible for exoteric and esoteric languages to coexist. Faith, in its higher aspect, is what is known as "*religio cordis*"—religion of the heart, or inner religion. Corresponding with this is *religio caeli*,[4] the expression of the eternal truth to which the discernible signs in the self and the outer world point. Faith can be satisfied with little, in contrast with intelligence, which requires precision and is never satisfied in its game of structuring expressions. Although it is constantly moving from one thought to another, from one sign to another, unable to dwell on anything, the faith of the heart can find reasons for acceptance and reinforcement in the most minute of manifestations, which thus meet its every need.

The differences between certain traditions, as well as the differences within each tradition, are expressed in the relationship of the individual self toward the external forms that make up the totality of the world. One's submissiveness, emotions, and intelligence depend on how one feels or interprets one's nature in relation to the self, desires, forms, and the world as a whole. These are the facts of human existence.

Governed by patience and submerged by it into the world of appearances, the submissive person accepts the world and selfhood as the will of the Absolute. This is the way of life that finds its purpose in sacred asceticism or sacrifice. For the submissive, the signs in the inner human selves and the outer world are not endless ladders leading to Infinity; doctrine holds, first and foremost, threats and promises. To the submissive, the metaphysical nature of existence is manifest in the smallest possible measure. For the intelligent person, the signs in the inner selves and the outer world are visible per se: they are limitless and transparent, and beyond them there is infinity and the unicity of truth, a detachment from forms and desires, and reality becomes that which can be embraced by this detachment. The emotional person is caught between these two possibilities, expecting to hear either voices or music in all manifestations. If the submissive person is defined by fear and will, and the intelligent person by knowledge, then one might say that the emotional person is defined by hope and love. Expressions of dedication will permeate this person's relationship toward both forms and desires; there is a feeling that life is based on predestination.

The dissimilarities between these types of self are not restricted to forms of tradition, language or race, although the way in which they are shaped may have the color and taste of the recipient and the exponent. One may thus speak of dissimilarities in the reception and expression of tradition from one individual to another, and of historical, racial or ethnic affiliations as the plurality of expressions of a single truth. In each expression, two apparently conflicting views hold good. First, the kernel of each tradition fulfills the demand that "not so much as the weight of an ant in earth or heaven escapes from thy Lord, neither is aught smaller than that, or greater, but in a Manifest Book."[5] Second, all expression of the truth in words is open-ended: "Though all the trees in the earth were pens, and the sea—seven seas after it to replenish it, yet would the Words of God not be spent."[6] The following three verses testify to this duality in plenitude and openness: "Indeed, We sent forth among every nation a Messenger, saying: 'Serve you God, and eschew idols'"; "We have sent no Messenger save with the tongue of his people"; and "Naught is said to thee but what already was said to the Messengers before thee."[7] Thus the truth is ever complete, in its concealment and its manifestation alike; and thus, too, the way that it announces for human perfection. On the other hand, this eternal potential can be actualized on a scale ranging from the consummate to the conditional, and may even shade into insignificance; it is linked to the relation between First Intellect and reason. In the traditional outlook, reason (*ratio*) is a lower expression of Intellect (*intellectus*): Intellect is of the first order, and reason of the second. Reason is not intellect, nor is it possible without intellect—but the reverse is not true. Although reason arises discursively through language, like a bridge linking two banks, the knower and the known, in so doing, it banishes neither the distance nor the river flowing between the banks. Intellect, however, knows intuitively, and equates the knower with what the knower knows, so that it is the cause of their unification. Or to put it differently, intellect is the manifestation of Plenitude in the human self. Intellect is in a sense the Breath of God in the body or, as Meister Eckhart has it, that which is "uncreated and uncreatable" in the self. That which appears as intellect in the mundane world has cognition of Plenitude—it is, in fact, Intellect as Plenitude-in-the-human-individual becoming perceptible in phenomenal consciousness. But the individual knows Absolute Plenitude only upon becoming It—that is, only in the resolution of the duality of self and Self through the utterance, not of the self, but of the *Self*. This is the perfect correlate of the testimony, in the Semitic expressions of the tradition: "There is no god but God."

Every sacred tradition claims that the human soul is immortal. Thus the sameness of knowledge and being: the true knowledge of immortality is immortality itself. But this raises the following question: how can this death-in-life and life-in-death be reconciled with freedom-in-enslavement and enslavement-in-freedom? It is here that one may turn to the question of the difference between the shared nucleus of every sacred tradition, on the one hand, and modernity, on the other. The outlook of every tradition, without exception, is of an order, a hierarchy that proceeds from the first principle toward its contingent manifestations. All these manifestations reflect the mirror image of the higher levels of being, arrayed in a great chain from the top down. But the mirror was abruptly broken, at a time that does not go back much further than the eighteenth century. The totality of existence was thus fractured, restricted to its material level: everything now begins with the material and must return to it for verification and confirmation. This raises the question: why, then, did the hierarchical outlook collapse? Huston Smith outlines the following response:

> As it had blanketed human history up to that point, constituting man's primordial tradition and what might almost be called the human unanimity, the force that leveled it must have been powerful, and modern science is the obvious candidate. The timing is right: Bacon, Hobbes, and Newton saw the writing on the wall in the seventeenth century, but it took another century for the scientific outlook to sweep the field. And the logic is inexorable: the structure of the two views is such that it was inevitable that they collide. Modern science requires only one ontological level, the physical. Within this level it begins with matter that is perceptible, and to perceptible matter it in the end returns, for however far its hypotheses extend, eventually they must be brought back to pointer readings and the like for verification.[8]

In such a mental world, the knowledge of the sacred and sacred knowledge lose their meaning. The different languages of tradition become inexplicable, just as the cosmos ceases to be the revelation of the inexhaustible Truth. Nor is this all. The different sacred languages evoke only fear, for there now exists an ignorance that cannot be overcome by translation. Diversity itself is thus blamed for tensions between traditions. The multiplicity of religious meanings, symbols, and languages develops through fear into hatred. It is no longer clear, even to those who adhere to them in the modern era, that temples are the sum or image of the cosmic totality, notwithstanding all their diversity. But in the traditional outlook, the hierarchy from the top down, from the higher to the lower, from the absolute to contingency, has as its consequence that subordination and proximity to the Supreme are one and the same. If the world and humankind are the manifestation of the Absolute, it follows that they can neither add to nor subtract anything from It. Human degeneration or debasement begins with the premise that the self may be able to add to or subtract something from the Self. This implies that the Self is not Perfection, is not Consummate. But, from this, it also follows that Perfection is not a human potential. Yet the magnitude and abundance of the heavens, in the traditional teachings, speak only of the Supreme: "Hast thou not seen how to God bow all who are in the heavens and all who are in the earth, the sun and the moon, the stars and the mountains, the trees and the beasts, and many of mankind?"[9] This state of submission and humility in the heavens and on earth is the glorification and praise of God, in which phenomena rise toward their first principle. This is the recognition of the consummate attunement and capacity of the human individual to understand and actualize itself in relation to the Supreme. Thus the signs in the outer world, from the highest heavens to the surface of the earth, correspond to the phenomena in the human individual as the image of God, from its basest physicality to the center that is directly illumined by Intellect. Accordingly, the worlds are a temple in which all is turned in homage toward the Truth. But the human individual is also the same in principle, albeit differently manifest. The cosmos and humankind are one and the same temple, but expressed in two languages. The temples built by humankind speak of this. But because the human individual's center is one and the same Unicity, the temple may take different forms, just as the cosmos has different outlooks. This diversity is in the proper order of things, and only with this diversity, with the diversity of languages, is the speech of Unicity sustainable: "Had God not driven back the people, some by the means of others, there had been destroyed cloisters and churches, oratories and mosques, wherein God's Name is much mentioned."[10] This "driving back" is none other than the right that derives from the duty of listening. Speech implies a listener. The self that has the right to speak to the "thou-ness" of the Other, which in this case has a duty to listen, thereby acquires for itself the right to reply. Conversation requires the assent of both parties to different languages, on condition that they are translatable in the "mention of God's Name." But if they are untranslatable, the conversation has neither purpose nor potential for response. Then the diversity of language has neither primal source nor confluence, and languages must compete by weight of force alone. The consequence of this is the denial of the Other, the Different. Monastery, church, synagogue, and mosque[11] are indeed different languages of freedom and submission, but not one of them is possible in all its fullness without the other, for, in translation from one to another, they reveal themselves as mention of the Ineffable Name of God in diverse ways. Any rivalry between them can have validity only in reestablishing the conditions for the relation of the self, the "I-ness," which has both right and duty, with the "thou-ness," which has duty and right, so that the diverse languages of their traditions might be intertranslatable and the remembrance of God therefore possible: "Fight them, till there is no persecution and the religion is God's; then if they give over, there shall be no enmity save for evildoers."[12] To lay the accent on proselytizing a Divine tradition also means that it may not be possible to do so: "'To you your religion, and to me my religion!'"[13] The two traditions cited here are, in fact, two outlooks or perspectives: one from below, from the lower to the higher, and the other from above, from the highest to the lower, which sees the temple as the congregation and speech of all that is "sent down" from the Truth via the Way to human virtue, and back again. In this order of the cosmos and humankind as *temple*,[14] the openness of both to Transcendence is witnessed and emphasized. But although there may be openness to Infinity and Eternity, it does not make possible our human actualization as such if, with the forbidden that Transcendence expresses, we do not remain ever in submission to the Truth. That submission is the human debt, or due. Thanks are due to the Bestower for all that we have as the manifestation of dignity—body, soul and association. The debt to the Bestower is invariably one and the same, and cannot depend on our will either to honor or to repudiate it. Human transience is evidence that the debt will be repaid, willy-nilly; it cannot be otherwise, for all the sacred traditions agree that God is Lord of the Day of Judgment. The repayment of the debt out of free will means that the self is engaged in praising the Bestower and is bound to Him through praise. Praise is complete only when within ourselves we constitute the sum of the praise of all the worlds. Our selves are then transformed into the manifestation of and union with the Self. All else is non-Freedom, or nonself.

3. The Apprenticeship of Submission and Freedom

Human potential derives from the existence or absence of interdiction in the openness of the self to Eternity and Infinity. But there are also two possible ways in which the self may be closed off—again, with or without interdiction. Each of these possibilities of the self is counter to the society that directs it or that it illumines, and in neither of them does the self evade suffering and death. It can resolve them in Absolute Plenitude, beyond the self and the outer horizons but also through them, as, indeed, it can all forms of suffering and disorder, of ugliness and evil, in transcendent beauty and good. Or it can repudiate this resolution and accept a role in the world of sickness and death, without the least submission to the transcendent absolute. Evil is manifest in every human modality, but the ways in which it is confronted and its presence explained are diverse. In the case of Bosnia, as in other similar cases, the issue of this diversity cannot remain apart from the quest for a response to the killings. Previous discussions have shed light on the three human types—those who are under the complete rule of First Intellect, who can advise themselves because they are open to God, Who places the interdiction upon them and thereby transfigures both them and the world into a temple; those who in their uncertainty and trouble see cause to seek and heed the advice of the first type; and those who have the nature of neither the first nor the second type, who lack inner self-examination and are as a result readily inclined to evil.

Aristotle's slave by nature and Hesiod's useless man belong—the latter at least partly—to a kind of social substratum, while our problem is that the useless man exists at all levels of society up to its highest ranks, including pastors, prelates, generals, industrialists, and so on.

So I would suggest the neutral expression "rabble" for this. There are men who are rabble in the sense that they neither have the authority of spirit or of reason, nor are they able to respond to reason or spirit, if it emerges advising or reminding them.[1]

In the ethnonational programs that are each structured by an elite, an ideology, and an organization, the "rabble" may even compose the very highest social stratum—and such a link from the top down to the lowest stratum produces an ethos of ruthlessness. For this reason, the issue of the collapse of the social framework that acts as a restraint on the rabble and its influence on the self, so that there might be a preponderance of the first two human types, is crucial to an understanding of the "Bosnian response" to the killings and destruction. The universal nature of the human self, in its relation to itself, society, and the cosmos, with all its inclination to evil, must be recognized in the all too familiar way in which neighbor turned on neighbor in a frenzy of killing. This, as Eric Voegelin sees it, is a matter "of the simple man, who is a decent man as long as the society as a whole is in order but who then goes wild, without knowing what he is doing, when disorder arises somewhere and the society is no longer holding together."[2] It then becomes evident how far humanity is held under restraint in the self of each individual and within the social framework. But if the relationships between the modern and the traditional language discourses as to the potentials of the self are to be defined, one must return to the issue of freedom.[3] This need is imposed by the modern notion that the traditional idea of servitude is unacceptable. To be free means to receive from someone or something a position that is so described. To embrace freedom means to eliminate the obstacles on the way to the goals set by human desire. But if the goal is the absolute, there remains the unresolved question of whether the totality of existence is an obstacle to this goal. And this gives rise to yet another question: is this world, as the self, society and nature, the only stage on which human freedom can be attained? Freedom that is accepted or embraced must be viewed from the perspective of submission to the First and Last as the repudiation of all other human subjugation. And this entails understanding that there is not a single phenomenon in the totality of existence, not even the human individual as the sum of all things, that transcends its own first principle. It is in submission to it that the bond is established and maintained with that principle. If the self isolates itself from the Self in any way, the bond is then ruptured. And this isolation means that freedom is a rejection of the incomparable, of that which has no equal, in favor of that which is comparable and similar. Freedom of this kind is limited, and so, therefore, are those who share in it. It is servitude to that which enslaves; as such, it can never be absolute freedom. Submission to the absolute makes union with the absolute possible, and this is the relationship with the Free.

De Tocqueville says that liberty is "the most arduous of all apprenticeships"; and perhaps this is so. The tradition, however, would take the view that the most arduous of all apprenticeships is that of submission. The most sublime freedom is that which is inexpressible. It is confirmed by pure being, as revealed in multiplicity and motion. This is the God of all the Semitic religions. He is not only the most sublime Self but also the only true self. Everything bears witness to Him. In Him all signs disappear: "Everything disappears save the Face of God." In Him there is no limitation; and thus, He is absolute freedom. Submission to Him is the freedom of the created; the greater the submission, the greater the freedom. If freedom is separation from motion for the sake of Peace, from multiplicity for the sake of unicity, and from the sign for the sake of the Signified, then freedom is submission. All phenomena participate in this submission or freedom[4]. God is Peace. Only in Him is there no dichotomy. There is nothing that can define Him. As a result, the totality of His manifestations neither subtracts from nor adds anything to Him. In this lies the unbounded multiplicity of a duality that is merely the inexhaustible potential for confirmation of Peace. Thus Peace alone is perfect freedom, and to be oriented toward Peace is to draw closer to freedom.

A path or link leads from God to all individuals, for He is present in everything, but there is no path to God from any individual, for all individuals are absent from Him. Thus the path expresses the relationship of the infinite toward the finite, a relationship that neither diminishes nor increases the finite. The potential of each individual for perfection rests on this relationship. The no-path, on the other hand, expresses the relationship of the finite to the infinite. This relationship is always nothing, as indicated by the words of the Revelation: "there is no creature that crawls, but He takes it by the forelock" and "Whosoever holds fast to God, he is guided to a straight path."[5] No other relationship is possible. Even the language of this relationship, which finds its complete expression in the doctrine of the covenant, points to the bond between people on the basis of their belief in God: "Only men possessed of minds remember, who fulfil God's covenant, and break not the compact, who join what God has commanded shall be joined."[6] (Here it is apposite to recall that the Latin root of *religion, religio*, means "renewed connection.") From this also follows a possible understanding of the explanation from the Revelation: "We offered the trust to the heavens and the earth and the mountains, but they refused to carry it and were afraid of it, and man carried it. Surely he is sinful [and] very foolish."[7] The important word here is *offered.* An offer can be either accepted or declined. The heavens, the earth, and the mountains rejected it. This does not mean that they should be designated as negative. Their submission is already complete: they have utterly submitted their will to the will of God. Their existence is completely in accordance with God's will. From the fact that the human individual accepts the "offer of trust" follows the conclusion that the individual is "sinful and foolish," violent and ignorant.[8] Here lies the difference between humans and all other created phenomena: only humans are free to choose submission or nonsubmission to God. This choice generates the rift between humans' being and knowledge. Given the contingent nature of human existence, the concomitant of this rift is conditional freedom. This kind of freedom is not possible unless its constituent elements are violence and ignorance. The presence of violence and ignorance is the touchstone of confidence. The essence of the traditional path to freedom is in its denial for the sake of its confirmation in the only true self. The human individual is always both with and counter to the Other. This is a relationship of motion and assessment, which means evaluation.

Although no perfect truth can possibly derive from the relationship between these two individual conditionalities, the I and the contingent you, confidence (Latin, *confidentia*) means the establishment of a relationship between individuals with the sense of responsibility before God: the face of the other manifests the face of God. The connection is maintained by the awareness that at all times "our God and your God is One." The betrayal of responsibility of one individual to another is a violation of what is owed to God. Confidence therefore maintains the recollection of God. It collapses into violence whenever the human individual forgets that God sees all that humankind is and does. That relationship between people mediated by their relationship with God, however, is reduced to "trust" in the modern world, where the self decrees the postulates of its autonomy as a sufficient source of moral decision.[9]

Thus the use of the concept trust can signify neither faith, as the relationship between God and humankind, nor confidence, as a relationship between people that derives from their belief in God. Its meaning can be understood only in terms of relationships between people that are not mediated by a shared belief in the Supreme Being. In this essay, this relationship is referred to as "trusting."[10] It has no potential for perfection, for it does not derive from the absolute nature of the Creator. Because it is a relationship of created beings, that is, of contingent or conditional existences, its inevitable feature is imperfection, as manifested in "violence and ignorance." The concept of trust is close to the modern notion of the social contract and representation. Its essence lies in the proposition that relationships between people can be maintained and harmonized by means of the human individual's orientation to a given social order, of which the self-image is constructed and developed by its members who rely solely on the authority of reason.

This preference for building a social order based on rational constructs embraces history as the underpinnings for future projections. In it are located both the artisan and the craft of shaping the world and humankind in line with rational blueprints and human desires. The human self is a building block, not a source and value that transcends the significance of any design for the mundane order. The human individual is no longer addressed by unicity with the demand to be heard and to receive from it the word that bestows meaning and purpose on existence at all times. Because a society that transforms self-awareness into nation becomes capable of discovering within itself and dominating some ultimate meaning, the same principled value cannot be accorded to those who are other and different. "Our God" can no longer be "their God"; that some are the elect, superior to others, necessarily manifests itself as a standpoint without which nothing can be learned about freedom. This raises the question of humankind's detachment from God and of God's proximity to all of creation. A constructed social order represents the other as our neighbor, and its transcendent principle as ever more distant from us as individuals and our links in society and the world.

Humankind is infinitely distant from God, but God is infinitely close to humankind:

[¶] We indeed created man; and We know what his soul whispers within him, and We are nearer to him than the jugular vein.
[¶] When the two angels meet together, sitting one on the right, and one on the left,
[¶] not a word he utters, but by him is an observer ready.[11]

The infinite distance cited by Holy Writ is manifest in the disjunction of the soul into its lower and higher levels. These form two contesting, opposing demands. Peace is their first principle; but as such it is inexpressible. In it the "whispering" evanesces. The relation between impulse and reason, soul and spirit, heart and intellect is expressed in words. In the word the human potential of attaining Peace through submission, love, and knowledge is assembled and attested. This attainment includes the impulsive force of the self, bestowed on it as its deepest nature, and the force that manifests itself as evidence of the states through which the self is passing. But all these states are determined by the relations between the two facets or faces of its disjunctiveness—the face that incites to evil and the one that reappraises, that is the fount of soul-searching. Their ever-present potential, the equivalent of the unparsability of silence in all speech, is Peace. This is not capable of expression in even a single one of these states, although it is their first principle and purpose: He Himself is aim of the return within which opposition of the wills of the self and the Self will disappear.[12] Individuality in the human self, as in the outer world, is disjoined into form and essence, space and time, beginning and end, interiority and exteriority; but the return to Peace is the most profound substance of every individuality. It is actualized in the final return of disjunction and disconnection into the original unity of earth and heaven, just as, at the end of time, heaven and hell will be one.

Equating the will of the self with the Will of the Self in this way may be presented through the three degrees of purification, perfecting, and unification. With the first degree, the self recognizes and affirms its own inability to direct itself toward actualization and realization unless the Creator, to Whom it owes its existence, guides it. This is the recognition and affirmation of its original potential. To seek God's forgiveness means to turn away from the unreal toward the Real, or to distance oneself from falsehood and approach the Truth. This is purification.

Contact with the impure, the unreal and the false is an intrinsic feature of the human condition, however; it lies between unreality and the Real. No self can be its own standard and arbiter. Perfecting oneself means to adopt, ally oneself with, and draw closer to the "best example," consistent with the prayer: "O Lord, unite me with the Praiser!" The attainment of human perfection is possible only in the self that is utterly humble, and thus entirely empty of all but the praise of God. Union, or the vision of the two worlds—this world and the other world—as the manifestation and corroboration of the primal oneness of the first and the last, the outer and the inner, the concealed and the manifest, flows from this union with the Praiser and the discovery of the Praiser within the self. The expression of this is the witnessing that there is no god but God.

With every moment everything existent changes, but the moment itself remains external to change. The immutable Unicity is present in all phenomena, whereas change manifests itself in the diversity of languages, symbols, and meanings. Thus it is that Unicity reveals itself in the diverse cultures that are the spatial and temporal manifestations, notwithstanding all their diversity, of the immutability that is never absent from the signs in the outer horizons and the selves. If culture is defined topologically, it becomes a series of translations and transformations of that immutability. Understanding this facilitates a clearer insight into the linguistic and symbolic motive force of culture, and of the differences that different languages and their "topological fields" maintain between themselves. Inner tensions in the translation and transformation of speech directed at the listener are perceptible in each of these fields. Different tensions pertain in different "topological fields." But in each of them there remains a tension toward Divine Unicity, or God: it transcends every horizontal connection between individualities and renders every self open to the Truth. This is the tension between the different orders in the world and within humankind.

Resolution of the tension between the terrestrial world, and participation in it, and the heavenly world, where lies redemption from finitude and death, always involves the relationship between God and the human individual as a call from the Former and a response from the latter. Inasmuch as both the call and the response take place in the finite world, they form the link of each individual with one and the same God. Strictly speaking, in the light of this it can be said that there are as many religions as there are human beings—though to embrace a revealed way means to join one of the many religious communities shaped over the course of history. Nevertheless, there can be no genuine religion without the discernment of the real from the unreal for which every individual has the potential. Nor can there be genuine religion without the acceptance of reality, which requires knowledge and a link with the best possible human mediation, on the basis of which different languages and rituals are possible. Confidence is possible between individual members of religions and among them taken together because the relationships between each individual I and the collective we are established through the supreme and only real I. This demands consensus as to the one and the same, perennial aspects of different sacred traditions. And from this consensus there derives the affirmation of the unity of humanity as a single community with the same Creator and ancestors. But because the signs in the outer world and the selves, in the macrocosm and the microcosm, those symbols of which the ultimate meaning lies in their link with Peace, are read by every individual, they become a language that people in a close relationship one to another can use to communicate. The relationship between people is thus determined by shared meanings, symbols, and language. Historically, they branch out into a plethora of communities, each with its own different meanings, symbols, and language. This in turn gives rise to two levels of relationship between people. The first lies within a given circle of meanings, symbols, and language. The second is the relationship between the different circles or communities. As already noted, these relationships depend upon the acceptance or rejection of the openness of the self to Eternity and Infinity. And on this depend the forms and interpretations of society. Whenever a particular form or interpretation is taken as final, the self, too, becomes sealed off, and the individual becomes subordinated to society and its interpretation.

The stability of Bosnian premodern society as a structure composed of different religious communities rested precisely on the confidence within those communities and between them. Each of those communities established its own structure. In each of them a doctrine and a way were preserved and developed, but the knowledge that its way would converge with all the other ways in infinity and eternity, in God, Who cannot be solely "ours" or "theirs," maintained the sense of responsibility toward all the other communities and their members, which is affirmed by the already-mentioned statement on the God's unity.[13] The differences between holy rituals and symbols were transcended in each of those communities by the connection between God and each one of its members. Without this, both rituals and symbols would have been idols. And this is the source of Bosnian tolerance: its reasons are neither those of realpolitik nor those of indifference toward the Other and the different, nor do they derive from the "right of all to freedom of choice." It is a qualitatively different outlook, rooted in the one and the same sacred that can and must manifest itself in diverse ways in time and space. To each community was accorded the principled recognition that it could be in communion with the truth by means of its own language, and the individual was located within the framework of the community. In the modern outlook, the individual is plucked out of the community, so as to eliminate the limitations that are the consequence of the bond between the truth and the group that is in communion with the truth through a set of uniform meanings, symbols, and language.

Among the changes to traditional society that have resulted in its taking on modern forms is secularization. Relationships between individuals are increasingly based on trust rather than confidence. In this context, the human individual ceases to perceive itself as created "in the image of God." It becomes the highest plane of being—all else is below it. The individual thus assumes the position of a being that "takes" or "seeks to take" itself and every other being "by the forelock," while both ends of the rope of its salvation are in human hands. This transforms the position of the human individual as creature into the illusion of itself as creator. The finitude of the individual and the apparent unconditionality of its *self* are expressed in its relationships toward others and those of others toward it as violence and ignorance. Our human knowledge becomes the acme of all potential, and speaking of the known takes precedence over all listening. For each of us can attain everything that is offered by our presence in the world. Desire becomes wholly focused on the subjugation of the Other through speech. The reasons for restraint or silence in a mode of speech that might be founded on virtue are vague and uncertain, for this would mean that the desire for recognition would be viewed in equilibrium with the duty to listen to the Other. The sacred tradition, with its many forms, becomes replaced by secular ideologies, the most significant of which is the ideology of the nation-state. Every religious community is left with its own structure and the language of its tradition, but now without God as absolute freedom and the source of individual redemption. In such circumstances redemption is shifted to the relationships among the people who are heir to the religious communities and their elements.

In an ethnonational program, this heritage is transmuted into the political structure of elite, ideology, and organizations. Holy rituals and symbols and all that is related to them no longer resemble bridges across which each individual is carried to the "other shore," to God. They become part of the overall set of instruments determining the relationships within a closed world. The installment of a political elite requires a coalition with the religious elite, whereby the latter is in a subordinate position. Ideology requires a restructured understanding of religion, which is placed within an ideological interpretation of history.[14] One-people-one-state becomes, in this perspective, a false god. Its destructive effect is demonstrated in the ontotopological project whereby ethnonational identity has to be equated to territory. And this means that the presence of those factors which represent a threat to the desired homogeneity, whether spatially or temporally, must be eliminated from the ideologically postulated territory. Thus elites, ideology, and structures become the mediators of trust between individuals. They take over the absolutized role of sustaining society, but do not also take over the satisfaction of the desires and needs of the individual. A course running counter to this, however, is that of a deeper understanding of human needs and of the fragility of social structures once all the links with the inner aspects of the historical identity of a society have been lost.

Human manifestation or liberation requires a doctrine and a way. This doctrine cannot be engendered by the individual, for it is nonindividual and supraindividual, and, as such, attuned to every individual. The doctrine is ever present; it is only the individual who can be absent. To be submissive or free means to find the primal self.[15]

> To grow into our mature better selves, we need the help of our nascent better selves, which is what common standards, authoritative education, and a sense of the public good can offer. Consumption takes us as it finds us, the more impulsive and greedy, the better. Education challenges our impulses and informs our greediness with lessons drawn from our mutuality and the higher good we share in our communities of hope. Government, federal and local, with responsibility for public education, once took it upon itself (back when "itself" was "us") to even up the market

and lend a hand to our better selves. Now via vouchers the market threatens to get even with public education. This sorry state of affairs is not the work of villains or boors. It arises all too naturally out of the culture of McWorld in a transnational era where governments no longer act to conceive or defend the common good.[16]

In this picture of the human position, the universal perspective of our original perfection, from which we may descend to the lowest of the low, has disappeared. But even there, in that potential for the greatest abasement, perfection remains the reason for our creation. Even at that point, the human self does not lose its consciousness of the *cube*, the Kaaba, the symbol of construction that includes the paradox of the simultaneous abasement and exaltation of every being.[17] The cube, box, and house—in all their simplicity—signify interiority and exteriority in space. Six directions of the objective world radiate out from the secret center of the human self—forward and back, right and left, up and down. Nothing that is revealed in those dimensions of exteriority can be anything other than the manifestation of that which is as one and the same in interiority, the first principle or seventh ray. Space receives phenomena with their names, and time corrodes and ravages them, that it may be clear through continual change that exteriority and interiority are a duality that manifest and corroborate Unicity. There is no knowledge that is not the expression of full knowledge: the knowledge that only God possesses. Changing this knowledge toward Knowledge is thus possible only by accepting that it is the best standpoint of the self that is a nonstandpoint. Whenever the bond that is remembrance between humankind and God is dissolved, the individuality of the self is turned into a lifeless, rationalized building block. But maintaining the living remembrance of Eternity and Infinity, with the interdiction at its center, links us with Absolute Plenitude, giving us cognition of the speech of truth through the signs in the outer world and the inner worlds of the self. Neither the Vedas nor the Torah nor the Gospels nor the Qur'an speaks of freedom in the way modern ideology does. It is only when both life and death are in perpetual association with the supreme through submission that we are liberated from "graven images." None of them is worthy of human potential, for the world in all its dualities is none other than the manifestation of Him Who has neither associate nor alterity. Only submission to God opens up infinite possibilities for us; in the most profound depths of our createdness, we are open to and designed for it.

4. The Lower Horizons of Freedom

The relationship between modernism and tradition parallels the relationship between trust and confidence. Traditional doctrine tells us that humankind is infinitely far from God, but that God is as close to humankind as can be: "and We are nearer to [it] than the jugular vein."[1] This is perfect proximity, with the unicity that confirms the mystery lying between the human individual and the individual's heart. The heart is eternity and infinity, and there is not one of its manifestations in the world but unicity is immanent in it. Every plurality of individualities is thus linked with confidence through the freedom of the human individual.

But when the self is limited to the quantifiable world, reason becomes its highest potential. God is then no longer "nearer . . . than the jugular vein," nor "between a man and his heart."[2] Confidence is thus reduced to a direct relationship between the rationalist worldview and the individual existences that are subordinate to it, in a world lying only between the starry heavens above and the moral law below. From this it follows that the material world, as the empire of multiplicity and motion, in which quantity is the arbiter of all, becomes the sole scene of human manifestation. In this supreme intellectuality, the sciences, skills, and rites that belong in this domain are regarded as the infirmities and naïvetés of the past.

In this worldview, speech takes primacy over listening, which is necessarily subordinate to it in the external world. In the traditional outlook, however, the reverse is true; silence is above all speech, reveals and confirms speech, is the beginning and end of speech. Indeed, silence, or the ineffable, is the inward and outward aspect of every phenomenon. Perfection in human language, therefore, is possible only on condition that listening is taken as a higher level of communication than speech. Listening is possible without speech, but taking the converse as one's principle instigates arrogance and violence.

Submission to true freedom, in which individual phenomena have their archetypes as primal and eternal potentials, is transformed, in a world that has forgotten such submission, into a freedom "subordinate to reason." In tradition, reason is the reflection of First Intellect in the world of multiplicity and motion. As the correlate of multiplicity and motion, it has no potential in the sense just mentioned. Reason is preoccupied with such potentials, but it does not reside in any of them, and therefore Plenitude, the one, is not possessed by reason. Though humankind wants plenitude, in this worldview, reason is the highest level of being, with nothing above it. Thus the world can permit its reshaping according to human elements "subordinate to reason." This is McWorld,

> a theme park—a park called Marketland where everything is for sale and someone else is always responsible and there are no common goods or public interests and where everyone is equal as long as they can afford the price of admission and are content to watch and to consume. McWorld as Marketland is, however, not a natural entity imagineered by some benevolent deity. It is fabricated and it is owned, and how it is owned tells us a great deal about its nature.[3]

This world is not concerned with the plenitude of our createdness, or with our potential for perfection. Its guiding force manifests and understands itself in transcending the boundaries of individuality through liberalism as embodied in the state, the market, culture, and the like. The supraindividual and the nonindividual sources of unity are forgotten and denied. Unification is imposed upon the world on the basis of power alone, and neither its acceptance nor its rejection is conditioned by place or time. This finds its reflection in the human self—the self that incites to evil, the self that is reproachful, or the self that is at peace.[4]

Although the greater part of the selfhood of the modern human is involved in economic issues—which at the level of society manifests itself as the rationalization of selfish interests in the acquisition of wealth, but also as the arena of the human struggle for recognition—contemporary economic theory remains for the most part powerless to account for the totality of human behavior. This is what Adam Smith suggested, noting that economic life was deeply rooted in social life, and that it could not be divorced from the customs, habits, and social behavior within which it functions. Accordingly, it cannot be divorced from culture.[5] Both economic life and culture can be seen as containing two simultaneous and contrary processes in one and the same reality: one that seeks to unite people in an ideological world, and the other in which they seek to "find themselves" in the consummation of their selfhood. When constrained by the first, people turn to the second. This results in the discovery of the "ancestral faith," most often in the form of dead symbols and modes that strengthen sentimentality and morality, but almost invariably lack a true intellectual doctrine. "Finding oneself" then mostly consists of blind resistance to McWorld and encouraging "development" in which the consciousness of the first principle only becomes weaker.

In connection with this discussion, it is worth drawing attention to the obsession with defining a civilization by classifying phenomena and their external interrelations. In such an approach, a civilization's higher essence, which is confirmed by the *totality* of its phenomena, becomes neglected or negated and replaced by an insistence on the peripheral. There is an obsession with the proliferation and relation of numbers, even as the fundamental nature of the principal unit is ignored. Civilizations thus become irreconcilable entities, material systems whose decisive factor is quantity. It was this understanding of plurality that gave rise to the theory of the "clash of civilizations"—a logical consequence of the amputation of all that is beyond human reason, when the one and the same center that is mystically present and absent in every phenomenon ceased to be the means through which even civilizations were seen to be only different manifestations of the Truth that is nonindividual and supraindividual.[6] In reality, there can be no civilization without a transcendental center, through which the symbolic meaning of all of its forms is maintained. Indeed, without this center, all the phenomena of civilization, including civilizations themselves, begin to take on the nature of condensed, concentrated forms that cannot be transcended by reason, and thus become material systems that stand in irreconcilable opposition.

The dynamics of these "civilizations" as opposed forms that have lost the consciousness of their transcendental centers is also indicated in the concluding remarks of B. R. Barber:

> What becomes apparent is that the confrontation of Jihad and McWorld has as its first arena neither the city nor the countryside, neither pressured inner cities nor thriving exurbia, but the conflicted soul of the new generation. Nations may be under assault, but the target audience is youth.[7]

This assertion is incontestable, though the labels adopted for definition of its contrasting poles—"Jihad" and "McWorld"—do not reflect the true nature of the conflict. No individual or communal reading of the holy doctrine, once it has been delivered in a certain language and ritual, can be obligatorily sacred for others as well. Each of us has both the right and the potential to find in our reading whatever helps us strive to overcome ignorance and the impulse toward violence while remaining rooted within our own self, and to establish ourself in the fullness of peace, in that same center without which no civilization is possible. This struggle bears the name "jihad" in the Arabic language, but despite—or precisely because of—its holy intent it has been subject to distorted readings and application. Accepting its distorted readings, however, only confirms the way of thinking that ignores and negates the true center of phenomena.

The struggle for self-recognition often leads to the discovery or intensification of ethnic or religious identity. But what does this mean for young people in the postcommunist world? Or for their peers in the "most developed" continent? In the wake of ideological collapses, frequently accompanied by the devastation of entire social systems and mass killings and expulsions, they are left facing confusion and disorientation. The defeated ideology is then replaced by ethnicized religion, religious language and symbols, and ethnonational programs. Religious organizations, with all of their available elements, become frames that separate and demarcate people while offering them no intellectual escape from the confusion. The guilt of others is intensified, as is the need to read history in a way that can give simplistic explanations for the causes of rising tensions.

This dichotomy, which contributes significantly to the fragility of social systems, is usually called "the conflict of tradition and modernism" or "the conflict of religion and secularism," although these concepts tend to be very nebulous and, for the most part, trivialized. When the advocates of modernism speak of tradition, and when traditionalists speak of modernism, they see it as the negative of their own world image. Thus the gulf between these two perspectives merely grows wider. A parallel process happens when formal religious language and organizations thrust their way into the secular world, where they become distorted. Conversely, this is also the case as the language and systems of modernism become increasingly present in religious organizations. These developments pose a difficulty for any dialogue that seeks to place the question of trust and confidence at the center of any discussion on the common good. Both sides have taken over the language of the other, distorting its elements, in order to use them in mutually irreconcilable negation. This tension in all modern societies has been termed the "trivialization of religion in the secular world."[8]

In this phenomenon, which can be regarded as a facet of the relationship between modernity and tradition, it is important not to lose sight of the crucial oppositions such as evil and good, falsehood and truth, matter and value. Without such oppositions, racial, linguistic, and religious differences are meaningless, and are treated as betrayals of some utopian or ideological image of humanity, society, and the world. The aspiration to respond to the question of unity in diversity by means of some simple surface comparison of race, language, and religion is doomed to failure but is frequently accompanied by quantitative judgments based on power. For the most part, there is no recognition in plurality and diversity of the prerequisites for a living process of distinguishing the unreal from the real. Notwithstanding all the similarities and constraints that derive from the comparability or quantifiability of the corporeal and biological aspect of humanity, only by viewing racial, linguistic, and religious differences relative to a center present everywhere and nowhere can the self be in touch at every present moment with Eternity, and find in every "death" more than the palpability of corporeal decay. The need for a singularity in which there is an incessant receiving from and giving to the Absolute Plenitude is so powerful that the superficial advantages of comparing and quantifying ostensibly malleable matter vested in racial, linguistic, and religious differences have never outweighed it. Humanity can retain its viability only in its division into a multiplicity of races, languages, and religions. But not one of these particularities is reducible to or separable from any other, and all of them together, in incessant dialogue—which means translation—bear witness to the ineffable Unicity without which none of them has an answer to the question of "now" and "death."

Two contrary and yet also similar modern phenomena, communism and fundamentalism, are of particular significance in the trivialization of the relation between unicity and multiplicity. Of course, there are essential differences between the fundamentalist and the communist vision of the world order. The phenomenological starting point of the fundamentalist vision is the individual's recognition of and loyalty to religious truth. In this there is a recognizable endeavor to apply the perennial order of tradition, as Truth approached by the human individual in humility and clemency (*hilm*), compassion and generosity, to a secular, ideological agenda that seeks to order the world by social and political action. Fundamentalist communities invariably equate their interpretation of the perennial wisdom with the Truth itself, presenting themselves as the guardians and agents of its application to the terrestrial order. For the most part, however, such communities are far from the living traditional current, which is largely incomprehensible to them. The true language, meanings, and symbols that this current conveys, in fundamentalism as in communism, are almost always disavowed. Such communities thus feel the need to define themselves explicitly in relation to the external, majority society, so as to protect themselves from the dispersion and erosion of values that are the result of "negative" influences around them. Every nucleus where purity is only external is a stage on which strut ignorance and confrontation. The proposition "Anyone who is not with us is against is" is the invariable catchphrase of that ideological nucleus, that elite. And given that they assert with incontrovertible conviction that they are "right," it inevitably follows that others are not—and not just wrong, but evil. They equate the truth, which is nonindividual and supraindividual, with its interpretation, which is invariably personal and conditional. It is here that the basic contradiction between fundamentalism and true tradition lies. There is no tradition that permits the individual, or a group, solely on the basis of its own assertion, to proclaim its own knowledge to be infallible and absolute. To the contrary, this is, for every tradition, the greatest of sins, the kind of overweening pride that is a barrier to our access to primal perfection.

The elite then decrees that the reconstruction of society on the basis of an ideological vision is the right and duty of that pure nucleus, to be effected by society's own institutions. In the case of communism, political organization and action were linked to a secular vision of the new order, which saw salvation as lying in society. Individuals were subordinated to the blueprint for the shift toward the construction of that new social order, although they were also regarded as corrigible, capable of being changed from their existing conditions to further the "march toward a new world."[9] Here, paradoxically, the Kantian postulate of the individual self as the source of morality is clearly recognizable, and because the "moral law" is not, and cannot be, a matter of negotiation, exchange, or barter, the self is thus endowed with an aura of sanctity. Once a Kantian project is sociologically framed, however, moral meaning becomes immanent in society, and society becomes the substance of moral action and evaluation. Society is thus the essential factor of success to the entire project of modernity. But this is a return to paganism, of which nationalism in all its diverse forms is the most complete expression. Although, in simplistic terms, fundamentalism and communism appear different from—and, indeed, opposed to—one another, they are similar in essence. Fundamentalism absolutizes the interpretation of a particular tradition and locates it in a pure ideological nucleus that seeks to change the social and political order. Communism aims to achieve the same end, but by absolutizing reason as a crucial and sufficient tool to perfect humanity through political and social changes.

In the fundamentalist vision, reshaping concerns the individual, above all, although success in this endeavor is inseparable from reshaping the social order. Whereas the communist aim is to bring about social and historical change, the fundamentalist aim is to bring this change to a halt because, in the fundamentalist view, change opposes "perennial" values. In both fundamentalist and communist movements, one encounters efforts to differentiate Western cultural values from science, technology, and economic efficiency per se: the former should be resisted and rejected, whereas the latter should be taken up, adopted, and applied.

The most significant differences between fundamentalism and communism lie in their attitudes toward modernism and its related political, economic, and cultural programs. In the fundamentalist outlook, human perfectibility is unacceptable. But this is contrary to the authentic Jacobin outlook, which is premised on such perfectibility, as are the Enlightenment and the communist and socialist visions related to it, as well as fascist, nationalist, and national-socialist regimes. The communist view goes further, emphasizing human perfectibility. Communist movements and regimes stress the primacy and crucial importance of instrumental rationality and technology—indeed, they represent themselves as the sole exponents of such an instrumental vision, of progress, technology, mastery over nature, and the rational, emancipatory restructuring of society. Fundamentalist ideologies, on the other hand, have repudiated certain of these Enlightenment postulates: they accord primacy to the understanding of God, or the metaphysical first principle, as the supreme Reality, and His presence in the world and in humanity. But notwithstanding the different ways in which their views are structured, both communists and fundamentalists fail to discern the true place of reason in the totality of being. Modernity rejects traditional intellectuality, but so does fundamentalism. Both fail to reverse the dominance of speech over listening, and thus to eliminate the absolutization of knowledge, because both lack a notion of the autonomous self that develops from imperfection toward the consummate.

In this respect, the issue of the relationship between reason and Intellect is fundamental. Though the Intellect is the prime manifestation of Unicity, the aspiration of human intellectuality to reduce it to just one of the levels of being is always present. In origin, the concept of religion denotes the establishment of a "bond" or connection between every phenomenon and the transcendental truth. Similarly, Intellect is that which unites all phenomena with the supreme principle. Thus the Arabic word *al-'aql*, which means, first, "intellect" and, second, "reason," derives from the verbal root meaning "to bind" or "to fetter"—for Intellect is the bond between humanity and the One, or God. In the words of the Prophet, God first created Intellect. Thus humanity is linked by Intellect with that created firstness and, through it, acquires the root of firstness, the greatest possible closeness to God. Knowledge derived from Intellect or its reflection (because it is in the greatest proximity to the oneness of knowledge and being), assigns to the knower unification with the supreme principle.

But in contemporary discourse there are numerous instances of lack of clarity and of oversimplification in the use of the terms "Intellect" and "reason," which are most commonly used to designate cerebral as opposed to emotional competence. In this discourse, "Intellect" (Latin, *intellectus*) is reduced to and equated with "reason" (Latin, *ratio*), thus reflecting the modern interpretation of the world and of humanity, and repudiating the traditional outlook. In the traditional teachings, the totality of the human individual is manifest at three levels—that of the body, that of the soul, and that of the Intellect. In this totality, reason lies between corporeality and spirituality, that is, between the body and the Spirit—it is a manifestation at the level of the soul, but is neither autonomous nor independent. It does not have its own light, but receives, like the moon, the reflected light of the Sun of Intellect. Reason thus operates in the world of forms, and its horizons therefore encompass conjecture and reverie, calibration and reflection, hallucination and illusion. It is the first principle of speech, through which it externalizes itself. Intellect, on the other hand, is supraindividual and beyond form. What is more, Intellect may be created or Uncreated, that is, of angelic or Divine nature. The First Intellect is the same as the Word of God or the Logos. Although immutably present in every phenomenon, including human individuality, which is created through that Word, from the heavens to earth, it cannot be attained in reverse, from the body through the soul. And this external and internal manifestation of the uncreated is what constitutes the human self.

Rational knowledge, therefore, cannot replace intellectual knowledge, and is thus ignorance, nonknowledge, for truth remains unattainable by it. In the traditional outlook, this fact calls for an acceptance of the potential of "tasting," or "putting to the test." This is sapience (Latin, *sapientia*) in the etymological sense of the word: from *sapere*, meaning "to taste." Knowledge that derives from *sapientia* is direct. It may be described, but it cannot be circumscribed by verbal expression. It is simply being in contact with the eternal and immutable treasury of all knowledge. Its completeness may only be hinted at in language or sacred art. Only through the acceptance that speech about such knowledge is nonknowledge can its potential be affirmed as the eternal wisdom that manifests itself in illuminated lives. The cognition of the senses is analogous to such knowledge; but this knowledge is not itself of the senses. The premise that there can be nothing in Intellect that has not already been in the senses is the basis of the modern secularization of knowledge. The true view, however, is the inverse: if everything were not in Intellect, nothing could be known. The reformulation of this premise in the modernist worldview has two crucial, mutually opposed consequences. The first is that values, which derive from Spirit and Intellect, must be rejected if full knowledge of the quantifiable world is desired. The second is the co-option of values by those whose agenda is to bring about the political reconstruction of humanity and the world, which in turn results in attitudes to evil and good being made dependent solely on the ideological matrix adopted.

Because no modern ideology accepts that the self is open to transcendence as the essential source of enlightenment of the political order, the isolation of the self is the most important feature, in a variety of ways, of the entire enterprise of modernity. The inevitable consequence is that the openness of every individual to Transcendence has to be replaced by the idea of the capacity of the nation itself to determine and attain its ultimate goal—which is none other than internalizing the nation as sufficient to itself. This self-sufficiency, this possession of "its own God," can be demonstrated only in the ability to conceive of and carry out one's separation from all others and thus construct a historical order that fulfills the ego that occupies and is evidenced in society and nature. This may be total separation because it renders the nation utterly isolated and imbues the self with the illusion of self-sufficiency. Those who are other and different are tolerated on the basis of numbers and power, not principled differences. Only after the horrific experience of widespread suffering in the nineteenth and twentieth centuries, evidence of the inevitable consequences of such isolation, was the question of tolerance of the other and different based on principle resurrected. If the question is taken to its logical extreme, every individual self and collective identity must be defined by the fundamentally other and different, which manifests itself at the most superficial level of identity as hostile and alien, as sick and helpless.

5. Pride and Humility

The issue of tolerance is becoming more and more salient wherever there is serious discussion about the tensions of contemporary society. There are three prevailing interpretations of the issue. The first is that those who are other and different continue to survive in a majority environment because, in the given circumstances, the means of excluding them are lacking. Tensions between "us" and "them," however, can all too readily deteriorate into denigrating and humiliating, persecuting and even killing the others. The second interpretation is that the nature of the culture of others is of no fundamental importance, and the attitudes toward them are without value judgment. It is unimportant to the majority what distinguishes the minority. But the nihilism and relativism of this narrow view of diversity can also easily turn to violence of the worst kind. Nor is this all: in such circumstances, few can adhere to values and meaning, and those few who can lack the conditions for the kind of dialogue and scrutiny that could lead to a reorientation and improvement of the situation. The concomitant of both interpretations is a self-contained, inward-looking notion of identity, which conflicts with diversity, and which can lead, at the end of the day, to complete degeneration and disintegration.

Advanced by the liberal, Enlightenment enterprise, closely linked to the Cartesian sufficiency of disengaged reason, and fostering freedom of choice as an unquestionable right, the third interpretation of tolerance is that the self is autonomous: its "Cogito, ergo sum" requires that the right to difference also be protected, but does not consider as equally valuable every particularity that proceeds from this right. Freedom of choice, on the basis of the sufficiency and detachment of each individual's own powers of reasoning, does not imply any recognition of the validity of a choice that is different. From this modernist perspective, values are regarded as a matter of secondary importance. Nor, as evidenced by many instances in the modern world, is there a bar to the majority deriving from this universal right the "right" to commit violence against an Other who has made a choice that does not suit the majority option. Be that as it may, in such circumstances, when heteronomous authority is excluded, the rule of quantity becomes absolute: the majority choice is always expressed as the greater value. In the politics of contemporary societies this manifests itself as the unchallengeability of ethnonational sovereignty. Once the totality of being, in all its hierarchy from higher to lower, is reduced to just one of its levels, confidence—as a bond between people that is simultaneously a vertical bond with God and a horizontal bond with the Other as individual—is replaced by trust: a direct, unmediated connection between people at the horizontal level of existence, without openness toward the Infinite. Society is thus reduced to the election and perpetuation of representatives legitimized by the co-opted advantages of "democracy." But representation and its associated institutions are without protection from incursions by even the basest potentials of the self, manifested as the distortions resulting from its self-referential character.

The issue of choice from the viewpoint of the tradition has an entirely different focus. Contrary to the modern view of the capacity to decide—which alone ostensibly leads to freedom—tradition proffers prayer, which is impossible in the absence of absolute freedom. Prayer of this kind does not exclude the potential for choice, but orients it to the Ultimate Determinant:

> When we set out after two concerns,
> one of which makes Thee pleased with us
> and the other of which displeases Thee,
> incline us toward that which makes Thee pleased
> and weaken our strength in that which displeases Thee!
> Leave not our souls alone to choose in that,
> for they choose falsehood
> except inasmuch as Thou givest success,
> and they command to evil
> except inasmuch as Thou has mercy![1]

Given that every tradition incorporates the multiplicity of being, and that the greatest and highest is the first principle for the lesser and lower in all the levels of being, heteronomous authority is the principle of all relationships of existence. The human individual is so constructed, through its uncreated and uncreatable substance, through its orientation toward Perfection, as to be an image of the multiplicity of all being. The hierarchy in this world from the earth via the heavens toward eternity is reflected in the human hierarchy from the corporeal via reason to the First Intellect.

From these two worldviews there derive two anthropologies—the evolutionary, in which the greater and higher is explained by the lesser and lower, and the creationist, in which the lesser and lower is explained by the greater and higher. In the evolutionary, humanity is the acme of existence, and human reason is the founding principle of being. In the creationist, humanity is fallen, but ever connected with perfection, which is its origin and its final recourse. These two perspectives engender differing attitudes of pride and humility in modernity, with its autonomous self, and in tradition, with its heteronomous authority. And because both are present in the modern world—though it is not without significance that the creationist worldview is probably espoused by the majority of humankind—it is of crucial importance to answer the question of how to promote discussion and seek assurance in the different forms of the tradition as a source of tolerance.

Although it seems that the outer world—society, nature, and the cosmos—is plainer to see than our inner nature, for all that, it is not hard to demonstrate that in fact everything that makes up the signs in the outer horizons is illumined and interpreted from the interiority of the self. Society and self, therefore, are far from identical. Society is illumined and interpreted through the individual selves that compose it, but each self has the truth of its soul, which can never be reduced to any societal truth. These two truths are perpetually in opposition. The openness of the soul to Infinity demands that there be seen in every social achievement only one of the possibilities of the contingent manifestation of the Truth in our inexhaustible discovery of our primal perfection. But the soul, too, is in a state of disassociation between its baser nature and the contact with the uncreated Intellect as its supreme potential. If that openness of the self to infinity, in which lies our redemption in Complete Alterity, is controverted or denied, the self becomes sealed off, self-referential, and only the truth of society exists for it. The totality of human redemption is then reduced to society, which becomes the god of human destiny as a whole. The symbolic bonds of society are turned into idols, for they have ceased to mediate between one contingent state and another: their role is merely to confirm the truth of society as the sole truth. Different social experiences and cultures—that is, different languages, symbols, and meanings—with which this absolutized truth comes into contact or relationship, can be neither accepted nor tolerated, for by their very existence they exclude the right to completeness. The openness of the soul to infinity enables discernment between forms of the truth, which does not mean denying the existence of society in which diverse outlooks and their diverse contingent truths vie one with another.[2] In the mental world of absolutized truth, however, there is no Unquantifiable to mediate and confirm the discernment to which it attests. Authoritarian governments attempt to deny and bar the openness of the individual in relation to the Truth. For them, different modes of illumination and self-interpretation of society are unacceptable because interiority as the transcendent source of the life of civilizations is neglected in favor of social exteriority. Symbolic differences in rites, clothing, or interdictions, within the whole hierarchy of the cosmic wheels of change and differing attitudes toward one's own community and toward others who are present in the world, cease to be different points of departure for the one and only Truth. The illumination from within fades and finally vanishes altogether in the hegemony of the external experience. Although each political society derives ultimately from this inner illumination and self-interpretation, it may disintegrate in two ways. In the first, it loses the link with internal openness as the enduring source of life and self-interpretation, turning into an operative singularity in space and time. Thus the openness of the individual self turns into a self-referential self, engendering in turn a self-referential society. This is what may also be called "loss of faith" or "loss of true intellectuality." The second way a political society may disintegrate may take several forms: its members may so disperse that it becomes physically impossible to maintain the bonds and links between them; the partial destruction of their tradition and their connection with it may erode resistance to the process of disintegration; political and intellectual leaders of that society may be persecuted, excluded, and repressed; its fundamental elements of identity may be desecrated and defiled, leading to or actually bringing about the breakdown of the society as an integral whole; or, finally, the entire society may be extirpated.

Given the ravages wrought on society throughout the modern age, it is essential, in the quest for an understanding of a differently grounded tolerance, to reexamine the relations between the truth of the soul and society. Only by doing so can we discover the main causes of our failure to understand that the plurality of interpretations of the truth is, by the nature of things, the confirmation of that very truth. If humanity is seen as the greatest and highest attainment of evolution and history, it must also be their supreme value. From this it follows that human aggrandizement and self-exaltation are a way of life. The world is accordingly subject to humanity's unconstrained domination and modification because it can have no meaning or purpose that is not subordinate to human authority. This is pride, in the full meaning of the traditional teachings. It is no longer an anomaly, but the normal expression of the modern worldview. This pride could be represented as the modern disenchantment with the world or its transformation from an enchanted garden into a human building site, in Max Weber's view, or as the death of the "real world," in the view of Friedrich Nietzsche. As Hannah Arendt puts it:

> Meanwhile, in increasingly strident voices, the few defenders of metaphysics have warned us of the danger of nihilism inherent in this development; and although they themselves seldom invoke it, they have an important argument in their favor: it is indeed true that once the supersensual realm is discarded, its opposite, the world of appearances as understood for so many centuries, is also annihilated. The sensual, as still understood by the positivists, cannot survive the death of the supersensual. No one knew this better than Nietzsche who, with his poetic and metaphoric description of the assassination of God in Zarathustra, has caused so much confusion in these matters. In a significant passage in *The Twilight of the Idols*, he clarifies what the word God meant in Zarathustra. It was merely a symbol of the supersensual realm as understood by metaphysics: he now uses instead of God the word true world and says: "We have abolished the true world. What has remained? The apparent one perhaps? Oh, no! With the true world we have also abolished the apparent one."[3]

If the predominant modern interpretations of tolerance are seen in this light, it is evident that pride—the unconstrained aggrandizement of the self by emphasizing its sufficiency for the attainment of its supreme potential—is its essential component. There can be no understanding of modern tolerance without understanding pride. This is a predictable outcome of the very nature of evolutionary anthropology. From the perspective of tradition, in all the forms that we in the West now know principally as Judaism, Christianity, and Islam, anthropology proceeds in the reverse order. The human individual is not itself the root, but a symbol of the supreme, to which it is open in its interiority. Humility in the face of the Perfect Self is humanity's way of freeing the self from the illusion of independence. It is only through humility, in all its many manifestations such as repentance, prayer, service, servitude, contrition, abstention, forgiveness, and so on, that the self opens itself to the diversity that is evidence of the unity and unicity of the Logos, the first confirmation of the Ineffable. There is nothing in the outer or inner worlds toward which humanity has reason to be arrogant, for everything is a sign of the only and perfect magnitude. All symbols are thus translatable into God. Tolerance is the inevitable mode of existence that derives from humility before the perfect Self, which says that there is no truth but the Truth.

These two faces of tolerance—one deriving from pride as the natural expression of the modern concept of the autonomy of the self, and the other from the self as a symbol or evidence of the Divine Self—are described by the following two verses (though the same message occurs in several other texts): "I shall turn from My signs those who wax proud in the earth unjustly; though they see every sign, they will not believe in it, and though they see the way of rectitude, they will not take it for a way, and though they see the way of error, they will take it for a way."[4] And the converse: "Is it not time that the hearts of those who believe should be humbled to the Remembrance of God and the Truth which He has sent down?"[5]

It is clear that the experience of the modern world, with all its fragility and the destruction and suffering that results from it, demands not pride but epistemic modesty, that is, abstention from pride. But even though many other and well-founded weighty reasons may be found for it, this abstention can only be principled, and consequently tolerance itself can only be principled, through active and unimpeded humility before the truth as one and great. The speech of the truth is then transmissible from every form, and tolerance of diversity is free from relativism and nihilism, though wholly imbued with the epistemic humility that maintains its connection with Knowledge.

This, however, raises the question of the self and authority. In every individual self there inheres every other self. The more fully aware it is, the greater the degree of its sameness with the "I in we and we in I." (In the Semitic revelations, this is indicated by the voicing of the Absolute I as "We.") This testifies to its openness to every potential in the contingent world, without its uncreated and uncreatable center ever being nullified. In the chain that links the worlds, tradition, bowing in prayer, and remembrance, there is an invariant thread that unites the entire multiplicity. Seen in and from the human individual, this is remembrance. It can never entirely fade away from either body or soul; and it is the only means of enabling liberation from enslavement to the contingent and finite and of restoring an outlook toward the absolute and infinite. Then, through remembrance, the self sees itself as the locus and subject of cognition that leads to the oneness of the knower and the known. "He who knows himself knows the Lord," said the Prophet. This knowledge of the self is total openness toward all human potentials, and it comprises the "we" of all individualities.

The greater the focus on remembrance, the greater the degree of unity. But the absolute is the Mystery confirmed by the unicity of being, and unicity manifests and confirms unbounded multiplicity. The Absolute I is thus equally present in the Mystery, in unicity and in multiplicity. To pray to that absolute is to address it out of a freedom without limit. But as long as there is prayer, there also abides within the self the entirety of human potential: "Guide us in the straight path, the path of those whom Thou has blessed, not of those against whom Thou art wrathful, nor of those who are astray."[6] It is the human individual that speaks that prayerful openness, expressing the openness not only for itself alone, but for all people.

Converse to the straight path, the upright path in which primal human perfection, or the "fairest stature," is actualized, there is the inverse direction, that of distancing from the first principle and decline into ever deeper oblivion. Movements from the conditional toward the absolute, and vice versa, are actualized on this path with its two opposite directions. Here, the vertical, the upright, enables one level of existence to dissolve, overflow, and spread out over every plane from the center of the human heart. When it becomes so oblivious of this level of existence that it is sundered from the center, and thus from the vertical that joins all the worlds, the human individual goes astray. Its mind is then able to measure and quantify with ever-greater accuracy but will never be able to attain the absolute. This is the state of unappeasable reason that, as it seems to the individual, is capable of everything except being at rest. To exist in these terms is to be perpetually in a darkness lit by the occasional flashes that the presence of Intellect imparts to every human condition. In being freed by the initiation into the upright path from its conditional freedom, the self as I in the self as we, or individuality in plurality, confirms the immanent and irrevocable presence of *confidence* as the bond that unites all people. This is the meaning of the shared exclamation "Amen!" that follows prayers and many utterances in the Psalms.

To the modern mental world, the signs in the outer world and the inner human self have ceased to proclaim the truth as the infinite and incomparable first principle of all that is. The quantifiable and calculable world is the sole stage of rationalization and intellectualization. This does not, however, denote an upsurge in general awareness of the real conditions of life, nor, to put it differently, does it mean that the answer to the question of meaning, purpose, and value is any closer. As Max Weber explains:

> It means something else, namely, the knowledge or belief that if one but wished one *could* learn it at any time. Hence, it means that principally there are no mysterious incalculable forces that come into play, but rather that one can, in principle, master all things by calculation. This means that the world is disenchanted.[7]

The consequence of this disenchantment is to sever the connection between the human individual and the perfection of its beginning and purpose, thereby reducing the individual to just some of the elements that comprise the totality of its being. As Huston Smith notes, "Values, like meanings, purposes and qualities slip through science like sea slips through the nets of fishermen. Yet man swims in this sea, so he cannot exclude it from his purview."[8]

Nor is this all. The individual is always there with its desire for the absolute. All the signs in the outer world and the inner selves are a response to the absolute only if they are transparent, if they cease to conceal Unicity. And speech about Unicity, also known in the Gnostic traditions as the "Breath of the Most Merciful," bears witness to the Ineffable. Were it not so, the world and all that is within it would be wholly self-contained, an end in itself, none other than a dungeon. The actualization of desire is thus focused beyond any boundaries. The proponents of desire may turn their gaze toward any sign, but, without a channel to the absolute, nothing they can find there can respond to the individual's aspiration to perfection.

The self lies in the consummation of speech of the outer world and that alone. Thus it is that abstention from speech is a prerequisite for the discovery of what has been said to it. If the human individual does not recognize in its purpose all that lies within the outer horizons and the inner selves, it is condemned to see it as unfulfilled. But if the individual can discern in all this the confirmation of what makes up the individual's deepest nature, the diversities around it must be translatable into that desire for perfection. And because the maintenance and establishment of the link with perfection are the essence of every religion, tolerance of different meanings, symbols, and languages is also its deepest substance. Although its own path is sufficient to the individual, even when it is not competent to translate into its own language the meanings and symbols of the Other, the individual must acknowledge the primal, principled validity of that Other. Rare are those who are able to translate different religious languages, but however narrow the confinement within the meanings, symbols, and language of a single tradition, translation is the essence of seeing through phenomena toward their supreme principle. The individual does not exist that can say it has freed itself from dependence on this need to see through phenomena. If that were possible, Peace, too, as the Ineffable, would be expressed in the world, and would no longer be the goal of human desire. It can thus be said of tolerance as an attitude toward diversity that it is essentially indivisible from religious intellectuality. With the atrophy of religious intellectuality, tolerance also ebbs away, metamorphosing into a balance of quantity and power.

This is true as well of the modern concept of the autonomous self, which is quantifiable and, in principle, mutable. In this model, life ceases to be disclosure of and actualization in primal perfection. The incomplete wishes to construct its perfection: existence itself, as a result, shifts from its essence toward conjectural and speculative images of humanity and the world. Confining itself to a space between earth and heaven, or between body and Spirit, the human individual becomes caught between boundaries that it cannot transcend. Within this confinement, it must turn to false gods, attributing to extant and conjectural phenomena that which they are not and which they will finally renounce.

6. The Dispute over Names

Muslims, Christians, and Jews have all contributed to the formation of Bosnia's complex identity in its historical entirety. It is from these religious affiliations that her diverse political and national identities have been drawn during the modern era. Thus today's Bosniacs are linked historically with Islam, Bosnian Serbs with Eastern Orthodoxy, and Bosnian Croats with Roman Catholicism. These religious components were an element in the formation of their distinct political and ethnonational identities, accompanied by the shifts in the role and understanding of religion that have been taking place ever since the Renaissance and that continue to this day. That totality of religious, national, and political identities covers a spectrum of affiliation from the ideological to diverse traditional forms, frequently intermingled, often blending and interchanging. An entire typology of the use of religion and religious language in the justification of modern concepts of tolerance and intolerance may be deduced from this fact. Here the focus is on the religious perspective of this issue, but its premises lie in the traditional approach, which is essentially different from the modern.

In any religious community, whether or not it is subordinate to an ethnonational or political ideology, two possible modes of affiliation are discernible. In the first, language, meaning, and symbol determine identity without being divorced from their authentic, primal tradition. Diversity and mutability in language, meanings, and symbols do not preclude an individual contact with the perennial unicity and its living content. In the case of Islam, Christianity, and Judaism, there is accord on the Unicity of God, the Last Judgment, and good deeds as the confirmation of belief in the first two principles. Humankind's consummation is subordinate, therefore, only to God's Unicity and to nothing else, for there is no truth other than the Truth, no reality other than Reality.[1] This alone is the first and last determinant of the destiny of all things. Its rejection takes the form of denial, hypocrisy, and associationism.[2] Every manifestation—whether it be passion or idea, individual, group, or structure, or anything else—is taken for God whenever it is deprived of its full dependence on the ineffable and supreme Reality. Manifestations themselves are then taken as gods, and this becomes an act of association with God or idol worship. In the case of Islam, Christianity, and Judaism, this is the greatest possible sin because it involves a denial that human nature is created in perfection and for perfection's sake. Denial of this kind is at the core of the dis-enchantment with and de-sanctification of the world, for it is then reduced to a perspective in which there is nothing other than contingency and mutability.

Neither witnessing nor repudiation of the Divine Unicity, as the first principle of Being, extinguishes uncertainty. Evil and disorder are ineradicable facets of existence. They are to good and peace as is darkness to light. By the very fact of their creation, phenomena are incomplete, and dependent on the Creator. Only with Him—in that they begin with Him and to Him they return—are they endowed with perfection. The supreme mode of human recognition of that plenitude lies in humility and generosity, with all their doctrinal and ritual elements, including testifying to unicity, prayer, abstention, purification, and focusing on the Center. Furthermore, this mode demands that the apparently proximate and dependable be made real, distant, and uncertain, and that the transcendent be made proximate. It is impossible to turn to God without affirming the uncertainty of all other than Him. Although no mode of submission eliminates fear or uncertainty, human submission to God relocates the source of fear and uncertainty from every phenomenon in the horizons and the inner selves, the macrocosm and the microcosm, to the transcendental unicity. In the language of the Qur'an, this is the "refuge with the Lord of the Daybreak from the evil of what He has created, from the evil of darkness when it gathers, from the evil of women who blow on knots, from the evil of an envier when he envies."[3] These forms of evil have substance and manifestation in immanence but never have mastery over the Lord of the Daybreak, Who alone is Absolute Certainty. There is thus no certainty without the

Certainty. To accept this means testifying to certainty in uncertainty. Only thus does the self include itself in the totality of being; this is its mode of witnessing and affirming itself in firstness and lastness. Imam 'Ali, too, notes this uncertainty and its concomitant fragility: "How wonderful is man that he sees with fat, talks with a piece of flesh, hears with a bone and breathes through a hole."[4]

This is merely a different expression of the truth about the human individual delineated in the paradox of exaltation in submission: "We indeed created Man in the fairest stature then We restored him the lowest of the low"; and "Recite: In the Name of thy Lord who created, created Man of a blood-clot."[5] Fragility and uncertainty lie in opposition to the present moment and death: in this relationship lies the reality of being.

But if the phenomena in the outer worlds (all that is created) and in the inner human selves (the gathering darkness, the women who blow on knots, and the envier) become disunited from the first principle of the Daybreak, the other possibility for overcoming uncertainty offers itself. Instead of distinguishing between the unreal and the Real, the individual adopts one of its conceptual images as the real, adheres to it and appeals to it. For this, the individual needs coercion, for the image alone is insufficient. But this is a mere delusion of power, constructed by the self in its distortedness: once verticality and horizontality, or the individual's understanding of itself in relation to God and to the world, are transformed into mere spatial and temporal presence without the vertical link with God, humility, and submission lose their meaning, and the delusion of power takes their place. Such conceptual images are always fundamentally erroneous, and the error can find no remedy in thought. Everything that is derived in this way cannot but be discordant with Reality and, as such, in opposition to God. The self, with its potential for thought, aggrandizes itself over the world, and in so doing repudiates all that is above it. The world and the self thus become, in principle, equal and separate. The other becomes, inexplicably, the essence both of itself and of the world. The self persuades itself of its potential to change the world by force so as to reshape its uncertainty into certainty. But this, too, is mere delusion, the delusion of certainty, in which either God is denied, or some phenomenon or delusion is associated with Him. The self then becomes ruled by its passions: they become gods, the motivation of humanity, with their continual exacerbation of divisions and antagonisms.

These two outlooks are differently reflected in language. If we accept that all being descends from God, as Absolute Certainty, toward humanity, as absolute uncertainty, the self is not the master of language—rather, language is our attendant. Language speaks; we begin to speak only after we have heard; in so doing, we respond to silence, a potential that lies in the language that we receive. But what we receive neither derives from nor is constructed by our own, self-sufficient potential. The Logos or the Divine "Be!"[6] is the first principle of every language and of all languages as a whole. The delusion of certainty imposes human action based on the illusion that we are the trustees and masters of language. This notion is contrary to the postulate that the Truth can be revealed in every language and that each language individually and all languages as a whole derive from the ineffable Unicity.

Direct and unconscious affiliation to a religious form, whatever it may be, does not automatically mean accepting and testifying to the perennial content of the tradition: this lies only in the individual relationship between humanity and God, which includes both awareness and being. From the religious perspective, the nature of that relationship determines the individual's ultimate attainment. The myriad particularities in the outer world all reflect the names of God. Orientation toward Reality, which is higher and greater than all phenomena individually and combined, means knowing that the names of God are revealed in all that lies in the outer world and the inner self: "To God belong the Names Most Beautiful; so call Him by them, and leave those who blaspheme His Names—they shall assuredly be recompensed for the things they did."[7] The denial of God's Unicity, by contrast, manifests itself in the use of His names for invective, which leads to distortions of notions such as justice and good deeds. Life, with all its languages, meanings, and symbols, becomes thereby transmuted into subjugation to phantasms that touch neither its source nor purpose: "If you call upon them, they will not hear your prayer, and if they heard, they would not answer you; and on the Day of Resurrection they will disown your partnership."[8] Because the world and humanity alike are created with a purpose, this separation between the primal nature of phenomena and their names is none other than a distortion of the self. In the final account, however, that separation will cease to be, for then every self will return to God: thus only primal perfection and the justice of the last judgment will enable the present moment to be mastered.

We encounter in the Qur'an both condemnation and praise of Jews and Christians. It is worth examining the reasons for each of these, so as to see the source of tolerance as lying at the very heart of the tradition. In the Qur'an, it is clearly stated: "Surely they that believe, and those of Jewry, and the Christians, and those Sabaeans, whoso believes in God and the Last Day, and works righteousness—their wage awaits them with their Lord, and no fear shall be on them, neither shall they sorrow."[9] From such a perspective, the position of each of us depends upon our belief in God and the Day of Judgment, and our affirmation of this in doing good deeds. The Qur'an's praise of the Jews is based on the recognition of this fact: "Of the people of Moses there is a nation who guide by the truth, and by it act with justice."[10] Or again: "and We provided them with good things, and We preferred them above all beings. We gave them clear signs of the Command, so they differed not, except after the knowledge had come to them, being insolent one to another."[11] Here "differ" refers to the divergence between those who show steadfast adherence to the essential and eternal elements of the tradition—faith in God and the Day of Judgment, and working righteousness—and those who show dissension, hypocrisy, or indifference, which are forms of adherence to gods without God. Both attitudes are possible among all peoples, Jews, Christians, and Muslims alike, and both praise and condemnation, respectively, relate equally to peoples of all three sacred traditions. Thus the Divine Unicity is announced by all God's messengers, but, in every generation, their followers may accept or repudiate, bear witness or dissimulate, transmit or misrepresent it. As a result, Muslims, Christians, and Jews maintain their link with Unicity through their language, meanings, and symbols, and see and hear the voice of Peace in the signs that lie in the outer world and the inner self. On the other hand, those Muslims, Christians, and Jews who, to outward appearances, use the same language, meanings, and symbols, but without any connection to Unicity, are complicit in the use of "His names as invective," which is an aspect of "taking gods other than God."

Humanity depends upon the Divine Unicity, and not vice versa. We are evidence of Unicity, but are not Unicity Itself. To be in submission and humility before Unicity is to draw nearer to It, and opposition means distancing oneself from Unicity and a distortion of primal human nature. The true names of phenomena speak the ineffable name. But whenever they are disunited from it, the names of phenomena aid the transmutation of the world into phantasms, into a place characterized by irreconcilable conflicts between names.

Although the immanent meaning of names is intelligible in all forms of traditional wisdom, they appear incomprehensible and, what is still worse, naive in the language of modernity. Names and their sacrosanct unity are both present in and absent from phenomena: as such, they express the oneness of being, which in the case of humanity is manifest as the truth, the way, and virtue. The hierarchy of modernism, as a blueprint for civilization, embraces Immanuel Kant's extremes: "the starry heavens above us and the moral law within us." This hierarchy is restricted to the material world: it lacks the vertical dimension that the tradition speaks of: "In the Name of God, the Merciful, the Compassionate. Praise belongs to God, the Lord of all Being," to again quote the opening words of the Qur'an. This true totality of existence is another word for the signs or speech of the Divine Self, arrayed through all the levels of being, where He is the First and the Last, the Inward and the Outward. These levels were created as the seven heavens, of which the lower or closest is adorned with stars.[12] All existence, accordingly, is speech of the Truth or, to put it differently, praise of the Truth.

The outcome of denying that the "starry heavens above us and the moral law within us" must be seen as that which praises is the notion of the autonomy of the self. The founding postulate of the tradition—"We shall show them Our signs in the horizons and in themselves, till it is clear to them that it is the truth"—then loses its meaning, although, finally, these signs are the speech of the Truth, and there is nothing that has not been endowed with speech.[13] The distinction between tradition's preference for speech, where words are primarily and essentially symbols, and modernity's preference for numbers, where words are designators of quantity, then becomes greater still.

In the Kantian view, transcendence can be represented only as transcendental reason, although it retains its authoritative nature and sacred halo, encompassing the material expanse from the cosmic heights to the human depths. In this view, transcendence is quantifiable, and thus forms a closed system, a dead end: "Those that cry lies to Our signs and wax proud against them—the gates of heaven shall not be opened to them"; "And those who cry lies to Our signs We will draw them on little by little whence they know not."[14] At once disavowal and pride, this tells of the acceptance of the human self as self-referent; as a result, the manner in which the self is structured, instead of confirming the openness of speech of the truth, is reduced to the absolutization of immanence. In other words, the signs in the horizons and the selves are made into existence per se, for the truth that they announce is repudiated. This disavowal is the condition of modern knowledge of humanity and society, as Ralf Dahrendorf also asserted, some forty years after Weber's discourse on the "dis-enchantment" of the world:

> As long as sociologists interpret their task in moral terms, they must renounce the analysis of social reality; as soon as they strive for scientific insight, they must forgo their moral concern with the individual and his liberty. What makes the paradox of moral and alienated man so urgent is not that sociology has strayed from its proper task, but that it has become a true science. The former process would be reversible, but the latter leads to an inescapable question. Is man a social being whose behavior, being predetermined, is calculable and controllable? Or is he an autonomous individual, with some irreducible measure of freedom to act as he chooses?[15]

In our aspiration for perfection, we seek Opening, the progression from duality to unicity. In our orientation toward the infinite and incomparable, we then eternally face the end of night, the daybreak. No matter how enmeshed in the material world we may be, none of our states can be an orientation toward darkness or evil, for these do not partake of the nature of first principle, but are merely contingent manifestations of Light and the Good: "By the dawn and ten nights, by the even and the odd, by the night when it journeys on!"[16]

In this verse, unicity and duality correspond to the relationship between "dawn" and "the night when it journeys on," confirming that the Light is not visible without its contingent mode; in other words, the presence of darkness. But here "light" is also the first principle that surpasses its contingent other—or, as God's words testify in the sacred tradition: "My mercy has prevailed over My wrath."[17] Here "mercy," as with "light," is another name for unicity, which nevertheless manifests itself in a myriad of dualities: "Glory be to Him, who created all the pairs of what the earth produces, and of themselves, and of what they know not."[18]

Every human condition is darkness relieved by the light of dawn; a perpetual journeying on through night, for what is to come overrules every manifestation, every beginning and every end. The denser the darkness, the more visible and impressive the daybreak, the passing of the night. Might this not explain many aspects of the structuring of traditional knowledge in the present age? It appears that traditional knowledge has never so much as now been expressed in speech and books, although individual and collective being, and general global trends, are radically uncoupled from it. Here, all the about-faces and changes are not a cycle in the temporal and spatial sense, but clearly express the truth about two radically opposing views of God, the world, and humanity. The traditional outlook stresses the meaninglessness of a quantifiable world without an unquantifiable first principle, that is, without that infinity and eternity that are like nothing else, and are comparable to nothing else. In other words, no speech can have meaning without listening, just as phenomena can have no meaning without the truth that is within them and external to them.

Every duality is confirmed by an infinite series of other dualities; and as such, all dualities are, in principle, one, testifying to the unicity to which everything returns in order to confirm the Ineffable. God is everything's Other, and everything is as nothing before God, for "He is the First and the Last, the Outward and the Inward."[19] In Adam, we were originally higher than the angels, for God taught Adam, but not the angels, the names of everything.[20] Moreover, all the angels have to submit themselves to God; but the same is true only of "many of mankind."[21] We are accordingly defined both by an angelic submission to God and by a satanic refusal. In our submission, we are higher than Satan; in knowledge of the names of everything, we are higher than the angels. In our potential refusal to submit, however, we are with Satan and his nature. As beings of forgetfulness,[22] with our loss of the knowledge of the names of everything, we descended to the level of the angels, and indeed became lower than they. We are thus beings whose potentials lie between the original "fairest stature" and the "lowest of the low."[23] The human self is riven by this duality, but wholeness may be attained in the response to the commandment: "Not equal are the good deed and the evil deed. Repel with that which is fairer and behold, he between whom and thee there is enmity shall be as if he were a loyal friend."[24]

The key question of transforming enemy into friend, stranger into kin, also embraces individuals who are from different sides of the border between religious communities and sects. The potential to transform enemy into friend and stranger into kin presupposes a shared core within diverse religious languages. At the level of principle, it is an orientation to unicity as the supreme confirmation of the Ineffable. In the world of appearances, it is defined by the "Noahide laws," "natural religion," "following the revealed Book," and the like. One of the participants in the "Colloquium of the Seven about Secrets of the Sublime" says:

> Indeed as I view the almost infinite variety of sects, Christians differing with Ismaelites and pagans differing among themselves, no standard of truth seems more certain than right reason, that is, the supreme law of nature, planted in men's minds by immortal God, than which nothing more stable, nothing more ancient, nothing better can be made or even imagined. Moreover, with this law of nature and religion Abel, Seth, Enoch, Noah, Job, Abraham, Isaac and Jacob lived, and they reaped the highest praise of piety, integrity, and justice from the most awesome testimony of God eternal, the only One whom they worshipped.[25]

Although this is a recognizably Renaissance view, in it can be discerned the most significant elements of the modernist outlook as it has prevailed over the centuries since then. Here reason is elevated to the level of criterion and arbiter. But the question of the verdict on it remains salient, for reason itself originates from somewhere. Someone bestowed or created it, and that someone is higher and greater than reason. Thus the faith and judgment that transcend reason can also provide the answer to the question of how to free oneself from the idol of modernity—from the belief that humans are self-sufficient because we are endowed with reason. Without recognition of the transcendent, this idol cuts us off from the supraindividual and nonindividual truth that would otherwise resolve the inability of reason to recognize the cause and purpose of human existence.

If the Mystery reveals the Word, if It speaks, and yet remains one and the same reality, It is also the eternal listener. Its revelation incorporates its listening, Its name is at one and the same time its presence and its absence. It is dispersed in the multitude of phenomena as loci, and concentrated in the human individual. Both dispersion and concentration require translation through speech and listening. Every prophet is an example of the listening and speech initiated by him. When mutuality of listening and speech is achieved, the Praiser is manifested in the messenger as the reason and purpose of creation. Even though there may be many responses around the Praiser to the Divine command "Say!" they are invariably translatable through listening to the one and only Ineffable.

7. The Word Held in Common

Ten years after the Hegira from Mecca, Muslims and Christians held a debate in Medina, in the presence of the Jews, on the tradition and its different forms.[1] During the course of the debate, more than eighty verses of the third sura of the Qur'an were revealed, addressing the relations between different phenomena in the tradition. Here it was stressed that differences in language, meanings, symbols, and their related teachings do not mean disunion from the Word that is common to all these external forms. Disunion from the Word involves denial or indifference, hypocrisy or distortion; and equally, no tradition is free of the potential for such divergence. The core of the tradition is the contact with the Truth, and all temporal forms are its manifestations, but they become lifeless when they are disassociated from that living heart. In that disassociation everything, even the entire content of the tradition, risks becoming adherence to an absolute that is external to the Absolute, or to a god other than God. This is "association with God," which is an unforgivable human mode because it derives from a will that repudiates the Divine and an adherence that is determined by hatred for the Absolute Plenitude.[2] It demands that the openness of the inner human self to the Truth be transformed into the Truth itself, to which everything must be subordinate, whereas it is itself subordinate to nothing. This is a denial of submission; it is its transmutation into self-aggrandizement. The order of things from God, as the highest and greatest, to humankind, whose realization lies in humility, has become inverted into an illusion of progress from nullity to human reason as the consummate good; and humankind has transformed itself from the image of God into an actual god.

Given its consequences for the human self and the world that is subordinate to humankind, such associationism is unforgivable: "God forgives not that aught should be with Him associated; less than that He forgives to whomsoever He will."[3] The most malignant form of associationism is the promotion of individual religious languages, meanings, and symbols, and of the structures connected with them, as the center of affiliation, accompanied by the relativization or forgetting of Unicity and the need for submission to it. Thus even speaking against associationism with God is turned into a god, absolutizing even the understanding and conduct that declares an orientation toward the Truth. In the modern era, such relationships reduce the tradition to ideology, in which the sacredness of the Supreme as the source of reality or the state of Being becomes lost. Therein lies the paradox of the modern secularization of religion. In an Enlightenment understanding of the self as perfectible, language is rooted solely in reason: it derives from the brain as its material source. In the traditional image, by contrast, the heart is the contact between the self and the Intellect/Spirit; the revealed Word is "brought down by the Faithful Spirit upon thy heart,"[4] and thus all its forms of existence in reason and the material world are but the reflections of this bond with the Intellect/Spirit. These interpretations lead to two understandings of the self: either as sealed and self-referent or as open.

Associationism is a denial of Divine Unicity, and is thus an impediment to humankind's unshackling from all that does not bear witness that there is no god but God, that is, from falsehood. In an associationist view, the human self is determined at birth, and reason locates the spatial and temporal origins of the self in one's parents. The worlds are thus reduced to the scope of reason, and origins are reduced to birth. And if one's parents are seen as the decisive determinants of the self, the parental connection is seen as the most important element in the shaping of the individual and society. From this, in turn, derives subservience to one's elders, obedience to the clan, the power of the tribe, and the like. There is a clear connection between subservience to one's parents and violence against one's children. Holy doctrine, by contrast, points to the need to distinguish between emotional and rational links, on the one hand, and submission to reality, on the other, for absolute submission to one's parents is also associationism with God. But the human freedom that is attained by the connection with Unicity through humility, the traditions teach us, is neither contingent nor limited. "Say: 'Come, I will recite what your Lord has forbidden you: that you associate not anything with Him, and to be good to your parents, and not to slay your children because of poverty; We will provide you and them; and that you approach not any indecency outward or inward.'"[5] The conduct we are called on to display toward our parents is that we be good, which is very different from being subservient to them; for only the nonindividual and supraindividual truth merits human submission. Faith in God and the Day of Judgment cannot be subordinate to parentage or to anything else; what is due to parentage is that which is "good and fine."

In the verses sent down during the debate between Muslims, Christians, and Jews, the Revelation appears to provide the founding principle of discourse and tolerance between the adherents of different forms of the tradition: "Say: 'People of the Book! Come now to a word common between us and you, that we serve none but God, and that we associate not aught with Him, and do not some of us take others as Lords, apart from God.'"[6]

As followers of the Book, participants in the debate proceed from the standpoint that this is the Truth. But they also testify to the existence of others with the same conviction: if they lack that conviction, in principle, they may repudiate those lacking the conviction, for that which does not attend to the Truth is falsehood. But if challenged to affirm their conviction by actually execrating those who seem to be in the wrong and who are participating in the debate, they will soon perceive, the more they become engrossed in the debate, that no individual can ever possess the Truth in its entirety. The answer to this conundrum is that every phenomenon in the world, which includes the different traditions, may be simultaneously not only diversity and plurality but also the Truth that testifies to the one and the same Word. Because they differ one from another and yet all have the same view of the absoluteness of what they adhere to, these differences call for a principled concord: that what they have is *from* God, but that none of them can say that it *is* God; nor can they ever know that it is, for if they were to accept it as absolute, they would be associating some other reality to that of God. All that they have are signs that point toward the one and the same God; and their debate can assist them in seeing and comprehending this more clearly. It is nothing to be wondered at, therefore, that the 1463 Letter of Covenant on which the Muslim Sultan and the Christian friar reached agreement should have had as its model the similar invitation and reply from the year 10 A.H.:

> The protection of God and the surety of the Prophet Muhammad, messenger of God, encompasses Najran and its surroundings, which is to say its wealth, its people, the performance of their rituals, those of theirs who are absent and those who are present, their families, their shrines, and all, great and small, that they possess. No bishop shall be displaced from his episcopal seat, nor any monk from his monastery, nor any priest from his parish.[7]

In both instances the covenant lays an obligation upon the more powerful to adhere to the principle of tolerance and commits them to the contractual protection of the weaker. The warrant for the obligation between them is their joint "witness to the Fairest stature" or submission to God. Indeed, any oath of mutual fealty between people is an oath of fealty to God, an oath based on the "Word held in common."[8]

In the Semitic traditions, God is that Common Word. But this also touches on the issue of the Name and the Names. In God's Name all is subsumed, and thus His is the Name that cannot be spoken. Hence the Name is absolutely open to all Names, but is also indefinable: "Say: 'Call upon God, or call upon the Merciful; whichsoever you call upon, to Him belong the Names Most Beautiful.'"[9] And therefore the Word must be held in common, given that everything has been given speech, and given the plurality and diversity of languages,[10] and the oneness of the Truth that they reveal. The diversity of beings and their languages cannot limit the Truth, which means that the openness or attunement to the Truth is available to every human being. The external forms speech and listening differ, but their uncreated and uncreatable center, to which primal human nature is attuned, remains the same: "So set thy face to the religion, a man of pure faith—God's original upon which He originated mankind. There is no changing God's creation. That is the right religion; but most men know it not—turning to Him."[11]

Thus the enduringness of the tradition is defined by the Word held in common, which is exhausted neither by the speech of all creation nor by the diversity of all its languages. The Word testifies to the perfect origin and purpose of human creation. It is a turning to the Truth, it is the remembrance by which the Self summons Its image: "So remember Me, and I will remember you."[12]

The tradition comes from God, who is the Truth. In the world of appearances, it is confirmed by the submission of all things: "What, do they desire another religion than God's, and to Him has surrendered whoso is in the heavens and the earth, willingly or unwillingly, and to Him they shall be returned?"[13]

Turning to that primal submission is the condition for love, which is the sense of the beauty of phenomena and the recognition that the signs in the horizons and the inner selves speak only the Truth. Virtue is submission to the Truth, which manifests itself in mercy and clemency, generosity and humility. But none of us can judge ourself to be better than another, for we would then promote ourself, that is, our self, to the level of absolute arbiter, and thus turn it into an association with God. Whatever the understandings and interpretations of the tradition, if its symbols, language, and meanings lose their link with the Truth, they turn the way into a truth in itself. But a way without the Truth is an idol, through which the self loses its clemency and mercy, its humility and generosity.

The central issue for the followers of Judaism, Christianity, and Islam, therefore, is that of the Word held in common and the center that makes them into different manifestations of the perennial tradition. Their essence is the Truth that has manifested itself throughout the past, in diverse languages and forms but always one and the same, and recognizable as such. And as it lies in every present moment, every "now," it is thus a condition for the actualization of every self.

The modern dis-enchantment and de-sacralization of the world have given rise to an unexpected rediscovery of the tradition. This is a miraculous response from the heavens, as the poet Martin Lings senses in his poem "Autumn":

> For though all seem lost, yet All is found
> In the Last who is the First. Faithful pageant,
> Not amiss is thy mime, for manifest in thee
> Omega is an archway where Alpha stands framed,
> The First who comes Last, for likewise art though
> The season of seeds, O season of fruits.[14]

Each of us is born biologically feeble, but we remain one and the same from beginning to end. Our upbringing as the "image of God" in the "fairest stature" stems from our Creator. The actualization of this lies in our particular tradition, through which the Truth gives us a way that suits the totality of our self. Yet, whatever our path, our human integrality lies in submission, loving, and learning, a triad that forms the essence of every tradition, all of which are grounded in submission as the pinnacle of freedom.

In the depiction of the tradition given in the famous questioning of the Prophet by the angel Gabriel, the hierarchy is defined as submission (love or fear), faith, and love. These last two degrees, faith (*iman*) and love (*ihsan*), manifest themselves differently, however, in different interpretations: at times one takes precedence, at times the other. In Protestantism, faith is promoted to first place, whereas, in Catholicism, the first place belongs to love. The interchangeability of these two places, in the depiction of the tradition, indicates the inevitability of love's being known and knowledge loved. Two ways of actualization derive from this: in the first, knowledge is attained through love, and in the second, love through knowledge. Jalaluddin Rumi is an example of the first, and Muhyiddin ibn 'Arabi of the second.

Faith (*iman*) is a prolongation or extension of knowledge. Without that knowledge, there can be no faith. But for that extension to be sustainable in human memory, it must manifest itself in beauty, that is, in the expression of the eternal in the world of motion and multiplicity. The attraction of beauty lies in this link with the essence of the world and its phenomena, where inwardness and outwardness are joined through faith. This is why faith and love are so close: faith confirms the potential to see the infinite in every finitude and the eternal in every present moment, whereas love is the yearning to achieve unification by this means. Nothing is hermetically closed to knowledge; but the openness to Absolute Plenitude through which knowledge continually changes as it draws closer to its goal, manifests itself as the "sacred halo" of manifestations, that is, as the presence of infinity and eternity in worldly phenomena. For this reason, faith (*iman*) can be interpreted through love and vice versa.

Nor is this all. Our primal human fragility, our beginning from a mere clot and returning to it through the ultimate subjection in death, is the confirmation of a first principle that belies the illusion of human strength and power. This fragility confirms that "there is no strength or power but in God." Promoting the illusion of human power thus implies seeing God as finite, or rejecting Him—in other words, tearing the "sacred halo" of eternity from phenomena, and reducing them to mere quantifiability, without their original and final purpose, their absolute values in terms of the Truth. And knowledge that deals with phenomena seen in such a light must therefore abjure all its higher values and purposes, reducing itself to a mere set of processes. Similarly, the Word held in common, which is ever one and the same, cannot have mastery over all phenomena, including humankind, if, instead of the Unicity to which the signs in the inner selves and the outer horizons should testify, we accept the illusion that phenomena may be self-sufficient. Self-sufficiency makes every language untranslatable into the Common Word, which ceases to be language's master. And thus there arises in humans the delusion that we are the masters of language, and meanwhile we forget that language is the evidence and revelation of the Mystery or the Ineffable. This Word held in common is one, but only through it may speech be translated, for all that it contains takes a multitude of shapes:

> Any model of communication is at the same time a model of trans-lation, of a vertical or horizontal transfer of significance. No two historical epochs, no two social classes, no two localities use words and syntax to signify exactly the same things, to send identical signals of valuation and inference. Neither do two human beings. Each living person draws, deliberately or in immediate habit, on two sources of linguistic supply: the current vulgate corresponding to his level of literacy, and a private thesaurus. The latter is inextricably a part of his subconscious, of his memories so far as they may be verbalized, and of the singular, irreducibly specific ensemble of his somatic and psychological identity.[15]

This is because each person is open toward Transcendence. The root of language is not in the person, but in that openness and its purpose, and thus the Intellect itself gives inner life to language. Only thus can language, which belongs to the world of quantifiable relations, remain in contact with the Logos or the Common Word. Although the ways in which the tradition manifests itself are innumerable, the Common Word is the inexhaustible wellspring of all these differences: they confirm the Common Word, and it confirms them as speech of the One Truth. It is only through the Common Word that languages are translatable into each other, and that every human individual can in principle have confidence in every other. The disassociation of language from the Word held in common and of people from the transcendent God reduces humankind, society, and the world to a closed system in which the limited is the arbiter of the incomplete, while representing the incomplete as the Truth.

The past two centuries provide a mass of examples of this restricted form of judgment that represents itself as absolute. This has resulted in a sharper disjunction between the advocates of the two outlooks—the traditional and the modern. To the modern mind-set, in today's era, traditional philosophers or sages are hard to countenance. And yet, in recent decades, many askers of intellectual questions have been drawn, suddenly and unexpectedly, to the tradition. It appears that this is becoming more explicit with the retreat of modern paganism, as symbolized by the Qur'anic motif of dawn and the passing of the night. For most followers of modernism, the postulate "Cogito, ergo sum" has divorced tradition from its living source, and tradition has become incomprehensible and redundant. But for a growing minority it is linked with the perennial wisdom that lies at the center of every religion: *Sophia*, the most sublime achievement of human life. With *Sophia*, the unity in the diversity of life becomes clear, and responsibility to the Truth in humility and clemency toward every being becomes visible. This is the virtue that bears witness to the way and the Truth; this is the way that leads to the oneness of being and knowledge.

Doing that which is beautiful and good is the expression of the harmony of being and knowledge known as clemency. The following Qur'anic verses point to this link:

> And vie with one another, hastening to forgiveness from your Lord, and to a garden whose breadth is as the heavens and earth, prepared for the godfearing who expend in prosperity and adversity in almsgiving, and restrain their rage, and pardon the offences of their fellowmen; and God loves the good-doers.[16]

Those who are always willing to assist the poor, who are slow to anger and revenge, and who forgive injury, are the embodiment of the virtue of clemency. The reasons that make them so in the world of diversity derive from the Word common to all speech and every language, the Word that is attained by pure intellect, in a fusion of love and knowledge. In sensing absolute beauty, in conformity to our primal human nature, we are beings of love.

Submission has five degrees—affirmation of that which is heard, prostration before the Absolute, self-purification by giving, restraint from taking, and turning to the center of existence so that the self may direct itself through the center toward the Absolute. As submission, this is also hearing.[17] Its correlate is listening, which involves a physical response and inspires listeners to conduct themselves according to the desire of the Speaker. And the speech is the revelation, the teaching by which humankind's original purity is reestablished. In fact, there is no tradition without submission. The sacred tradition returns humankind wholly to God. Examples of this are the prophets and messengers of God: their nature is identical with that which they heard, and to which they submitted; their praise derives from their fidelity to what they heard, and orients them toward the Word and its Speaker; and their response, through their submission to the heard, confirms the expectation that God will hear the one who praises Him. The core of this listening and submission is summed up in the command of the Decalogue: "Bind them upon thy fingers, write them upon the table of thine heart."[18] The distribution of the Ten Commandments on the five fingers of the right hand and the five fingers of the left, and upon the upper and lower tables of the heart, signifies their sequence from higher to lower. The upper table of the heart is the domain of the higher potential of the self, of Intellect, corresponding to the commandments of the first tablet, namely, those concerned with prayer to God; the lower table relates to the lower part of the self and instructs us how to control anger, abstain from passion, master our desires, and guard our mind, eyes, and hands from the property of others.

Our original human nature was in harmony with submissiveness. With the fall, however, it was obscured. The Decalogue is a sign of God's mercy to us as fallen beings, an offer to renew the original light of our human self. On this, Muslims, Christians, and Jews agree. Differences in their attitudes to the Decalogue may thus be regarded as different languages speaking that which is one and the same.

8. Wealth in Poverty

The only way toward Reality lies in humility and generosity. The greater the humility and generosity are, the greater the remembrance of God or the openness of the self to God. This does not mean that suffering and death can be avoided or disregarded, but that their role is different, and the attitude toward them more direct and active. They are inevitable in the appearance of the world but cannot be resolved there. For this, distance from the world and infinite closeness to God are needed. Conversely, the notion of their immanent resolution or the reduction of transcendent Perfection to the terrestrial order demands, above all, an image of humankind, society, and the world in which some of its essential attributes are disarranged or restructured. Distortions or fundamental flaws of this nature can readily be found in any modernist program aimed at changing humankind and the world. Given their salience, and the fragility of any edifice constructed on such foundations, their root causes must be sought in spiritual divisions and tensions. Here the attitude toward the real is radically disturbed by the exclusion of the elemental essence of reality. The reason for this lies in the hegemony of the will to power over humility and submission to the entirety of Being. But whatever form that will to power may take, Being remains what it is—and is the only true power. Human arrogance and pride cannot enable us to transcend the boundaries that define us humans. It is impossible to rule over Being, though programs that are a priori founded upon error give the illusion that it is possible. And out of this there emerges an illusory satisfaction.

Affirmation of human pride in a world in which reason is supreme, on the one hand, and rejection of humility as the testimony and means of attaining the eternally and ubiquitously present truth, on the other, also find expression in the modern attempt to promote human life to the dominator of the world. Tradition, by contrast, demands acquiescence, which evinces the cosmos as the revelation of the Word. God reveals Himself through His names: "To God belong the Names Most Beautiful."[1] For He is Beautiful and loves beauty.[2] They are all comprised in Him as Peace.[3] The active stance toward Peace (*al-salam*), as the natural, absolute, and only goal of the self, is thus humility or acquiescence (*al-islam*), a stance that repudiates all that is not linked with Peace, as the source and confluence. All that does not support the orientation toward that perfect Peace can be seen as associationism with God, which may take the form of human passion: "Hast thou seen him who has taken his caprice to be his god?" or the memory of one's forefathers, which in the broadest sense can mean the worship of one's ancestors and one's nation, may become a substitute for the remembrance of God.[4] Taking one's ancestral roots, which can also mean ethnonational ideologies, as the determinants of the final source and consequence of human destiny, also implies seeing one's descendants as wholly under the rule of their parents—as told in the verse on nonassociationism, doing good to one's parents and not killing one's children because of poverty.[5]

Seeing poverty as a reason for violence is also an element in the inversion of the hierarchy from the higher toward the lower into one from the lower to the higher. Poverty is primal human nature, and thus its acceptance implies human actualization in the relationship toward God: "God is the All-sufficient; you are the needy ones."[6] But in the reversal of the natural order, poverty is a source of violence. No situation that results from a hierarchy in which the human being is the highest point of existence and of the world can be considered as sufficiency: it can only be poverty, which in the absence of God cannot be resolved without the denial of and violence against others. And yet human poverty in relation to God implies human acquiescence to God. When the hierarchy is not inverted, poverty reveals the boundless wealth of the uncreated and uncreating human center instilled in it by God. Indeed, only in the acceptance of poverty as the elemental human position, through which our original and final Perfection is consummated—

which also means the rejection of all gods other than God—are all forms of violence and distortions of human nature banished.

From this perspective, the acceptance of the other, regardless of the other's situation, becomes an element of the universal poverty before God's mercy, for everyone is poor before the Truth. Because Truth is the arbiter for every individual, each of us is closer to the Truth when we deny ourself the right to pass judgment on others. Thus programs that, though intended to establish perfection and peace on earth, are rooted in the will to power, deny the real nature of humankind, society, and the world, no matter how far they provide their "creators" and adherents with an illusory satisfaction. Nor can the sought-after power be achieved anyway, for Reality cannot be reduced to any one of its interpretations.

The question of the source of such needs and expected gain cannot be answered without addressing the rifts and tensions within the inner self, as Eric Voegelin notes:

> It would appear that this gain consists in a stronger certainty about the meaning of human existence, in a new knowledge of the future that lies before us, and in the creation of a more secure basis for action in the future. Assurances of this sort, however, are sought only if man feels uncertain on these points. If we then inquire further about the reasons for the uncertainty, we come upon aspects of the order of being and man's place in it that do indeed give cause for uncertainty—an uncertainty perhaps so hard to bear that it may be acknowledged sufficient motive for the creation of fantasy assurances.[7]

Modern-day Gnostic speculations are prompted by human uncertainty, and in them the issue of fear, love, and knowledge finds resolution in an illusory uncertainty. This shifts the response to that element of the self that lies between body and intellect, or between earth and heaven. Humility is excluded here, for the self sees itself as an essence that shapes itself, society, and the world: in other words, humility is lost in the illusion of power. But the true hierarchy of being, from above downward, presents humans with the potential for a different resolution.

Humility before God is linked, therefore, to the requirement to actualize human nature as the tradition sees it, and to resolute refusal to associate any phenomenon with God. The Prophet is the paragon of submission to and praise of God, the concomitant of which is a relationship with other human beings essentially characterized by humility and clemency. As God says of the Prophet: "It was by some mercy of God that thou wast gentle to them; hadst thou been harsh and hard of heart, they would have scattered from about thee."[8] Poverty is human nature, always and everywhere. If it is in relationship with anyone or anything other than that which is Absolute, neither acquiescence nor Perfection are human potentials, and we are not what the tradition teaches about us: that we are created in and for the sake of Perfection. Poverty that is linked to Peace is in itself acquiescence. But poverty that is linked to anything else, is nothing other than a false reading of the signs in the outer horizons and the inner self, which in their original and final meaning speak of the Perfection of the uncreated human center.

Inherent in the notion of the I-self as right-minded and the thou-self as flawed, which is the most common mode assumed by the human individual, is the proposition that the I-self is rich and the thou-self impoverished. As a rule, fear is the reflection of the sense that this attitude is untenable, as it is imprisoned within the dualities by which reason incessantly measures one against another. If the possible attitudes of the self to others, in terms of the second and third person—the thou/you-other and the he/she-other—are considered, the picture becomes more complex. The absolutized self judges itself to be superior to others. But because the attitude toward another is inevitably witnessed by a third, the I-self may seek confirmation of its absolutization by recognizing the you-self, the second selfhood, with whom it is in direct contact, adjusting its speech so as to obtain from the you-other its support in the denial and attacking of the third selfhood. This is the inevitable consequence of the self taking itself, in its own estimation, to be rich, which means that it must demonstrate this by denying the same quality to the third, a process witnessed by a second who is invariably addressed insincerely.[9]

In examining the links between the traditional and the modern image of the world and of humankind it is important to remember that the relationships between people in the traditional are invariably mediated by a third selfhood in the form of a reality that overlies the orientation of the I-self to the you-self. Here confidence—which means the shared sense and testimony that this third selfhood is always the higher presence—is reduced to trust, where individuals are trapped in their own reason, thus in a society and a world where the capacity of reason to quantify and measure is the supreme human achievement. As a consequence, the sublime and transcendent third selfhood must be reduced to the ontological enemy of the ideologically constructed community. Human relations, defined and governed through the covenant with God, become entirely reduced to the horizontal plane of social barter. This is the inevitable consequence of the reduction of the multiple levels of being to the material and temporal plane. When the instatement of the self through First Intellect (or reason as its derivative mode of existence) or the Revelation becomes distorted through various deformations in the individual and society, human brutishness then appears as (illusory) gain or (cruel) cunning.[10]

If the I-selfhood and the you-selfhood become a closed system, and thus a suitable subject of reason, their ontological poverty is described as wealth. They may actualize themselves in an antithesis whose only resolution is the dominance of one by the other. Even the orientation of the I-self toward the third selfhood, however, means denying the thou-self because its role is purely to take part in the ritual of denying, disowning, and annihilating the third selfhood. It is intrinsically impossible to accord any value to the thou-self, for the I-self is itself a god that judges itself as the highest good, for it is not oriented toward the supraindividual and nonindividual truth as the final and absolute arbiter. Wealth is thus the sole response of the I-self to the fear of being extinguished by the thou-self.

The outcome of this is a preoccupation with acquisition, as in these words of the Revelation: "Gross rivalry diverts you, even till you visit the tombs. No indeed; but soon you shall know. Again, no indeed; but soon you shall know. No indeed; did you know with the knowledge of certainty, you shall surely see Hell. Again, you shall surely see it with the eye of certainty, then you shall be questioned that day concerning true bliss."[11]

The preoccupation with acquisition, as the outcome of the fear that is inseparable from measuring the I-self and the thou-self within the limits designated by "Cogito, ergo sum," implies avidity for greater wealth, tangible or intangible, real or illusory. This is the human aspiration for greater comfort, more material goods, greater power over others, the dominance of nature, and continual technological advance. The avid pursuit of these, to the exclusion of all else, deprives humanity of all spiritual insight and, consequently, of the ability to accept any constraints or prohibitions based on purely moral values. The outcome of this is the gradual loss by both individuals and society of their inner existence, and thus of any potential for bliss or beatitude. For human corporeal finitude cannot lead to perfect plenitude, any more than the material worlds can be conceived as infinity. The concomitant of this is that human actualization cannot be achieved through the corporeal expression of the self alone. Only in an inversion of attitude toward the Truth to which we as human beings are attuned is it possible to speak of actualization—by recognizing the center of the human being as perfect, and that in this center lies the homeland of remembrance of, return to, and union with the Truth. But this view is contrary to the modern view of our origins and ultimate potential.

> Far from denying life's progression, tradition provides a reason for it (in its own order of explanation, of course). Microcosm mirrors macrocosm, earth mirrors heaven. But mirrors, as we have noted, invert. The consequence here is that that which is first in the ontological order appears last in the temporal order.
>
> Not that the higher appears after the lower but that it is produced by the lower—this is what tradition denies. In doing so it counters the dominant mood of our time. Order from revolution (Marx), ego from id (Freud), life from the primal ooze (Darwin); everywhere the reflexive impulse is to derive the more from the less. Tradition proceeds otherwise.[12]

The two conceptualizations of freedom—the modernist and the traditional—may also be viewed in these terms, as may their respective understandings of the world and the self, and of the relations between them. In the first view, the human individual is free, and rich, for it is itself the first principle, determinant, and holder of authority over the disposition of phenomena and their development. In the second, all phenomena in the outer horizons and the inner selves are signs or symbols of the Perfection that forms both reason and purpose for the world and for humankind. Submission to that Perfection transfigures the self into bliss in its ownership of nothing other than submission, prayer, and appeal to the Truth. The self that is humble and generous is not so as a result of regarding itself as good. On the contrary, it does not regard itself as better than any other self. For this self, good is the principle that makes its poverty absolute: as Jesus Christ said: "Why callest thou me good? there is none good but one, that is, God."[13] This sums up the truth of all beings: whatever the difference between them on the scale of existence, they are always insignificant by comparison with the first principle. Being is always dependent on the first principle, without which it cannot be. The actualization of being into the first principle lies in the attainment of Peace, the liberation from all contradictions and tensions. And only from the viewpoint of Peace do phenomena in time and motion become comprehensible: only the being at the center, and outside multiplicity and motion, can know all the worlds. Thus humility in the face of the absolute, as a conscious and active expression of the self, leads to the principled recognition of alterity.

These two views of freedom are indistinguishable until one realizes that modern rationalism, in terms of its opposition to traditional intellectuality, refers to a duality that does not confirm unicity, that necessarily remains without the authority necessary to resolve a calibration without end, and must therefore be the cause of continually growing fear. The traditional view, which has as its explicit starting point the premise that the world of multiplicity is apparently alive only if it lacks transcendence and the authority of that which is one, equal and comparable to none. The consequences of these two views to the world in plurality are essentially different, and only by bringing them both into the picture is it possible to tackle the question of the incessant killings in which modernity has become embroiled, although it began with the promise that modernity was the only way to preserve life. The promise declared itself to be knowledge but proved to be ignorance. This fact indicates the need to reexamine both knowledge and its opposite.

Human desire for knowledge derives from the essence of the self, and its ultimate aim is the absolute, the one and only, without which there can be no distinctions, but which cannot be the object of anything. This is the meaning of the Prophet's response to the question whether he had seen God: "He is Light: how shall I see Him?"[14] All that we can see directly in our desire to see God is our own ignorance, for that is truly ours. Discussing Job's words on how wisdom is concealed from all that lives, Nicholas of Cusa says:

> We may be compared to owls trying to look at the sun; but since the natural desire in us for knowledge is not without a purpose, its immediate object is our own ignorance. Nothing could be more beneficial for even the most zealous searcher for knowledge than his being in fact most learned in that very ignorance which is peculiarly his own; and the better a man will have known his own ignorance, the greater his learning will be.[15]

Our relationship with the world and its diversity, including all forms of tradition, is an encounter with the unknown. The untranslatability of what lies beyond the boundaries of the intelligible manifests itself in the individual being as fear. Its translation on the level of relations between individualities to whom God is not Wholly Other cannot lead to a final response, for this would only be a measure of finitude. It is only in regard to the Ineffable that one may speak of the translatability of all its names. With the Ineffable everything becomes translatable; without it the fear of quantifiable phenomena develops into hatred. Regarding phenomena as translatable in terms of the ineffable transforms human relations into ones of confidence, and shifts fear into one's relationship to God—a fear that cannot be a source of hatred, but is the very root of wisdom. Knowledge derives from and guides, but is not the same as, wisdom.[16] Intellect is reason, but it is not correct to say that reason is Intellect. Job's words on wisdom clearly delineate the hierarchy of being from above downward, in which Wisdom belongs to God alone, but from that source permeates the Intellect or Spirit and, through them, descends to the individual human self. All the signs in the outer world thus comprise something of Wisdom, but only in the merging of the self with the Self is wisdom actually attainable. Recognition of one's ignorance about wisdom is thus a stage on the path to its attainment.

- [¶] But where shall wisdom be found? and where is the place of understanding?
- [¶] Man knoweth not the price thereof; neither is it found in the land of the living.
- [¶] The depth saith, It is not in me, and the sea saith, It is not with me.
- [¶] It cannot be gotten for gold, neither shall silver be weighed for the price thereof.
- [¶] It cannot be valued with the gold of Ophir, with the precious onyx, or the sapphire.
- [¶] The gold and the crystal cannot equal it: and the exchange of it shall not be for jewels of fine gold.
- [¶] No mention shall be made of coral, or of pearls: for the price of wisdom is above rubies.
- [¶] The topaz of Ethiopia shall not equal it, neither shall it be valued with pure gold.
- [¶] Whence then cometh wisdom? and where is the place of understanding?

[¶] Seeing it is hid from the eyes of all living, and kept close from the fowls of the air.
[¶] Destruction and death say, We have heard the fame thereof with our ears.
[¶] God understandeth the way thereof, and he knoweth the place thereof.
[¶] For he looketh to the ends of the earth, and seeth under the whole heaven;
[¶] To make the weight for the winds; and he weigheth the waters by measure.
[¶] When he made a decree for the rain, and a way for the lightning of the thunder:
[¶] Then did he see it, and declare it; he prepared it, yea, and searched it out.
[¶] And unto man he said, Behold, the fear of the Lord, that is wisdom; and to depart from evil is understanding.[17]

9. Other Gods but Him

Whenever the presence of wisdom is displaced by oblivion, the self embraces poverty as wealth and ignorance as knowledge—and passion then imposes itself as a god. We see the world as subordinate to us, rather than ourselves as subordinate to anyone else. The weakness of the other is something to be desired, for it seems to prove the power of the self-deluded self, which avoids poverty and humility, seeing them as the very negation of itself. If the self in this state is considered from the perspective of the modern sense of the sufficiency of reason, it will be seen that greed finds its most brutal expression in the assertion that there is no intermediary between the self and God. The self then ceases to be susceptible to redirection or rectification, the Praiser is no longer its supreme exemplar, and the meaning of the Unicity of God fades to nullity in the multiplicity of phenomena in the outer horizons and the inner selves. Such a self locates all values, all standards within itself. The weak, the poor, the sick, the stranger have no rights. But these are the very people whom the Recitation places at the top of the scale of the human debt to God. The weak, the poor, and the stranger are fundamentally other in the totality of the world; God is on their side. On the Day of Judgment, then, when every phenomenon will be restored to its true name, God will ask, and we shall respond:

> "Son of Adam, I was sick, and you did not visit me." And he will reply: "How could I visit Thee, when Thou art Lord of the worlds?" and He will reply: "Did you not know that this My ser-

vant was sick, but you did not visit him? Did you not know that had you visited him, you would have found Me with him?"[1]

The totality of existence remains in utter poverty by comparison with Him Who renders it indebted through revelation. What must be repaid is the fullness of the Word that has sacrificed itself from Unicity to multiplicity. As a result, the worlds, the loci of the revelation of the Word, cannot be identical with the Word itself. Gathering around it means acknowledging the signs in the horizons and the selves as its speech. And this recognition opens the world to its transcendent first principle.

It is possible to come together around the unifying Word because it is primally one, which means that its primal authenticity cannot be lost in manifestation through multiplicity. The Word and its manifestation are dual, for the Word is always both other and prior to all multiplicity, but as its externality and interiority, testifying to the nonduality that manifests itself in an illusory duality. If this illusion is not resolved in nonduality, then the phenomena through which Unicity is manifested become seen as self-generating, and not as signs. Unicity is then masked by a multiplicity in which every individual takes on the Divine nature. This is not ascertainable in the phenomena themselves, that have become disunited from their primal names, but, once again, in the Word that is eternally in the phenomenon and outside it: for the Word is the first principle of creation and its evidence. The unresolved duality of the Truth and its manifestation leads therefore to a refusal to believe or accept the Word sent down to the Prophet: ". . . thou hast not brought us a clear sign, and we will not leave our gods for what thou sayest: we do not believe thee."[2] With the loss of the original meaning of the Word, the speech that is sent down becomes mere poetry, and the Prophet a poet, and the deniers cry out: "What, shall we forsake our gods for a poet possessed?"[3] To accept signs with no connection to that which they manifest is to deprive them of life; taken in this way, they seek to sustain and explain life without awareness of its source. This leads to neither Eternity nor life, but condemns the taker to death, for nothing in the taker has power: "Yet they have taken, apart from God, gods; haply they might be helped."[4] The human taker is thus caught in the snare of the duality between true power and its illusion—and yet this generates the question that restores the taker to awareness: "What, shall I take, apart from Him, gods whose intercession, if the All-merciful desires affliction for me, shall not avail me anything, and who will never deliver me?"[5] In reality, prophecy is the descent of the Word into the center of creation, eternally and everywhere in order to resolve the duality of Unicity and multiplicity, of God and the worlds: "God says, 'Take not to you two gods. He is only One God; so have awe of Me.'"[6]

This potential to take "two gods," however, and the concomitant interdiction permeate the totality of human nature: they are the relation between Truth and falsehood. But can there be speech about the Truth without falsehood? And where is the final absolution? If "now" and "death" are both incontestably real, the illusion of their duality confirms their mysterious Unicity—for there cannot be two Realities. It follows that all that is not the present moment and death is their manifestation through the signs in the outer horizons and the inner selves, the macrocosm and the microcosm. All that lies outside the present moment and death must, then, be only the shadow of Reality, a manifestation of it, but not Reality itself. If what lies outside is separate from Reality, it is false; and if what lies outside is taken for Reality, the appearance of that reality is also falsehood. The totality of language reflects that relationship between Truth and falsehood, revealing and deceiving at the same time. But because no single speech is absolute as the Logos, falsehood must invariably also be inherent in it: only with Silence as its fount (of which neither too little nor enough can ever be said) can speech not be falsehood. Without the awareness of this fact, either discrimination is meaningless, or it treats falsehood and Truth alike. Only in returning wholly to Reality, which is to say, to the immeasurability of the present moment and death, does speech abandon falsehood. The ultimate answer, the return to Reality, consists in the judgment by which all phenomena, all signs in the outer horizons and the inner selves, reject or refute their every attribute except for their manifestation of the Truth. All this makes itself known in time, which has the semblance of duration in comparison to the present moment, and in life, which has this semblance in comparison to death. On the other hand, to distinguish the false from the true may also entail regarding everything beyond and other than the world as false, while seeing the impulses of the imagination and their linguistic forms both as a prolongation of life and as a bulwark against death. The nature of the material world then becomes acknowledged as absolute reality, and imagination as its disguise. Then humankind, society, and the world come to regard speech as dissociated from the pure language. As Nietzsche asserts in *The Will to Power:*

> The antithesis of a real and an apparent world is lacking here: there is only *one* world, and this is false, cruel, contradictory, seductive, without meaning—A world thus constituted is the real world. *We have need of lies* in order to conquer this reality, this "truth," that is, in order to *live*—that lies are necessary in order to live is itself part of the terrifying and questionable character of existence.[7]

In other words, without its first principle, the world is nothing but a cruel and ugly lie that can be mastered solely by a greater, crueler, and more monstrous lie. The postulates and conclusions that are the essence of the tradition, however, point to entirely the opposite meaning from Nietzsche's conjecture: that there is a plurality of worlds; that all the worlds are signs that point to the Truth; that falsehood must be distinguished from the Truth, and the Truth must be adhered to; and that this calls for rites and doctrines that are not engendered by the contingencies of existence, although they coexist with them. The world is inferred from Meaning, and the illusion that it has concrete reality must be repudiated, so that it may be seen in the light of its true dependence on the Real. This is the meaning of "discrimination."[8] If one is trapped by the illusion of a concrete world in which poverty takes the guise of wealth and humility becomes a spectacle of power, it becomes impossible to resolve the duality between the present moment and death. The insurmountability of the present—which is the same as the unresolvability of death—is turned into a mental vision of an unbroken chain of cause and effect throughout the course of history. Thus an interpretive cause-and-effect model of the past is proposed in which humankind is sole arbiter, and this interpretation is adopted as a reliable response to future events. The insurmountability of the present is thus turned into the blueprint for a secure future.

Sacred rites renew humanity's primal trust in God: "He is the Truth, and that they call apart from Him—that is the false."[9] This is the connection between knowledge and being, in which the remembrance of God not only parallels our preoccupation with our forebears, but also transcends it. Departure from sacred ritual entails a fading of memory and a further descent toward seeing one's parents as the original and final determinants of human destiny. Thus the purpose of holy ritual becomes lost. Opposition to this decline is the task of human consciousness, in accordance with the call: "And when you have performed your holy rites remember God, as you remember your fathers or yet more devoutly."[10] The relationship with one's parents—broadly speaking, with one's family, social, and historical environment—then becomes superseded, through good deeds, in favor of the real source and real sea, which is eternally one and the same. All differences meet in this transcendent Unicity: they are its confirmation, and to fail to understand the differences or to deny them is also to break the link with Unicity, as manifested in associating gods with God and in the execration of His names. Neither religion nor ideology remains immune to this risk, for the loss of connection with the first principle may take any conceptual or material form. The relationship of transcendent Unicity with phenomena cannot be compared with relationships of birth or lineage. It is what it is, and it is only in the repudiation of all that is associated with or attributed to it that the potential for human perfection is to be found.

It can be said that the contingent self, as the image of the Absolute Self, takes on the semblance of duality, which manifests itself in the propensity to evil.[11] But also inherent in the contingent self is the voice of perpetual admonishment or censure.[12] This duality of self is analogous to that between heaven and hell. But even though heaven is the dominion of good over evil, hell is never the entire dominance of the ugly over beauty, or of darkness over light. Were this not so, duality and its rational image would be incapable of resolution. The good, however, is the first principle, and in consequence, evil is insignificant by comparison. Heaven is the manifestation of the Good, and must eventually overcome hell. If it were otherwise, there would be no unicity that is like nothing else, and to which everything bears witness with its beginning and its end. The potential of returning to Unicity, after all the contingent manifestations of the absolute, embraces every self and every phenomenon.[13] Bearing in mind that humanity reflects the totality of creation, it is evident that the self may experience all the states of all the worlds, from the most extreme contingency to the most direct link with infinity. Whatever it attains in that experience, the self is with the Truth, and to the Truth it returns. Its primal call, which is its uncreated essence, includes the return from each of its potential states to the Truth: "'O soul at peace, return unto thy Lord, well-pleased, well-pleasing! Enter thou among My servants! Enter thou My Paradise.'"[14]

This return encompasses every self. Regardless of the depth of its amnesia, regardless of the extent to which it is enmeshed in multiplicity and motion, its center, being uncreated and uncreatable, cannot be annihilated. This is the Name of which the expressions are the Merciful and the Most Merciful, the mercy that prevails over wrath. There is nothing that can have mastery over its elemental nature, as the Prophet has so clearly said:

> God, who bringeth whom He will into His Mercy, shall enter into Paradise the people of Paradise, and into Hell the people of Hell, Then will He say (to the angels): "Look for him in whose heart ye can find faith of the weight of a grain of mustard seed, and take him out of Hell." ... Then they will take out a multitude of mankind and will say: "Our Lord, we have left therein not one of those whereof Thou didst command us," and He will say: "Return and take out him in whose heart ye find an atom's weight of good." Then will they take out a multitude of mankind and will say: "Our Lord, no goodness have we left therein." Then will the angels intercede, and the prophets and the believers. Then will God say: "The angels have interceded, and the prophets have interceded, and the believers have interceded. There remaineth only the intercession of the most Merciful of the merciful." And He will take out from the fire those who did no good and will cast them into a river at the entrance to Paradise which is called the River of Life.[15]

This saying of the Prophet's attests to the duality of doing good, as humankind's discovery of the primal nature of the self and of that uncreated center that cannot be disrupted by any merits, for it is absolute and thus outside all duality. Without this, the duality of the self cannot be resolved. This follows from the testimony that there is no god but God and everything returns to Him. In other words, the measurable and quantifiable world can have neither meaning nor purpose without transcendence to the immeasurable, unquantifiable or infinite. Only with a view to infinity and eternity can reason liberate itself from the cunning with which it is always seeking to deceive the absolute by means of the contingent. In this game of deception, power becomes both goal and model. Here sycophancy is never used in order to accept the elemental value of power, but in order to acquire it. Any powers or possessions that are attained merely become a platform from which to look down contemptuously on the lower and lesser and to look up, with even greater envy, on the higher and greater. This formula helps to clarify the causes of war, which are inseparable from the overall experience of modernity, with its democratic forces and weak statesmen. After any eruption of killing and destruction, the solution found cannot but be incomplete and interim, for the root causes of violence are still present. Such fragile social circumstances are invariably met by inadequate theoretical responses. From crisis to crisis, efforts are alternately initiated and abandoned to oppose a reality that is deeply rooted in the feelings and thoughts of the majority in modern societies. These are the symptoms of a wider phenomenon, which may be called "the crisis of the modern world."

But this calls for a reexamination of prevailing attitudes toward first principles so as to restore the human potential for a different interpretation of the cosmic and the social order. To restore, however, does not mean to return to some historical golden age. It means discovering that lost awareness of the first principles that might prevail over the ravages caused by modern-day paganism. A reexamination of these causes leads to two hypotheses. The first, implied by the dazzling advances in the natural sciences, is that the methods used in the mathematized sciences of the outer world have "innate" virtue and that all other approaches to academic analysis would be equally successful if they were to adopt and apply the same methods. The second hypothesis is that the methods of the natural sciences constitute a universal criterion of theoretical validity. A number of interpretations of academic research follow from these two hypotheses, the sole condition for which is to use the methods of the natural sciences. Any other approach to the discovery of reality is thus contested or ruled out. Metaphysical questions that permit of no answer by means of scientific methods can thus no longer even be raised. And the outcome of this is to gainsay the significance, and even the very existence, of all levels of being that cannot be attained by research using the methods of this paradigm. Neither humankind nor society, however, is a simple fact, amenable to study and research as a mere natural phenomenon. Although it has an external expression, the human individual is an entire cosmos, with an illumination that comes from within. This is the crucial source of his actualization, and this in itself may engender a developed symbolic universe at various levels of connection to or disjunction from society, ranging from ritual to theory. The modernist outlook delineated here is contrary to Jesus' call to seek first the kingdom of heaven, and only thereafter may one expect to gain all else. This call is the very opposite of the modern mind-set, where material power is taken as the supreme value, human deeds are both means and ends, where the crucial meaning of faith as the bond with the redemptive finality is disrupted. Here the call to "believe and do good" is transmogrified into the order to evaluate and acquire still more, leading in turn, almost invariably, to disorder and weakness:

> It is easy to be astonished at the haste shown by the most artistic peoples of the East in adopting ugly things of the modern world; but it must not be overlooked that, apart from any question of aesthetics or spirituality, people have in all ages imitated those who were strongest; before having strength people want to have at least the appearance of strength, and the ugly things of the modern world have become synonymous with power and independence. The essence of artistic beauty is spiritual, whereas material strength is "worldly," and, since the worldly regard strength as synonymous with intelligence, the beauty of the tradition becomes synonymous not merely with weakness, but also with stupidity, illusion and the ridiculous; being ashamed of weakness is almost always accompanied by hatred of what is looked on as the cause of this apparent inferiority—in this case, tradition, contemplation, truth. If most people—regardless of social level—have not enough discernment to overcome this lamentable optical illusion, some salutary reactions are none the less observable in some quarters.[16]

This implies a different way of attesting to the same Mystery. Every human individual, however oblivious of the center for which the warrant is heaven, receives from the world, through other people, or by some lucky chance, benefits and experiences for which that individual expresses gratitude. In this there is a triple relationship: the thanker, the thanks, and the thanked. But the self that thanks, that gives praise in relation to itself and worldly phenomena, has cognition of the signs in the outer horizons and the inner selves that praise the createdness of the Uncreated and the multiplicity of Unicity. This is the innate sense that manifestations in the outer horizons and the inner self are not mere *forms*: beyond the quantifiable and definable is an immeasurable interiority that manifests itself through the exterior. Thus whatever it encloses with form is a sign of the infinite. In giving praise to the worlds, the universal presence of the Praised is renewed. And thus the self, in and through praise, returns to the Praised, fulfilling its primal purpose. Bearing witness to the Praiser, therefore, means drawing closer to the primal and ultimate purpose of all the worlds. Praiser, Praise, and Praised are the manifestations of Unicity, of the omnipresence of Truth in the Praiser's life. In this way, and only this way, do the signs in the inner and outer worlds, the microcosm and the macrocosm, speak clearly of the Truth.

Speech begins in and returns to silence: the Ineffable is the first principle of all speech. Speech materialized through language is made known through reason; but reason is not its root. If reason is postulated as the highest principle, however, language is sundered from the Logos that, as tradition tells us, contains the true meanings of all the signs in the macrocosm and the microcosm; then the symbolic content of language evanesces, reducing its scope to the quantifiable world. Two names demonstrate this reduction particularly well: "Messiah" and "Muhammad."[17] The root of the first is the verb *to anoint* and of the second, the verb *to praise*. In the holy scriptures, the meanings of these names are inseparable from the various forms of these verbs and their derivatives. The refutatory, and often abusive, attitudes toward the bearers of these names, and conversely their defense, acquire a wholly different aspect when considered in the context of the scriptures as a whole.[18]

Bearing witness that there is no god but God is inseparable from the testimony that the Praiser is the Messenger of God. If this is translated into the relationship between contingent selves (I and you), praise of God attests to the elemental equality of the interlocutors in the "conversation." Their speech expresses the presence in the world of multiplicity, that is, of relations between phenomena that can never be reduced to being identical: for only the Absolute Self is identical with God Himself, being infinite and eternal, and thereby One. No affirmative expression can describe Him; only negative concepts can do this.[19] The Self to which all Praise belongs cannot be defined, for anything taken from the Self in order to define it is not the Self, and would therefore be contrary to it. But this is impossible, given that this Self is infinite. Nor can anything be similar to it because it embraces every individual phenomenon. Relations between human individuals, between the I and the you, in which there is no denial or attempt at annihilation of the other, thus assume the recognition that all can praise God; and thereby the presence of praise in every individual is confirmed. Both the I- and the you-self have a praiser within them, namely, that which is imbued with the first principle in a relationship between dependent and independent, between poor and rich. Praise is accordingly a mode by which the infinite is made enduringly immanent in every finite manifestation. None of the participants in this relationship, in conformity with the reality of all that endures, may deny this condition without simultaneously distorting the contingent form of their self, as suggested by the words of the prophets when speaking of themselves as those who repent and thus, from their poverty and dependence, turning toward wealth and independence. In praising the Selfhood, the Praiser takes into himself God's Praise as the source and purpose of presence in the world.

All that lies between the self as image and the Self as Reality is merely the womb that praises God, which is why the name of the Merciful befits it.[20] In the words of the Psalmist: "Let the heaven and earth praise him, the seas, and everything that moveth therein."[21] Praising both measures and resolves the dichotomy of the self: "Why art thou cast down, O my soul? and why are thou disquieted in me? Hope thou in God; for I shall yet praise him for the help of his countenance."[22]

10. Two Histories

The testimony that there is no god but God leads to the question: who utters those crucial words? Every response is arrayed between the I of the human individual and the I of God. The testimony is thus the mysterious relationship of the human I and the Divine I; and it proclaims that there is no I other than the Divine I. Because all praise belongs to the Self, the totality of creation is but its revelation. The impulse for this is the love of being known. All that is dispersed in the worlds praises the Self. The link between them, the Self and the worlds, is praise. At the center of all creation is humankind, in which is concentrated the entirety of creation, so that we are the image of the Self. Our aspiration to self-realization is none other than love of or union with the Self. The self and the Self thus regard one another through the other, remaining in their first beginning and ultimate end, their exteriority and interiority of the one and the same mystery that manifests itself in the limitlessness of multiplicity and motion. The totality of the human predicament is our presence in the duality of the self and the world. In all our isolation and loneliness, we have our faith as knowledge and love, but our presence in the world is a taking and a giving, or the history of the people to which we belong. Our faith is invariably in now, but history is out of now.

With our "self," each of us defines a duality—ourself and our desires; and the world with all its forms. Our present moment allocates a past and a future, both to us and to the world. There are two essentially different outlooks on this duality: in one, we see the past as better than the future, and in the other, we see the reverse. The adoption of the first view of the future, as a time in which suffering will increase and overwhelm us, makes us concerned and more responsible. This view is extremely rare in our time, and is regarded as unconvincing by the predominant mode of thinking, which sees the future as an accumulation of good will and harmony in which evil and conflict will be resolved and cease to be. Historical progress is a credo of Hegelian and Marxian societies, which are based upon two ideologies. In one, society is moving toward "the end of history" in which liberal democracy will resolve all social tensions; in the other, the ultimate condition is one of full freedom and classless harmony.

In a different conceptualization of humanity's movement through time, the increasing distance from the first principle obscures and weakens the primal human nature, which is one of perfection. There are ways of preserving it, but also of destroying it. In relation to that primal human condition, development represents a distancing from the principled center, which the sacred traditions see as transcendental over the world, with the world itself as an image of this center. Moreover, the question of the origin and purpose of man has taken on diverse expressions and met with diverse responses. The Hellenic philosophers of the classical period propose the human as a being instated by nous. In the Semitic traditions, the human is a spiritual being to which God has uttered His Word, and as a result is open to that Word. The First Intellect, namely, nous,[1] and the Spirit are two expressions of our instatement as humans. That our existence is established by Intellect and Spirit is evidence that we are not self-created, but exist in a given world of which the first principle is an ineffable mystery, whose name is God. The major questions of philosophy are inseparable from the relationship between existence and that mystery. In the traditional outlook, the Mystery speaks to us as humans, who are attuned to hear and accept it, and to maintain our self as the image of God. In this lies our authentic dignity—the "image of God" and the "fairest stature." But there is the potential for this authentic, vertical relationship to be subjected to human distortion, which manifests itself as the loss of primal dignity. This occurs when the link with God is rejected and humankind itself is taken as god, which, because its instatement lies in the relationship of God to humankind and of humankind to God, results in its disavowal. This, in turn, leads to humans' becoming sealed off from Reality or, in other words, to their denying Reality. Humankind and the world alike are then reduced merely to their quantitative expression, with no connection with Reality. Thus the understanding and interpretation of time take on two possibilities. The first is the acceptance of each present moment as Divine will and presence, by which mastery of the present makes possible the mastery of the past and the future.[2] With the second, the denial of Reality, of every present moment as the presence of Eternity in time and of Infinity in finitude, duration is reduced to the horizontal dimension: the present moment is a mere point through which time passes from events in the past to events in the future. The eternal and infinite presence of God, by Whom humankind is instated, vanishes from this picture; matter and time are stripped of all immeasurable "otherness." Thus, if the present is not mastered, it is impossible to master the past or the future.

Losing awareness of this primal dimension of being, humankind enters an ever deepening alienation that René Guénon refers to as the "crisis of the modern world."[3] Guénon's view of the crisis of the world does not accord with the prevalent view of "historical development" moving toward a comprehensible goal. The experiences of suffering and death, of disorder and defeat throughout history, contrasting so sharply with transcendental peace and order, induce many interpreters to see their goal as building peace and perfection on earth—though, ironically, the roots of such aspirations may be found in tradition-based views of transcendental perfection. The modern era has witnessed various social and political movements that have attempted to actualize this reduction of the heavenly to the earthly order, all of which have been part of an enterprise to destroy the integrity of being, rooted as it is in the transcendental Unicity of God. This has been replaced with a terrestrial order of being, where perfection lies in the reality of human action, which entails changing the structure of the world because humankind and society do not yet conform to this perfect image.

This view sees a "better future," with death and destruction ever less probable. Suffering and destruction are seen as features of the past, of a lower level of development. This prompts naiveté in the face of such events as Auschwitz, the Gulag, and the war against Bosnia. For those who take this view, such events always represent some sort of aberration that runs counter to the laws of history. In the other view of the human presence in time, by contrast, death and destruction are a consequence of our turning away from, and forgetting about, the first principle of humankind—thus the future brings increasing, rather than decreasing, danger. These two views of humankind and the world can be seen as the correlates of two character traits: the first an optimistic naïveté, the second a pessimistic wisdom. When the first is at work, it seeks happiness and a variety of ways of finding enjoyment, but at the same time is unwilling to make sacrifices for the sake of a better future. In the second case, future events are evaluated on the basis of the worst-case scenario, which encourages changes in mind-set and efforts to prevent the bloodshed and destruction.

Both approaches to the human presence in time, in fact, are attempts to deal with the issue of development. Development may apply to any present human moment. It is irrelevant where that present moment may be situated—in some real past time or at a point in time attested to not only by knowledge but also by the whole of one's being. Development is the distancing from that present moment by means of change, which decreases or increases some quantity present in the initial state. But as human societies become ever more complex, their inherent fragility carries with it the danger of increasing bloodshed and destruction. The response to this, by those who subscribe to the illusion of power, is to seek still greater power. In the traditional view, by contrast, killings and destruction turn humankind toward itself, by which saving a single soul is equal to saving the whole of humankind.

This present moment can be shifted beyond humankind toward some starting point in time, which is thereby turned into specificity and contingency, leaving humans without an inner present moment that is in touch with Eternity and is thus both beginning and end. Without this, reason is seen as the supreme human potential, by which humankind's original imperfection is progressing toward some imaginary happy ending. The Ineffable, and all its manifestations, are denied; reason is taken as the source of knowledge, and revelation either reduced to reason's level or rejected outright. The relationship toward the comparative other that shapes the self, therefore, determines the disjunction between modernity and tradition. The human of the axial age, the traditional human, knows that there is an uncreated center to its self and, in consequence, is open to Absolute Plenitude. Its present moment is in touch with Eternity, enabling this human self to see both the Beginning and the End in the world. Its individuality is defined by the Ineffable, which is the source of all knowledge, and thereby of moral discrimination. Modernity, by contrast, is characterized by the rupture of this link between the individual and transcendence. The self no longer sees itself in relation to Otherness, but regards itself as self-sufficient. In the modern mindset, quantity and power are seen as higher than the first principle; in the traditional outlook, they are seen as subordinate to the first principle. If intolerance is the aspiration to use quantity and power to subjugate or annihilate the other and the different, then the notion of human perfectibility is inevitably intolerant, as the entire experience of modernity testifies. The enterprise of building a "new world," which is the essence of modernity, becomes feasible only if humankind is able to alter or modify the entirety of being. But the world remains what it is, for humans are obviously incapable of altering it in its entirety. Advancing agendas to change the world is primarily a rational enterprise, from which the essential attributes of being are excluded, or rendered meaningless and foolish by the proposed. Thinkers who advocate changing the world deny or exclude the essential element of reality in order to construct a picture of humankind, society, or history that corresponds to their desires. The evidence of this in the physical world, as manifested, for example, in threats to the environment, is only the reflection of the distortions within the human individual.

The history of everything that precedes modernity also provides a mass of examples of violence against others. In this case, however, one must say quite explicitly that such intolerance is not grounded in the first principle, which manifests itself in and is confirmed by difference. Disjunction and tension in the self can be resolved only in relation to transcendental peace; and only in that peace does the self attain consummation.

> These experiences [of transcendence] become the source of a new authority. Through the opening of the soul the philosopher finds himself in a new relation with God; he not only discovers his own psyche as the instrument for experiencing transcendence but at the same time discovers the divinity in its radically nonhuman transcendence. Hence, the differentiation of the psyche is inseparable from a new truth about God. The true order of the soul can become the standard for measuring both human types and types of social order because it represents the truth about human existence on the border of transcendence. The meaning of the anthropological principle must, therefore, be qualified by the understanding that what becomes the instrument of social critique is, not an arbitrary idea of man as a world-immanent being, but

the idea of a man who has found his true nature through finding his true relation to God. The new measure that is found for the critique of society is, indeed, not man himself but man in so far as through the differentiation of his psyche he has become the representative of divine truth.[4]

Modern humans see the resolution of their tensions as lying in society or in the world order. Differences between individuals, communities, societies, and states are seen as a call for a rationalization of human needs and rights. But today's world consists of approximately two hundred nation-states, a minority of which are ethnically homogeneous. It is a surprising fact that less than 10 percent—approximately twenty—of the nation-states in the modern world are truly homogeneous in that, like Denmark and the Netherlands, they could not become smaller unless they were to break up into tribes or clans. In only half of these does one ethnic group constitute more than 75 percent of the population. As the interrelatedness and interdependence of the world's nation-states becomes ever greater, the question of national self-sufficiency has long since ceased to have any meaning. The global market demands a unified approach, consensus, and standards.

The laws of economic development in this interdependent world impose the principle of the dominance of quantity demonstrated numerically, where the dominant hold the most economic power. This demands the expansion of a system of governance that will ensure the supremacy of the leading nation-state. From this follows the accumulation of state power, but also an ever greater exhaustion of resources. The most powerful take an ever more resolute stance toward the least wealthy, whose resources are not exhausted. Development thus leads to an inevitable dichotomy between those who are most distant from the "original condition" and those who are closest to it. The most distant tend to view the world in terms of liberalism, democracy, economic development, the free market, human rights, and the rule of law; the closest to see the world in terms of tradition, in which development means distancing oneself from primal perfection, forgetting fundamental human values, and disregarding human inadequacy in seeking knowledge of perfection and the path that leads to it. The second view of existence incorporates a very clear relationship between the transcendental and the mundane, where society has established doctrines, interpretations, and systems designed to resolve the conflict between this and the next world. The impossibility of perfection of the mundane can, in this view, be resolved in the redemption that is possible through transcending the world.

For those living in the most developed societies, their physical reality gives rise to disillusionment and alienation. The highest achievements of development do not necessarily allow a fulfillment that would be manifested both as responsibility toward oneself and the world and as the attainment of human desire. For the members of the underdeveloped nation-states, however, in which tradition is an integral part of the way of life, the highest level of social development, identified as social well-being and freedom, becomes no less of a model to aspire to. But it is precisely this model, once attained, which is blamed for the differences between developed and undeveloped and the impossibility of eliminating them. Thus even the developed nation-state of the modern world itself becomes a measure of the deprivation of the "underdeveloped"—and hence, to others, the developed nation-state may be viewed as a hostile ideology, one that can be understood and overcome only by rejecting and resisting it.[5] In both ways, therefore, modern arrogance denies the dignity of the other, and otherness thereby becomes a spur to an angry response.

The power that is generated by the prevailing worldview can never meet human needs. On the contrary: greater power leads to considerably greater needs, and the balance between human desires and what the world has to offer becomes ever more disturbed. The understanding of the cause and purpose of the human presence in the world erodes at an ever faster pace, as the measure of human power constantly increases. As already mentioned, this exacerbates the differences between the "developed" and the "underdeveloped," which also means an ever more marked confrontation between liberalism and traditionalism, for liberalism is on the side of the "developed" and their power, and traditionalism is on the side of the "underdeveloped" and their supposed powerlessness. The borders between nation-states become more and more permeable, in response to the demands of the flow of people and goods imposed by interdependence. Of course, this also means that there is an ever more salient presence of that outlook on the world that is defined as traditional. Yet the strengthening of democracy in some countries weakens not only those institutions of government that make government possible, but also the traditional links between members of that particular society. In this process, traditional intellectuality retreats in the face of modern science, and tradition becomes increasingly a matter of mere morality and sentimentality. These aspects of tradition, however, cannot compete with the laws of economic growth based on globalization, and as a result they are readily vulnerable to ideologies obsessed with autarchy.

These two conflicting and overlapping elements in the politics, culture and economy of the modern world have been designated as "modernity" and "tradition." Understanding the circumstances in which humanity finds itself implies and calls for a clearer insight into the differences between these two interpretations of the world and of humanity. For modernity, rooted in the Enlightenment, humankind is perfectible. Not discovering the perfection of the world and itself, humankind constructs it by change and mastery. The starry heavens above us and the moral law within us are the sole constraints on our attempts to reshape the world. This conforms to an evolutionary image of the world and of humankind, in which the lower precedes the higher, and the lesser precedes the greater: as humans, we are always at a higher level of development than our forebears. We are therefore prepared, in given circumstances, that is, once we have acquired a sufficient development in quantitative terms, to implement a revolutionary change in order to found a new society as the basis of a tension-free mundane order. This revolution is based on the premise of the autonomy of the self and its total capacity for freedom of choice on the basis of rational criteria. It is from this that all ideological promises derive—liberalism and communism, nationalism and fundamentalism alike. All are inseparable from the will to achieve the greatest possible power in a world reduced to a single plane, in which the multifaceted nature of being is denied. This power is material, and proclaims itself to be the supreme value, whereas all forms and modes that do not conform to such hegemony are presented not only as weak but also as intellectually incongruous or meaningless. In this mind-set, tradition is reduced to the mere past, to old, outdated modes of thought and behavior. The diversity of civilizations and religions is also stripped of meaning because their living source and heart is denied. Instead, they are reduced and distorted into old-fashioned liturgical shells, from which the primal, authentic intellectuality and the perennial wisdom are almost wholly absent. In this process, the meaning of life, the values and purpose conveyed by faith are reduced to simplistic forms of moralism and sentimentality, powerless in the face of a world dominated by the rationalization and uncheckable growth of structures of power, with their heightened desires and more powerful methods of fulfilling them. Moralism and sentimentality, in this view, must be repressed into the private sphere because they hinder the establishment of the public sphere in which, or so it is believed, the greatest effectiveness would be achieved if individual and collective behavior were reduced to a traffic control problem—where green, amber, and red lights dictate standard responses: accelerating, decelerating, and stopping.

The traditional outlook is wholly contrary to this. Its hierarchy is a vertical one, from the truth, the way, and virtue downward. Everything that is in existence is derived from a higher model or paragon, and bears witness to it; and all these levels of being are manifestations of the absolute truth in the contingent world. Humans are created in and for perfection, and remain so even when we fall to the lowest of the low: even when our primal nature is forgotten and obscured, it is not lost. And so it is with the world, which is also created as the image of perfection and with full openness toward it. The truth, which is independent of any individuality, reveals to each of us the way by which we can actualize our self in accordance with its authentic, primal nature. The way testifies to the truth, and virtue to both truth and the way. They may be expressed in a plethora of languages, meanings, and symbols without ever betraying the wisdom that always remains the same, which is dependent on neither time nor place. None of this can be said of any society, however, because every society is the product of a number of individuals that are oblivious or aware to varying degrees of the absolute truth. The meaning, values, and purpose of life lie first in humankind, and then in society, and owe their existence to the unlimited presence of transcendence in humankind's every present moment. Without this, the riddle of the duality of evil and good cannot be deciphered. Giving precedence to society means a priori accepting and promoting man's thrall to the finite. In the Semitic traditions, this is tantamount to association, that is, to attributing the quality of finitude to the truth. Because this entails the exclusion of perfection as the reason and purpose of the human presence on earth, so that the human can no longer be the image of absolute truth, such association, or idolatry, is regarded as the worst of all human conditions. It is engendered by the human desire for and feeling of self-sufficiency, and is thus regarded as a sin of which the price is guilt and responsibility. Only by seeing the human potential for perfection, and in bringing the primal human nature, as revealed and defended by tradition, onto the stage of the world, is it possible to speak of human reflection in society. As Confucius notes: "If there be righteousness in the heart, there will be beauty in the character. If there be beauty in the character, there will be harmony in the home. If there be harmony in the home, there will be order in the nation. If there be order in the nation, there will be peace in the world."[6]

This view of the world and humankind has manifested itself like an underground river welling up, suddenly and unexpectedly in the contemporary world, at a time when modernity envisaged the victory of masonry without a heteronomous architecture. Hence the contradictions between the promise of modernism and the unexpected worldwide reemergence of tradition and the quest for a different intellectual outlook call for new interpretations. The relationship between modern thinking and traditional wisdom, it seems, may help humankind to break out of the constraints within which it has isolated itself.[7] Indeed, the statements of certain leading contemporary sociologists, faced with the rising human call for a traditional outlook on life that is manifesting itself throughout the world, also testify to this. This phenomenon of the unexpected and widespread return to tradition dramatizes the conundrum that these two outlooks—the modern and the traditional—are irreconcilable simply on the basis of facts derived from the current state of the world. All that is visible on the public stage is better seen as the reflection of complex rifts in the individual self, and of the quest to find in an orientation toward peace a solution to the enigmas of human evil. The tragic experience of Bosnia, which more than any other marked the end of the second Christian millennium, underlines these rifts and this quest.

11. The Ideology of Nation

The tragic experience of Bosnia as a country that has for centuries been defined as unity in diversity prompts two opposing interpretations. In the first, the killings and ravages of war are an anomaly in modern evolution, and are explicable and resolvable from that perspective. In the second, these horrors are the inevitable consequence of the modern preoccupation with nation as the higher and more conscious level of existence of every society. The ultimate achievement of this mind-set is the notion of freedom without God, Who is the Lord of all the worlds, and thus of all the nations. Every nation, from this perspective, has all that it needs to define its ultimate goal, outline the way it will achieve it, procure the necessary means, and finally attain it in the history of this world. This goal and the capacity appropriate to it are none other than the secularization and nationalization of God and the exclusion of human orientation toward utter alterity. The consequence of this is to compel the self to realize its every purpose and intent within this world of finitude as the only reality. As a result, every nation, in one way or another, has its own god, which is always right, as against the flawed gods of others. In fact, national ideology and authority become idols upon which is bestowed the capacity to define and achieve the goal. The creators and executors of such an ideological blueprint elevate themselves to the highest degree, from which they determine both the goal and how it is to be achieved. They refute their mediating role between the supraindividual and nonindividual truth and its realization in society and the world. For this reason, they need national cults and myths of state. Religion and its heritage are degraded to mere material to suit the national ideology. They are used to inflame egoism as the source of imagination and idealism. In this mind-set, peace and dependability between nations are not, and cannot be, based on a principle that transcends all differences. All their forms are no more than ephemeral states in relation to differences of quantity and power. Whereas in every tradition the attitude toward the Lord of all the worlds is the source and determinant of every individuality and collectivity, in modernity that model has been transmogrified into a new ideology with god in the people. This is the ideology of modern nationalism, although it represents itself as something wholly exterior to traditional rhetoric. The interpretation of these signs in the modern age deals largely with relations within and between societies as the mutuality of quantifiable amounts. In this, the drama of the self, coerced in every ideology of nationalism into isolation and subjugation to the national blueprint, is ignored or repudiated.

The self stands between past and future; its only absolute certainties are its present moment and death. Its underlying essence is determined solely by this double certainty. Although this underlying essence, which could also be called the "primal human principle," is immutable, its manifestations are both mutable and unique. They may reveal themselves in chaos or order, decline or advance, but whatever form they take, they are inseparable from the readings of the past and future that are inscribed within the self.

Both past and future are uncertain, and therefore both are accompanied by speculation and, as a result, by illusion. The self's yearning for the future in terms of "progress" is denied by the certainty of death. Because the mental world is marked by the desire to escape or forget death, the "end of history" is divorced from the certainty that is the innermost nature of the self. This results in a need for ideology as a substitute for tradition. "Freedom" is the name most frequently given to this choice: neither the present moment nor death is seen as binding any longer. Confirmation of this choice is found in "externalization"— the human need that the Prophet describes as "competing to build huge edifices." The greater the externalization, the weaker the consciousness of one's primal inner nature. This is analogous to a law of inversion: what is outwardly the greatest is the least in terms of the first principle.

This rule of esoteric doctrine is indicated by the symbolic relationship between circumference and center. Any circumference is a peripheral manifestation, and thus evidence, of one and the same center. Neither an individual circumference nor all circumferences together—and there is a limitless number of circumferences around a single center—can add to, or subtract anything from, the center. Without the center, there can be no circumferences, but the converse is not true. Similarly, the fundamental innermost nature of humanity may have a limitless number of manifestations in time and space, but these neither add to nor subtract from it.

In the secular and liberal worldviews, human history is reduced to a multiplication of the manifestations and an acceleration of the dynamics of historical relationships. In this image, one of constant change and development, the history of humanity is a progression from the depths toward ever loftier heights. The traditional view of the human presence in time is, however, precisely the opposite: humans were originally perfect, but we have, over time, distanced ourselves from our primal purity, ever more obsessed by externalities in the shape of luxury and worldly glory. This distancing blocks our sight of the Center in the human self, which is equivalent to forgetting it. We are thus subject to constant temptation, torn between "goodness with God" and the riches of the world.

Tradition sees this temptation as ending decisively in favor of "goodness with God." We see this in the dialogue between Satan and Jesus: "Again, the devil taketh him up into an exceeding high mountain, and sheweth him all the kingdoms of the world, and the glory of them. And saith unto him, 'All these things will I give thee if thou wilt fall down and worship me.' Then saith Jesus unto him, 'Get thee hence, Satan: for it is written, Thou shalt worship the Lord your God, and him only shalt thou serve.'"[1] The Prophet reiterates the same message in various different ways, as in this tradition: "God gave one of His slaves the choice of what he wanted: to have the glory and luxury of life in this world, or to have goodness with God. And he chose goodness with God."[2]

Worldly riches are to be found in the domain of multiplicity and motion: their opposite is Unicity and Peace. Multiplicity and motion demand libertarianism because none of their states can ever be complete. Libertarianism is the measure of their illusory tendency to growth and acceleration, and it is paradoxical to expect that full and final harmony can be reached by way of such multiplication and acceleration. Unicity and Peace, however, are the province of submission. Submission means turning away from multiplicity and motion toward the inner depths, and forming a bond with the heart—the *religio cordis*. Taking the opposite direction leads to alienation from the Heart and the self's fading away in multiplication and acceleration. But this course is not without limits. Its certain end is the Hour implicit in "competing to build huge edifices."[3] The Hour is an absolute certainty, although it does not seem to be so; the "huge edifices" are seen as evidence of durability and power, but this is a delusion. Both illusions are the result of denying the multifaceted nature of being and of inverting the image of the world as a result. These two outlooks determine two interpretations of the self. In one, the self is imperfect in principle, but perfectible through the free choice of the "best" out of a mass of different possibilities, with reason as a sufficient arbiter for the self. In the other outlook, the self is perfectible in principle, but invariably distanced from that primal perfectibility. Reason may serve to remind it of this, and to redirect it in various ways toward its primal nature. Whenever reason is sundered from the perfect first principle, however, it can neither be oriented nor serve as a means of orientation. This first principle is both within and external to every manifestation, and only such choice as lies in it and derives from it will enable the self to "return" to its primal nature.

Tradition implies a steady focus on the first principle, Unicity and Peace, as the wellspring and purpose of every self and all the world. Tradition is the revelation of that one source in creation, the entirety of its manifestation in multiplicity and motion. The return toward that source, which is tradition, transgresses the bounds of multiplicity and motion. The innermost depth of humanity is its goal. It is therefore in tradition, and through tradition, that confidence becomes possible in and between communities. If the self is focused on the world of multiplicity and motion, which it sees as the only possible arena for humanity, it demands definitions and distinctions. When it tries to establish and maintain a diversity of forms, the result is an all-embracing structure of ideology, propped up by sentimentality and morality. The customary title for such all-embracing structures is "civilization." Its most basic characteristic is the desire to increase its own power and scope, which is inevitably accompanied by a process of internal division and restriction.

This is reflected in the various forms of bond between the individual and society as a whole. The self invariably has an affiliation of some kind, and this trait, which becomes more pronounced in the aspiration to reinforce the self through separation, engenders its distinctiveness in relation to the outside world as a whole. A form of exteriorization of the individual, society cannot itself be an object of study, unlike the phenomena of the outside world, which are subject to scientific procedure; society is in a continual process of enlightenment and interpretation springing from the inner selves of the individuals that compose it. The difference between modernity and tradition, however, is discernible in the issue of how society is illuminated and interpreted by each of the selves that compose it. In modernity, the self alone is the source of that illumination and interpretation, whereas, in the traditional outlook, illumination and interpretation show the presence and reflection of Transcendence. The disassociation from transcendence of the self and its authority so as to locate humankind's whole being within society is usually known as "secularism." Authority is thereby differentiated into two possibilities: one that lies wholly in the self, and the other that lies in the interdiction to which the Transcendent testifies. One's moral view depends on the issue of this interdiction, which the self is free to accept or to violate. If the interdiction were dependent solely on the human self, it would be reduced to the quantifiable, and the self would become definable in relation to another quantity. It is on this proposition that the modern notion of human improvability through social change is premised. Human experience as a whole, however, clearly indicates that the self may be measured solely by the Immeasurable. Of every form of civilization, even when secularized, it may be ascertained that its center is one of the sources of Transcendence in immanence. Even when the openness of the heavens to that source ceases, the symbolic language that is present in every traditional form renders contact with it possible.

Each of the two contrasting views of humankind, society, and the world—modernity and tradition—has its own appropriate language. Although these views are not homogeneous (there is plurality in both modernity and tradition), they are reducible to the essential elements that determine them and maintain them in diversity and opposition. This imposes the need for debate to prompt and maintain the translation of their languages so as to reduce or eliminate the fear and hatred of diversity. For such debate to be successful, differences and areas of discord must be determined; but more significant still is the need to recognize the languages and forms that provide the stimulus and context for the dichotomies in this debate.

Because the modern phenomena of nationalism and fundamentalism are both characterized by their hypocrisy toward tradition and modernity, it is of particular importance for the present-day world that they be understood, with the corollary that hypocrisy is worse than denial. Although nationalism in its full expression is a modern phenomenon, comprising the essential characteristics of the Enlightenment (which form the ideological foundations of modernity), it cannot be understood without addressing the eternal distinctions within the self. For without taking into consideration the ability of the self to range from evil to good, from hatred to love, from confusion to knowledge, from cruelty to clemency, from fear to tranquillity, as well as the various conditions that result from the continual clash of these extremes, it is impossible to interpret social phenomena. The relationships between the members of a traditional society are mediated by the supreme principle, and their individual and collective differences are justifiable in terms of that transcendent will. Confidence between diversities is determined by the vertical, as the relationship to the Absolute, and the horizontal, as the relationship between individuals; and the reasons for diversity are thus principled. To endanger others is to betray and violate the commandments that are based on the transcendent principle. In the modern outlook, confidence is reduced to trust: links between people are merely direct and horizontal. The sovereignty of the traditional absolute is replaced by the modernist "sovereignty of the people." Although modernist movements and ideologies find their justification in the countless betrayals and violations of the principled acceptance of diversity in tradition, they also actualize themselves by means of violence and the denial of otherness.

An integral part of modernity is the emergence and expansion of the market and industrial economy, the bureaucratically structured state and the rule of the people. In the world as a whole, this has led to the breakdown of societies, areas, and nation-states into "developed" and "developing." Looking to the future fulfills the promise that the developing will catch up with the developed, or that the current living standards of the developed will also spread to the developing. It appears that the expansion of the market and industrial economy and the establishment of bureaucratically structured nation-states are accepted by all those who form part of the world's diversity. But the expectation that this will undermine traditional forms of confidence, as the essence of cultural diversity, meets with resistance. Developed societies and nations are expanding their power, along with the promotion of their culture as a whole, implying, overtly or indirectly, that this culture a priori takes precedence over others. The chief proof of this is the power their culture wields. Faced with this pressure, the developing nation-states resist the devaluation and denial of their culture, which they regard as a point of departure in their "progress" toward becoming developed nation-states. They seek, in the area where they enjoy real or imaginary power, to establish the same homogeneous, ideologically determined cultural formula. This gives rise to different understandings and forms of applications of the original pressure on the developed world, which expresses itself in turn in a host of modern nationalisms and fundamentalisms.[4] Nationalisms and fundamentalisms thus accept the notion of "development," in the sense of inclusion in the trends of the market, the industrial economy and the structure of the state that would serve this end, while adopting different cultural and political models for the homogenization of society. The political elite promotes an ideology that both includes and undervalues ethnonational culture, and attempts to use state resources—education, the military, the media and state organizations—to make it universal. Those others whose identity does not fit the model advocated and underpinned by the ideological "center" are left to sink or swim. Resistance takes the form of tensions and conflicts managed by realpolitik, which is the de facto shadow and expression of the will and power of the wealthiest. The decisive factor in these conflicts is the balance of power or, to put it differently, the dominance of quantity. Given the inescapable need to link individuals horizontally, in conformity with the postulate of "national sovereignty," and to control this process from the center of society or state—which arises from the inevitable increase in power that this process requires—the vertical, or orientation to the Transcendent, becomes redundant. The notion of the autonomous self and of reason as the sufficient guide and arbiter is demonstrably more appropriate to the undertaking of building a new world, and is accordingly given precedence. The necessary outcome of this is that the individual selves that are drawn into this undertaking ebb and dwindle into shallow superficiality. The frontiers and contacts with the other, the relations between people, are reduced to mere trust, in which cultural differences are left without their transcendental oneness, and are defined as obstacles for which the notion of the autonomous self provides no explanation.

All traditional forms of civilization derive from the living contact between eternity and finitude, whether through the supreme metaphysical principle and the doctrines based on it, or through the word of the Revelation and its embodiment in the book, prophet, or paradigmatic community. But this living source or unquestioned center has no place in the "civilization of modernity." This can be most readily demonstrated in terms of morality, as Adam B. Seligman explains:

> In the philosophy of Immanuel Kant the privileging of the intention (of that internal state that directs the action) over the course of the action itself, and hence over the opacity of its necessary outcomes, is wedded to the moral virtues in a manner that has come to define most modernist understandings of the term. Morality is thus located within the individual, in individual intentionality. However, if morality is located within the self, the source of moral authority cannot be far afield. For if the morally authoritative is that which is beyond negotiation, beyond the play of barter, contract, and commerce, beyond the realm of meager interest (to use the language of the eighteenth-century moral philosophers), if it is, as noted above, essentially an aspect of the sacred, it is also, in this modernist reading, located within the self. The sources of moral authority are, hence, internalized within the person. Here we turn to Durkheim's famous statements on the individual as being the "touchstone of morality," where the sources of moral action rest on the cognizance of the individual sanctity of each member of society.[5]

As soon as the Kantian project is framed sociologically, the moral sense takes on an element of immanence, for society becomes an element of moral action and evaluation. Society is thus the essential factor in the success of the entire project of modernity. But this is a return to paganism, of which nationalism is the most complete expression. The openness of the individual fades away in society. The outside world as a whole ceases to be oriented toward the individual as the image of God and the "fairest stature," which the individual can no longer be in the full sense because this would necessarily entail society's losing its drive to constantly reconstruct itself. In this conundrum, there takes place a further obscuring of the *world*, which becomes ever less visible as an array of outspread knowledge that praises its Lord.[6] It is unimportant whether the origins of humanity are to be located in the vast expanses of the cosmos or within the human individual itself. What is important is that they will cease to be the eternal and infinite truth that speaks in every present moment and every individual, ever giving the opportunity of fullness and the return from contingency. Phenomena in the outer horizons—and, in particular, nature itself and its manifestations such as the sun, the moon, the wind, thunder and lightning, and the heavens and earth that encompass these and other signs—cease to be read and praised as the visible revelation of the Divine. In this mental world, the outer horizons and the inner human self become wholly divorced from Reality, and are reduced to their own self-referent meaning, values, and purpose. Humanity is further alienated from itself on the one hand and the outer world on the other. The human self, with reason as its supreme potential, arrogates to itself the capacity to interpret and dominate the world, thus entering into combat with it and continually assuring itself that it can foresee its own victory.

There is not a single piece of evidence to justify this key supposition. The blueprint of the human as an imperfect yet perfectible being thus becomes a game of all or nothing, where it is the human hypothesis that humans are endowed with reason and freedom of choice, whereas the cosmos is not. Here, however, the indisputable weakness of the first premise is disregarded: taking the human as no more than a material fact, whose existence is summed up as "Cogito, ergo sum," reduces the entire drama to the ratio between two finite quantities—the human as a minute quantity and the world as a very large one. To see this ratio as being in favor of humankind is naive indeed in the context of the propositions on which the entire notion rests. The interpretation of the world that results from this notion is reflected in the dualities between being and knowledge, word and meaning, and letter and spirit. The adoption of the proposition that the self is sealed off from infinity imposes an insoluble dichotomy between form, as finitude, and meaning, which invariably dominates and surpasses it. But only with the duality of sign and significance, and its resolution in the Uncreated Intellect, is it possible to understand how one language may be translated into another, how contingency may be seen as a manifestation of the Absolute, and how humankind may be open to Eternity. This does not mean, however, that translatability makes the self directly open to another; it is open only to the other as the Absolute. Every translatability thus involves both a bond and a disjunction between interlocutors. If meaning is reduced to a sign and equated with materiality as the ultimate reality, there can be no translatability, no openness of every self to the Absolute. The ideology of nation persists, overtly or covertly, in this isolation, this imprisonment of the self. Meaning, which continually transcends form, is thus itself hermetically sealed off, and humanity as otherness is thrown off balance or condemned as an impediment to the limitless will for power of the other. Even if the translatability of one form into another through orientation to their meanings in terms of the Absolute is not wholly excluded, it is at most an attitude of equivocation toward the first principle of humanity.

Be that as it may, the human condition in the era known as "postmodernism" calls for a strengthening of awareness of the potential of these two different outlooks—the modern and the traditional. The fact that each of them starts from the premise that it is complete, and is able to resolve human embroilment in disputes over the past, present and future, is not proof that they are what they claim to be. The human condition is proof that there is no explicit, incontrovertible proof, as strongly evidenced by the continuation and universality of tensions, falsehood, and killing. Passing from one disillusion to another, even if designated as a return to "old-time religion" after disillusion with the project of the autonomous self, resolves nothing, but merely accelerates the downhill slide. There is no return in the spatial and temporal sense; return is possible only by looking to the outer horizons and the inner self. Here the fissures and imperfections that can arise solely in the human outlook become whole. This is the condition of the self as outlined by the Revelation: "Thou seest not in the creation of the All-merciful any imperfection. Return thy gaze; seest thou any fissure? Then return thy gaze again, and again, and thy gaze comes back to thee dazzled, aweary."[7]

Thus the experience of modernity engenders the need, instead of a mere return to the "old-time religion," for a revival of a truly traditional intellectual outlook on God, the world, and humankind. This means that the entire notion of the world as a single, closed ontological system needs reexamination. But changes in outlook of this kind cannot be achieved out of pride. They call for epistemic modesty. Only thus is it possible once again to draw near to the primal human perfection for which tradition descended and endures. Both these expressions of the One have their root in infinity, which lies at the center of humanity. Infinity cannot be attained by reaching out for it; if it could, it would not be infinite. It can only be demonstrated, in knowledge and being, in connection with the contingency of the human presence in the world. This demonstration is infinite and never exhausts the succession of repetitions that always contain both perfection and its clear or obscured reflection. In terms of one of the traditional expressions, this is the Breath of the Most Merciful, His new creation in every moment. Our human being is never without the potential to manifest beauty—which means the continual presence of the infinite and absolute truth in a finite and contingent world.

12. THE CHASM OF THE FUTURE

Every form engendered by modernity denies the possibility that a single truth may be handed down throughout time, in every historical imprint. In the traditional outlook, however, there is no period of history, no sign in the outer and the inner worlds that is not suffused with the truth. Each of them praises the truth, albeit in its own specific way: for, as humans, we have always been perfect and will always be perfect, and exist only for this. In this view, no single period can be better, in principle, than another, for neither the Truth nor human openness to it can be reduced to the temporal. Modern ideologies, however, regularly interrupt this continual expression of the truth in the outer horizons and the inner selves, proclaiming a "new beginning." In so doing, they repudiate the fundamental traditional stance that the Truth is beginning and end, always and everywhere, and that not a single phenomenon—whether in the past, the present or the future—is possible without it, though of course none can be wholly and solely the truth. Thus one can say that tradition is steadfast in the art of transmission—unlike modernity, which denies any meaning to it. None of God's prophets, all of whom speak different languages, have brought any new substance to what they reveal. The eternal novelty of what God reveals may have innumerable expressions, but it is always immutable. The fact that there are differences of expression does not refute the Unicity of the Truth that is transmitted through them, as the saying of the Prophet indicates: "Learn the transmission and teach it, for it is half of knowledge and will be forgotten; so that it will be first to be lost from my community."[1] This link between the manifestations of the absolute truth in its contingent modes, that is, the signs in the horizons and the inner selves, however, presupposes human submission and openness to the oneness of the praiser, the praise, and the praised. The transmission, therefore, is the acceptance of the diverse manifestations of the irrevocable Unicity. What is expressed is inseparable from what is thought, though the thought is not exhausted by the expression, yet attempting to know a certain phenomenon while ignoring its primal cause is tantamount to denying it. The matrix of thought is more direct, more fluid, and more powerful than the matrix of language, but neither exhausts the absolute, for both are but signs in the outer horizons and the inner selves, respectively, signs that are empowered to speak of the Truth. The conception of thought and language as signs that both derive from the first principle and are oriented toward it has vanished from the modern mental world.

Yet, even though the horrors of the twentieth century—with its world wars, the Holocaust, gulags, Bosnia, Kosovo, and Chechnya—elude verbal description or comprehension, what they prompt, perhaps, is Silence, for, as humans, we are but seekers after Reality. It is our deepest hope that in Reality we will find our place in the sequence that goes from silence and listening to speech, and from speech to writing and reading; and then back again, speaking what is written, and reorient ourselves back toward listening and silence, thus remembering and turning again toward the perfection of our human origins. Speech is the confirmation of Silence; Silence is both the beginning and the end of speech. The unsaid is the essence of what is. Holy Writ testifies to the endless light that surrounds it. The ink absorbs the speech that reaches it from Silence, testifying, in its insignificance, to First Intellect as the infinite halo around each letter. But forgetting this eternal and infinite halo around speech and writ, breaking with silence, reduces us to nothingness. Knowledge then appears to us as sufficient in itself and divorced from the Ineffable, and in that rift the human self is sealed off, the necessary consequence of which is the isolation of society and of the world. Faith, on the other hand, is seeing and acknowledging that in all knowledge there is also a higher potential through which it is but a sign pointing to the Absolute. Through faith, the isolation and disjunction of the self, society, and the world from Reality is prevented.

But when the self is receptive to the Logos, it is in a state to hear the Self and, in what it hears, to restore itself to its original rectitude. The Self then speaks to and in the self: "Say: 'My prayer, my ritual sacrifice, my living, my dying—all belongs to God, the Lord of all Being. No associate has He. Even so I have been commanded, and I am the first of those that surrender.'"[2]

The command "Say" is uttered by the Self to the self. The Self thereby, with Its command, which is the Word, locates the bond with the absolute in the contingency of the self. Both the bond and the sacrifice, life and death find their recipient, who is the original bestower, from whom the debt is incurred. Out of this we are granted the potential of being in the world with our orientation toward that which lies beyond and of which the signs in the horizons and the selves are evidence. The skill of listening thus demonstrates the supreme human potential. Every other skill—speech, writing, reading—derive from the fact that, as humans, we are designed to hear and receive.

In modern civilization, speech and writing, on the one hand, and silence and the blank page, on the other, are seen as mutually exclusive, thus reducing the multibranching tree of the world to its visible and quantifiable element. The recognition of this state in the human self symbolizes the need to point to the *daybreak*, to write in white on a black ground. Assigning creativity to the inner self manifests itself as a denser darkness, as envy, as a sorcerer's apprentice—as the evil of the human self's rupture from the Lord of the Daybreak. Moreover, the human self lives within bounds defined by its relationship with the other. This is the matrix of the self's individuality, but redemption also lies in and with the other; for this living boundary defines both sides—the self and its other. This is an intricate topology, however, not susceptible of resolution without continually being alert to the other and striving to translate the other's language, symbols and meanings into those of the self, without reaching out "beyond the boundary." To experience alterity, to feel the resistance and materiality of that which is different, is to breathe life once again into one's own identity. Every individuality is delineated by what is external to it: its own integrity derives from the contact with and pressure from the exterior; it exhales into otherness and, in inhaling, takes in and adopts that otherness. The present moment manifests itself more clearly through the purity of the language of alterity. At the level of principles, every sign in the outer horizons and the inner self carries the message of otherness, and for this reason the openness of the self to the other side of its boundaries—which means to other languages, symbols, and meanings—is the only way in which it can discover its primal perfection, in which it can maintain life in the twin realities of the present moment and death. Imprisonment within the pale, and thus seeing otherness as darkness and nullity, transforms impulses and conjectures, passions and hallucinations into the illusion of reality, to which the present moment and death appear as terrifying, invincible dragons. Indeed, the more insignificant the difference between one self and another, the greater becomes the urge to define, preserve, and defend one's own distinctiveness. There are two possibilities here: one is to seal oneself off hermetically within the boundaries that separate one from the otherness, the foreign that is seen as having no language, nor symbols, nor meaning, and that must therefore be repudiated and rejected; the alternative lies in the translation of all that lies outside the self, so as to render its life stronger and more durable in terms of a principled difference that is oriented to the first principle.

The fundamental dichotomy between the outlooks of modernity and tradition thus lies in their understanding of the human self. In the traditional outlook, the self is open to Infinity, whereas, in the modern mental world, the self is a closed system, determinable only in relation to the quantifiable world. These different understandings have crucial consequences. In the traditional outlook, if the self is open to Transcendence, Transcendence can act as a theoretical touchstone for the interpretation of human existence in society, and as a source of authority. The openness of the soul to transcendent reality provides it with a source of order that is of a higher degree than any structure established in society. Moreover, as we have seen, otherness is a feature of the Supreme Reality, and thus the aspiration of the truly open soul.[3] The closer the soul's ties to the quantifiable world, by contrast, the more distant it is from the first principle. Every truth that society attains through symbolic self-interpretation can be only provisional, for it can be only one of the innumerable host of potential manifestations of the Absolute Truth. No social achievement, accordingly, justifies turning humility and modesty toward the Truth into pride by appeal to any of its interpretations. Fear of poverty, as the primal human mode, is nothing other than a turning away from Perfection toward one or other of the specters that represent themselves as Perfection. The sole touchstone of the openness of the soul is the Unfathomable God, and from this there follows the notion of the universal human community—a reality that has little to do with that of "civil society." Each of us is part of that community through the universal mediation of Intellect or the Logos, bringing to it the openness of our soul.

If, by contrast, the antitheses and tensions of the truths of soul and society become set in stone, and the soul becomes fixed in finite terms—the second model signaled above—this premise requires the soul to be sealed off from its counterparts. Otherness is reduced to contingency, and all its properties are seen as conquerable by the self, as attainable in the material world. This entails the reduction of the transcendent order to the mundane, and gives rise to the postulate that a "new human" can be created through social change. This leaves the soul without a higher interdiction, however, which means that a fissure opens up within it, for it can never be so hermetically sealed as to be protected from the power of transcendence. The quantifiable world, by definition, supplies the missing sense of principle that has formed this fissure. The self must therefore produce its own first principles; but as they are closed off from everything that lies outside it, from the first principle, the totality of being is thus reduced to imprisonment in the quantifiable. Such latter-day solipsism manifests itself in Marxism, progressivism, positivism, scientism, and fundamentalism, whereby eschatological redemption is replaced by the promise of the earthly paradise—an inchoate mass of possibilities that lack the final arbitration of Unicity.[4] But tensions between the truths of the soul and of society cannot be eliminated by the rejection of either, and the human self does not lose its primal "fairest stature," no matter how decisively it rejects this stature—in other words, at any level of its descent to the "lowest of the low." If, however, the self is closed, the existence of the fissure that replaces the interdiction predicts an inevitable explosion.

The contradictions between these two views is summed up paradigmatically and strikingly in the conclusion to Max Weber's essay "Science as a Vocation":

> To the person who cannot bear the fate of the times like a man, one must say: may he rather return silently, without the usual publicity build-up of renegades, but simply and plainly. The arms of the old churches are opened widely and compassionately for him. After all, they do not make it hard for him. One way or another he has to bring his "intellectual sacrifice"—that is inevitable. If he can really do it, we shall not rebuke him. For such an intellectual sacrifice in favor of an unconditional religious deci-

sion is ethically quite a different matter than the evasion of the plain duty of intellectual integrity, which sets in if one facilitates this duty by feeble relative judgments. In my eyes, such religious return stands higher than the academic prophecy, which does not clearly realize that in the lecture-rooms of the university no other virtue holds but plain intellectual integrity. Integrity, however, compels us to state that for the many who today tarry for new prophets and saviors, the situation is the same as resounds in the beautiful Edomite watchman's song of the period of exile that has been included among Isaiah's oracles: "He calleth to me out of Seir, Watchman, what of the night? The watchman said, The morning cometh, and also the night: if you will enquire, enquire ye: return, come." The people to whom this was said has enquired and tarried for more than two millennia, and we are shaken when we realize its fate. From this we want to draw the lesson that nothing is gained by yearning and tarrying alone, and we shall act differently. We shall set to work, and meet the "demands of the day," in human relations as well as in our vocation. This, however, is plain and simple, if each finds and obeys the demon who holds the fibers of his very life.[5]

Weber wrote this at about the same time as Maks Levenfeld was speaking in Andrić's short story "A Letter Dated 1920," referred to in the introduction to this volume. These were the first decades of the final century of the second millennium, with its high expectations following the darkness and desperation of the First World War. This was a period that saw the predominance of the modern image of the world, and a rejection of the traditional view. If this philosophical path is scrutinized from the perspective of the start of the third millennium, it can be confidently stated that only epistemic modesty and lenience testify to the fact that the promises have remained unfulfilled, and that it is necessary and possible once again to instate an order in which the truth might manifest itself as salvation for the human openness toward the signs in the outer horizons and the inner selves.

The arrogance of science, reduced to method and thus divorced from values, can be of no assistance in this, and has no answer to the issue of its resulting deafness to the question of evil and good. Weber characterized the return to the "old churches" as an "intellectual sacrifice." Contrary to this he proposes an "intellectual integrity" that is summed up in science as the reduction of the world to the quantifiable. This resembles Levenfeld's confusion, in Andrić's story, when confronted with the nighttime image of Sarajevo, its roofs overtopped by minarets and church towers and its silence broken by the striking of clocks keeping their different sacred times. To solve the riddle of this image, Levenfeld offers atheism, and Weber science. But from the experience of the entire century just elapsed, it is evident that neither a return to the "old churches," which is taking place unexpectedly and contrary to the prophecies of modernity, nor intellectual integrity, defined as the power of science, can heal the gaping fissure in the human self. Out of this fissure have emerged the idols of modernist agendas, with their ruling elites and ideologies that offer to construct paradise on earth, and structures in which the inexhaustibility and indefinability of the individual is denied for the sake of the new social and political order. Nor is this all. The killings have continued, despite all the promises and entreaties—as both a science without values and the entire experience of Bosnia testify. The killings have been repeated, although the forecasts were otherwise. They are there, no longer in the past, but are a present reality of the failure to respond to the question of good and evil. That science can prevent such events has been shown to be a flawed and failed hypothesis. This is due in part to a misconception of science's true role in human understanding.

> If the adequacy of a method is not measured by its usefulness to the purpose of science, if on the contrary the use of a method is made the criterion of science, then the meaning of science as a truthful account of the structure of reality, as the theoretical orientation of man in his world, and as the great instrument for man's understanding of his own position in the universe is lost.[6]

This is not merely a matter of the distortion and denial of the traditional outlook. The malignancy of it is more complex when "old churches" that lack traditional intellectuality find common cause with "intellectual integrity," in which the inevitable wiles of reason are directed by the scientific method to the quantifiable world as the sole point of departure and return. The linkage between distorted traditional narratives and modern rationalism has never been so fallaciously and systematically encouraged and developed—and to such dangerous ends—as in modern nationalism.

The ideology of nation defines a collective I, which it names "nation," on the basis of its differences relative to the other. The nation is presented as an essential need of the elite who embody the collective I. It demands an organization, which can be properly fulfilled only in the form of a national sovereignty that reflects the betrayal of the "covenant with God" for the sake of an "alliance of people." Others can be accepted into this sovereignty only if they have no true power, if their only rights are those granted to them by the indisputable authority of the sovereign nation. And when the unavoidable reality of ethnic plurality is projected into the past, then hatred and conflicts between the different groups are constructed as the desirable and all-pervading image.

McWorld is one such image, which is presented as the acme of development from chaos into a peaceful and harmonious system. McWorld is defined in its own terms as the crucial development made possible by the innovations in technology and communications that arose toward the end of the twentieth century, in a way, the culmination of the modernization process that some refer to as "Westernization." This development began with the birth of modern science in the age of the Renaissance and its accompanying paradigm of knowledge as power. In this respect, Benjamin R. Barber notes:

> There is little in McWorld that was not philosophically adumbrated by, if not the Renaissance, the Enlightenment, its trust in reason, its passion for liberty, and (not unrelated to that passion), its fascination with control, its image of the human mind as a *tabula rasa* to be written on and thus encoded by governing technical and educational elites, its confidence in the market, its skepticism about faith and habit, and its cosmopolitan disdain for parochial culture.[7]

This view of McWorld entails a negative attitude toward history: history, according to Voltaire, is almost nothing but an inventory of human mistakes and stupidity. The psychology of the Enlightenment, on the other hand, starts from the premise of a single universal human nature rooted in proper reason set against tradition as an order reflecting the nonindividual and supraindividual truth. From this follows the confrontation between McWorld and tradition, wherein both sides see each other in the light of their negative manifestations in the social order. Nationalism is a syncretism derived from the reductionism of both McWorld and tradition. By contrast, McWorld sees nationalism as outmoded and retrograde, a throwback to the past, and tradition sees it as a modern, antitraditional degeneration.

When confronted with Bosnia's tragic experience at the end of the second Christian millennium, marked by mass killings and expulsions, the ravaging and burning of villages and cities, increased distrust and confusion, and the incapacity of the outside world to act as a third party in preserving and strengthening the components of society that enable its survival in peacetime, it is reasonable to ask: does the prevalent culture of liberalism have the ability to recognize its purpose in the structures of tradition? And do traditional worldviews have the ability to recognize in liberalism a reflection of that same human perfection in which they see their own roots?

If, however, liberalism and tradition see themselves as two languages that announce two truths, then their speakers are in irreconcilable hostility. Yet the future of all of us, both individually and jointly, depends on the resolution of this duality. The promise of the Enlightenment that human power and dominion over the world would increase is not to be challenged, as the modern world testifies. But in the very core of these phenomena lies an awareness of the decline of Western culture. The human quest for the transcendental fount of authority, for the inner illumination of the self and through this of society, is growing again, despite predictions that it would wane. Human worldviews thus contain images of both progress and decline, of both order and disorder. Neither image of the orientation of the cosmos and humankind—neither the ascent toward the end of history nor the closing of the circles of eternal inhalation and exhalation—can be safely taken as the more explicit. And yet both these images are present in the human outlook. They are also two languages, and only by translating one into the other can we prevent fear from growing into odium. And this is the fundamental challenge of the relationship between modernity and tradition.

If this difficult, but crucial challenge is not met, two conflicting future developments can be predicted. In the first, despite ever greater concern with social and economic structures, an ever larger number of weak individuals will be more and more frequently and brutally exposed to slaughter, expulsion, and destruction arising from the ever-widening chasm of violence and ignorance of the inner self. This chasm will be obscured by an obsession with idolatrous images of the reality. In the other development, an ever smaller number of individuals will be isolated in their belief in their potential for perfection and their resistance to an ever more overcrowded, yet ever more empty, world. The position of these rare individuals and their attitude toward such a world is reflected in the words of the poet Mak Dizdar:

> Ye who are pure shall be scoured all the more and shall by the sword be slain
> And loud will they laud the hour of thy flight away into silence and pain
> So take up thy buckler and shield and smite with thy sword that harrying horde
> Let death slay death that the one true life might stand
> For the time is at hand.[8]

EPILOGUE

It seems that news about Bosnia has touched everyone. It is hard to say what dominant quality is evoked by the word *Bosnia:* harshness or clemency, suffering or healing, arrogance or humility. In these dualities of opposing qualities lies the tension between the phenomenon and its name. What will the phenomenon itself and its name, once both are reunited, have to say in some final judgment about all the lies that have been associated with it and attributed to it? What is the truth in which justice can be shown for the humiliated, the displaced, the dead on the Promised Day? The violence that erupted from uncomprehended tensions in that country was to do with interpersonal relations, but it was also more than that. It was violence against the Truth itself. Investigating this violence is therefore linked to the universal question implied by seeing humankind as the full summation of all of creation, or, as the sacred traditions say, in the image of the Creator.

They say that in Stolac, an old town in southern Bosnia, a boy asked an aging and revered singer to teach him his skill. But the singer said, "No one can teach you better than the winds and the water, the birds and the beasts. They will direct you to listening as the most exalted of all skills. Through them, perhaps, you will know Silence. Silence is limited by nothing, but everything that it is not is a symbol of it. Anything I could teach you might distract you from listening. And distancing yourself in this way would lead you away from the peace and tranquillity of mind without which you lose the connection with your primordial perfection. Violence against God and yourself is nothing other than going astray in that way."

The boy accepted this refusal, withdrew, and continued on his way with the teacher's unexpected lesson. Several years later, the same teacher offered him the lesson he had previously denied him. "I have already found what I was seeking then," replied the youth. "I have received it from the Silence and what it has to say about everything. And it was you who directed me to that." The old man then asked him, "If it was really I, can I also turn you away?" "What was then your 'I' to me," replied the youth, "was soon transformed into the 'I' of the Silence. It was spoken by the milk and the wind, by the birds and the scents. Since then reason has showed itself to be a link to Silence, and song as the potential for knowledge to show itself through creation as being, and vice versa. What you said returned to the peace of the eyes and the innerness of the voice. The will is powerless in the face of that." The old man then continued: "Forgetting is contrary to Certainty, too. If the Plenitude is first, then it cannot be second. But the proclamation of Certainty is impossible without forgetting. The Plenitude is outside and within us, but the proclamation of Certainty is within us only. And there is no forgetting that can wholly vanquish Certainty. When the human condition is at its worst, when oblivion is at its greatest, there remains the seed of remembering. The human orientation toward Plenitude can never be wholly destroyed. Indeed, as humans, we are creatures of forgetting; for this reason, Certainty is wholly other for us. We face Certainty always and everywhere, for humankind is distant, but Certainty is near. And thus it is that in forgetting there is always the seed of remembrance. In everything that has been destroyed, in each of our scattered greetings, in every darkness however dense, there remains the fact that 'there is no truth but the Truth.' And there is no moment in which the dispersed is not being gathered together and illuminated in defiance of forgetting. Remembering, then, is the discovery of what was lost. This is none other than the self's drawing closer to what Is. Remembering is the measure of this. The truth is ever present, and only humankind can be absent."

Notwithstanding the plethora of narratives about Bosnia, listening offers itself as a better way. It is the skill of inheritance, of transmission. Our present moment inherits the perfection without which no single moment can be. And this is the meaning of tradition: to inherit and to transmit perfection in the plenitude of its present moment. This inheritance is not, however, a transference from the dead to the dead. It is the greatest life skill—on condition that receiving and transmitting it, and participating in it, comprises the remembrance of the will and link to plenitude. To break the connection with that stream of perfection is a failure of knowledge. "The first teachings that will fail are the teachings of the transmission," the tradition says. And everything we have, other than distortions of thought and interpretations of the world, is received or inherited. It is so with life and language, nature and temples, skills and rituals. In their perfection, they are received from the Word, and they are sacrosanct. Their primal perfection in the creative Unicity of the Word cannot be altered. Only human feelings, thoughts, and deeds in relation to their manifestation, or the signs arrayed in the outer worlds and the inner self for the sake of the clarity of the truth, can be different. And that difference transmutes feeling, thought, and action into profanity, which is none other than a forgetting and separation from the primal perfection and its potential in every present moment. Such separation engenders pride and arrogance, and the destructions and dispersions that are called "affluence" and "independence," "freedom" and "enterprise." A reversal of sequence then occurs, whereby "the slave gives birth to his mistress." The teachings of transmission are repudiated, and their contents transformed, in the form of parody, into pageantry and museum exhibits. Everything that is received in the chain of transmission is understood as deficient and unworthy. From the perspective of such feelings, the eternal presence of God's Will fades away. Our potential freedom of choice on the basis of rational discernment becomes the supreme value. As humans, we are interested only in the present moment and the morrow, and everything is transferred from the certainty of the present moment to the uncertainty of promises for the morrow. Thus we transmit that which we shun: we do not adopt the perfect pledge from the chain of transmission, but seek to convey it from our own feeling of magnitude and self-sufficiency, which needs, so we think, neither the truth nor its revelation. Our freedom means the subordination of the world, but not our own submission to the Truth of which humankind and the world, in the traditional view, are but signs. Thus Judaism, Christianity, and Islam become untranslatable one into another. From this point of view, their assertions of the self as perfectly all-embracing and sufficient are thrown into disarray by the impossibility of their testifying to this and of fully translating them from one language into another.

The killings and destruction, the dispersal and humiliation of Bosnia's people have given rise to many questions, many interpretations, but to no answers. Today, this has become a debate between tradition and its repudiation, between transmission and promise. If an answer is sought to the issue of intercommunal violence and obstructiveness in Bosnia, which to a greater or lesser extent concerns everyone, investigation should be directed toward every horizon, both outer and inner. Even if modernity strives to direct thought and deed toward the outer and future, experience compels it to acknowledge the inexhaustible openness of the horizons in which it locates the "definable individual." From this finitude derives the ever more salient need to return to the pledge of tradition. This is not and cannot be a retrograde step, for if time flows and derives its flux from Unicity, the human self returns to it in the direction of that flux. Tradition, therefore, is an affirmation of the inexhaustibility and indefinability of human individuality. Nothing that occurs in the outer world is separable from the inexhaustibility of the human self. Its freedom is complete, but only in relation to the Unicity to which multiplicity bears witness.

Is it possible to relearn the skill of transmitting Bosnia's authentic pledge? If it is, then we must find its authenticity in patterns that depend neither on time nor on the manner of their expression. We must see the eternal wisdom and lasting tradition in them. Thus, too, every complexity may be expressed as a "no" or as a "yes." In other words, this is the accuracy of logical judgment on multiplicity and Unicity: Mystery, Unicity, and multiplicity, on the one hand, and nothing, unicity, and duality, on the other. And this draws together and opens up the testimony that there is no god but God.

Because visible hatreds derive from the alienation between different languages that attempt to address one and the same issue, the intricate wealth of narratives about Bosnia, comprising languages, meanings, and symbols, calls for translation. Yet hatred is a condition of individuality by which languages, meanings, and signs are believed to be untranslatable, and that belief is no more than a deficiency in the skill of listening in order to translate. It is only through translation between languages that alienation is transformable into proximity; the best way of clarifying unclear meanings is first to collect, compare, and correlate all words. The Bosnian issue is, therefore, an acceptance that everything in every language is translatable because the one and eternal Truth lies behind and within every sign. The one and only God has announced to every nation its own right way and open path, and each of us has our own direction in which to turn and be called to advance in good deeds. But all these ways, paths, and directions testify to the eternal One and Only. In each of them resides the one and the same Beauty, which manifests itself in unlimited diversity. But to recognize this fact, we must learn to listen and to translate.

The Bosnian unity of differences, however, calls for a listening and translation not only from one form into another, but also from modernity into tradition and vice versa. The tensions that threaten and banish peace cannot be resolved in the arrogance of imagined knowledge, whereas modesty in the applying of knowledge manifests itself as a willingness to overcome the ignorance that is the reality of every individual.

Notes

Foreword

1. Voegelin, *Modernity on Endless Trial,* 256.
2. On the Lodi incident, see "Lodi, la lega alla guara santa," October 15, 2000.
3. Jaspers, *Reason and Existenz,* 100.
4. Ibid., 103.
5. Ivo Banac, "Foreword," in Mahmutćehajić, *The Denial of Bosnia,* x.
6. Buber, *I and Thou,* 157.
7. Cohen, *The Religion of Reason: Out of the Sources of Judaism,* 120.
8. Tawney, *Commonplace Book,* 54.
9. Cohen, *Religion of Reason,* 114.
10. "Liberalism" refers here to philosophical liberalism, not political liberalism.

Prologue

1. Throughout this work, the term *"jastvo"*—literally, "I-ness"—is used in both the singular and the plural. Later in the text, *"jastvo"* is on occasion contrasted with *"tistvo"*—"thou(you)-ness"; *"onstvo"*—"he-ness"; and "mistvo"—"we-ness." To avoid the clumsiness of these constructions, except where the apposition/opposition of one with the other is demanded by the original text, "self" is used throughout this English translation, with the variants of "selves" (where a plural seems clearly called for) and of "inner self/selves" to highlight the apposition with the outer world or, as it is almost invariably called in the original Bosnian, *"obzorja"*: "horizons" ("inner self/selves" and "horizons" are, of course, equivalent to the terms "microcosm" and "macrocosm," which, for the most part, were rejected as too impersonal compared with "I-self").
2. Coomaraswamy, *The Bugbear of Literacy,* 120.

INTRODUCTION: THE ACHIEVEMENT OF BOSNIA

1. Bosnia is the name of a country, a history, and a culture that have existed for more than a thousand years. For centuries a part of the Ottoman and Austro-Hungarian Empires and later of a Federal People's Republic of Yugoslavia, it has once again achieved the international recognition as a sovereign and independent country it enjoyed in the medieval era of the *bans* and kings. Bosnia is now a member state of the United Nations, although its name has recently been officially modified to "Bosnia and Herzegovina."

2. From Šanjek, *Bosansko-humski krstjani i katarsko-dualistički pokret u Srednjem vijeku,* 61. The English translation of this quotation and, unless otherwise noted, of those from other foreign-language sources is by S. R. and F. R. J. The Latin version of the abjuration reads as follows: "et nullum deinceps ex certa scientia manicheum vel alium hereticum ad habitandum nobiscum recipiendum."

3. From Šabanović, "Turski dokumenti u Bosni i Hercegovini iz druge polovine XV stoljeća," 192. For a more extensive treatment of the spiritual implications of this encounter, see Mahmutćehajić, *Windows: Words and Images,* 11–45. The content and form of the 1463 Letter of Covenant (*Ahdnama*) should be viewed through the prism of the teachings and praxis established by the Prophet Muhammad in his attitude toward Christians; for more on this, see Hamidullah, *Muhammed a.s.: Život* (*Life of Muhammad a.s.*), 467–86.

4. There is no conflict of attitude between the two Christologies—Muslim and Christian—in the case of the Bosnian Muslims. It is fair to say that the Christians of the medieval Bosnian Church listened to and read the Qur'anic accounts of Christ/the Messiah, and found therein corroboration of their looking forward to the Paraclete of the Gospels, whom the Muslims understand to be Muhammad. Muslim readings of the Gospels also testify to this continuity.

5. Various works refer to the reading and study of the Gospels by the Bosnian Muslims: Paul Rycaut, *The Present State of the Ottoman Empire . . . ,* 2:131; Vinaver, *Prve ustaničke borbe protiv Turaka,* 39. A more thorough study of these comparative readings leads one to those Bosnian manuscript translations of the Gospels that have been preserved (see Kuna, *Srednjovjekovna bosanska književnost*) and, in particular, the 1563 translation *Prvi i drugi del Novoga Testamenta,* printed in Bosnian Cyrillic (see Jambrek, *Hrvatski protestantski pokret XVI i XVII stoljeća*).

6. It is only in the modern era that it is possible to see with greater clarity—particularly in poetry and the visual arts—how that general heritage of Bosnia was incorporated into a single identity where diversity and singularities were not erased. Examples of this may be seen in attitudes toward the earliest written heritage of Bosnia (see Dizdar, *Stari bosanski tekstovi*) and its resonance in poetry (see Dizdar, *Kameni spavač/Stone Sleeper*).

7. Qur'an 6:109. Qur'anic citations, drawn from A. J. Arberry's translation *The Koran Interpreted,* are designated with two numbers, the first being that of the sura and the second that of the verse (*ayat*).

8. From Nametak, *Rukopisni tursko-hrvatskosrpski riječnici,* 252–53.

9. From Dobrača, "*Tuhfetul-musallin ve zubdetul haši'in* od Abdul-Vehaba Žepčevije—Ilhamije," 66.

10. From the "Resolution of the Nationwide Anti-Fascist Council of the People's Liberation of Bosnia and Herzegovina," adopted on November 27, 1943, in Mrkonjić Grad, published in *Prvo zasjedanje ZAVNOBiH-a (The First Session of ZAVNOBiH)*, Sarajevo, 1953, p. 62.

11. Seligman, *The Problem of Trust*, 4–5.

12. The history of Bosnia over the past two centuries is, however, part of the persecution and slaughter of the Muslims of southeastern Europe, which has to this day been largely passed over in silence. Between 1820 and 1920, more than five million Muslims were killed in this part of the world, and still more were forced out of their homes. (See McCarthy, *Death and Exile: The Ethnic Cleansing of Ottoman Muslims, 1821–1922*, 339.)

13. Although the etymological root of *grehota* is the same as that of *grijeh* (sin), *grehota* refers to one's ever present individual responsibility toward oneself and toward all other beings in the world. A breach of this responsibility cannot be justified in any way and is in conflict with the innermost values and nature of human beings.

14. See Seligman, *Problem of Trust*, 63.

15. Andrić, "A Letter Dated 1920," in *Deca*, 183–84.

16. Ibid., 186.

CHAPTER 1: THE FORMS OF EXPRESSION OF A SINGLE TRUTH

1. See introduction, note 13.

2. The word *džamija,* from the Arabic root *jama'a*, "to assemble," also designates a mosque used for the communal Friday prayer, hence the extended meanings "a place of prostration," "a place for attaining sublimity through humility."

3. See Mahmutćehajić, *Bosnia the Good: Tolerance and Tradition*, 154–57.

4. According to the 1991 census of Bosnia and Herzegovina, Bosnian Serbs were present in 95 percent of the territory, Bosnian Muslims in 95 percent, and Bosnian Croats in 70 percent.

5. Even though interpretations of "ancient hatreds" were propagated in parallel with the war against Bosnia and Herzegovina, any serious study of the country's history provides ample evidence there had been no such hatreds. See, for example, Malcolm, *Bosnia: A Short History;* Kovač, *Bosnie: Le prix de la paix;* Lovrenović, *Bosnien und Herzegowina: Eine Kulturgeschichte.*

6. Eisenstadt, "Heterodoxies and Dynamics of Civilizations," 111.

7. Qur'an 5:32.

8. Durkheim, "Individualism and the Intellectuals," 52.

9. See Balić, "Zur Geschichte der Muslime in Österreich."

10. For an in-depth discussion of the concept of modern rationalism, see Guénon, *Le règne de la quantité et les signes des temps,* esp. "Les postulats du rationalisme," 91–96, which is a study of Western rationalism from the point of view of perennial wisdom (*Sophia perennis*). See also Schluchter, *The Rise of Western Rationalism.*

11. Marx, "Nationalökonomie und Philosophie," in *Der historische Materialismus: Die Frühschriften,* 333.

12. See Voegelin, "Science, Politics and Gnosticism."

13. As used here, the word *interdiction* has the meaning of the Arabic *haram,* that which is forbidden, prohibited, interdicted because it is sacred—in the same sense as, in the Bible, the tree of the knowledge of good and evil is forbidden; *haram* is also used to mean a sanctum or sacred precinct.

14. Genesis 11:4. All biblical citations are from the King James Version of the Bible.

15. Genesis 11:7.

16. Qur'an 30:22.

17. Qur'an 16:77.

18. The terms "being," "knowledge," and "bliss" are the correlates of the Sanskrit *sat, chit,* and *ananda;* or the Arabic *qudrah, hikmat,* and *rahmah* (respectively, faculty or potency, wisdom or sagacity, and mercy or compassion). They are also among God's Names. In the metaphysical view, they are related to the triads "object-subject-union," "known-knower-knowledge," "praised-praiser-praise," "loved-lover-love," "called-caller-the call," "remembered-rememberer-remembrance," and so on.

19. Or as the Qur'an (21:30) says: "the heavens and the earth were a mass all sewn up, and then We unstitched them." This original oneness or wholeness remains in the primal human nature or the Divine paragon *(fitrat allah),* mentioned in relation to the Perennial ("right") tradition (Qur'an 30:30): "So set thy face to the religion, a man of pure faith—God's original upon which He originated mankind. There is no changing God's creation. That is the right religion; but most men know it not."

The "Perennial tradition," then, cannot be either invalidated or exhausted by the decomposition or perpetual expansion of the universe, of which the Revelation speaks (Qur'an 51:47): "And heaven—We built it with might, and We extend it wide. And the earth—We spread it forth." The expansion, the spreading forth, which begins with decomposition, is a distancing from the first principle, but never a loss of the link with It. Humankind is part of that decomposition, expansion, and spread. The root of both humankind and the heaven is external to them. It is only as "theomorph" and as *imago Dei* that the human individual knows itself in and is linked with God. There are various answers to the question, why humankind and the world? The root of being is in the sense of the first cause (Latin, *prima causa,* or Greek, *prōton aition*) with which the self is linked, philosophically through seeking and pneumatically through listening to the Word as revelation. And in the quest for God, in loving, in reaching out beyond the self for God, in the philosophical experience, and in loving and encountering through the Word, in the pneumatic experience, the human individual partakes of the Divine.

20. Qur'an 26: 192–94.

21. Imam al-Bukhari, *Sahih al-Bukhari,* 8:336–37. These words are comparable to the interpretation of John Scotus Erigena, a significant transmitter and teacher of the sapiential content of Christianity. In his view, human perfection and the quest to attain sacred knowledge, which is in fact the purpose and final end of that perfection, begins with the awareness of human thought

that all causes are from God. Above that level, *scientia* (knowledge) is transformed into *sapientia* (wisdom), and the human soul becomes illumined by God, Who in fact contemplates Himself in the selves He has illumined. (See Trouillard, "Erigène et la Théophanie créatrice," 99). For Meister Eckhart, the eye with which the human individual sees God is the eye with which God sees the individual. And this eye is none other than the supreme intellect or intellectuality that directly links humankind with the sacred and enables knowledge to become the center of the means of approaching the sacred. (See Vladimir Lossky, *Théologie négative et connaissance de Dieu chez Maître Eckhart,* 130.)

22. Because the original Hebrew meaning of *satan,* in Greek *diabolos,* is associated with opposition, resistance, denial, repudiation, and the like, it can therefore be considered to relate to the first principle, whose presence in the created individual might alone lay down the right to plenitude in itself. The names "Lucifer" and "Phōsphoros" for Satan also suggest this.

CHAPTER 2: SUBMISSIVENESS, EMOTION, AND KNOWLEDGE

1. Qur'an 29:46.
2. On the connection between understanding and belief, see Schuon, *Logic and Transcendence,* esp. "Understanding and Believing," 198–208.
3. Of universal importance in this regard is Perry, *A Treasury of Traditional Wisdom,* an inspiring summary of various holy scriptures arranged according to the "stations of wisdom."
4. Schuon, *Logic,* 206.
5. Qur'an 10:62.
6. Qur'an 31:27.
7. Qur'an 16:36, 14:4, and 41:43.
8. Smith, *Forgotten Truth: The Common Vision of the World's Religions,* 5–6.
9. Qur'an 22:18.
10. Qur'an 22:40.
11. The Qur'anic phrase *sawami' wa bye' wa salatun wa masajidin* is translated in similar ways by A. J. Arberry ("cloisters and churches, oratories and mosques") and by 'Abdullah Yusuf Ali ("monasteries, churches, synagogues and mosques"). Although four sacred languages are here in question (Arabic, Aramaic or Hebrew, Greek, and Latin), the etymological roots of the words *rise, link, bow, prostrate* indicate the mention of God's Name as the living core of their meaning.
12. Qur'an 2:193.
13. Qur'an 109:6.
14. Arabic *haram*; see chapter 1, note 13.

CHAPTER 3: THE APPRENTICESHIP OF SUBMISSION AND FREEDOM

1. Voegelin, *Hitler and the Germans,* 89.
2. Ibid., 105.
3. Among the chief issues this book addresses is the relation between the traditional and the modern outlook on the self. For more on the first, see

Schuon, *Language of the Self,* and Abu Bakr, *The Book of Certainty: The Sufi Doctrine of Faith, Visions and Gnosis;* for more on the second, see Taylor, *Sources of the Self: The Making of Modern Identity,* and Benhabib, *Situating the Self: Gender, Community and Postmodernism in Contemporary Ethics.* For a reexamination of the European structuring and interpretation of the self from a Buddhist perspective, see Keiji, *The Self-Overcoming of Nihilism.*

4. See Qur'an 22:18.

5. Qur'an 11:56 and 3:101.

6. Qur'an 13:19–21.

7. Qur'an 33:72. Although "trust" in this translated verse corresponds to the original *amanah* in Arabic, the root of *amanah* is the same as that of *iman* (faith). Because tradition (*din*) is defined, according to the famous narrative (*hadith*) on the angel Gabriel's teachings to the Prophet Muhammad, as threefold—submission (*islam*), faith (*iman*), and doing that which is beautiful (*ihsan*), this is a matter of the establishment of relations on the basis of confidence (Latin, *confidentia*).

8. The triliteral roots of the Arabic words of Qur'an 33:72 translated by Arberry as "sinful, very foolish" are, respectively, *z-l-m,* "to do evil," "to tyrannize," and *j-h-l,* "to be ignorant, irrational, or foolish." In his translation of the verse into Bosnian, the author opts for the meaning "violent and ignorant."

9. The author's preferred translations of his original "*povjerenje*" and "*pouzdanje*" are "confidence" and "trust," respectively. The derivation, in the case of the former, is similar in both languages: *vjera,* like the Latin *fides,* means "faith"; the Bosnian intensive prefix *po* means "altogether," "completely," as can the Latin prefix *com/con* (from the classical Latin *cum*). The author notes that *pouzdanje,* translated as "trust," is related to the word *uzda,* "reins"—the implication being a direct, unmediated relationship like that between a horse and its rider.

10. The meaning attributed to the concept of trusting is close to the definition of the concept of trust and its connection with that of confidence, in Seligman, *Problem of Trust,* 43.

11. Qur'an 50:16–18. Although the author as a rule favors Arberry's rendering of the Qur'an, *The Koran Interpreted,* which is therefore used throughout the English translation of this work, for his rendition of Qur'an 50:16–18, he used Muhammad Asad's rendering, *The Message of the Qur'an,* 797–98, which reads: "Now, verily, it is We who have created man, and We know what his innermost self whispers within him: for We are closer to him than his neck-vein. [And so,] whenever the two demands [of his nature] come face to face, contending from the right and from the left, not even a word can he utter but there is a watcher with him, ever-present."

12. See Qur'an 89:27–28.

13. See Qur'an 29:46.

14. On readings of history within the framework of the ideologies that were involved in the destruction of Bosnia, see Mahmutćehajić, *Bosnia the Good; The Denial of Bosnia;* and *Sarajevo Essays—Politics, Ideology and Tradition.*

15. The root of the Slavic word *sloboda,* "freedom," and of the Latin word *slavus,* "slave," is most likely present in the possessive pronoun *svoj* and

suus, respectively—meaning "one's own," which points to the connection of both words with "self."

16. Barber, *Jihad vs. McWorld,* 117.
17. See Qur'an 95:4–5.

CHAPTER 4: THE LOWER HORIZONS OF FREEDOM

1. Qur'an 50:16.
2. See Qur'an 8:24.
3. Barber, *Jihad,* 136.
4. These three possibilities of the human self are taken from Qur'anic definition of conflicts and their resolution within man: "Surely the soul of man incites to evil" (Qur'an 12:53); "I swear by the reproachful soul" (Qur'an 75:2); and "O soul at peace" (Qur'an 89:27). See, for example, Lings, *Muhammad: His Life Based upon the Earliest Sources,* 356. These traditional definitions can be conditionally linked with the modern interpretation of the three motivating aspects of human individuality, with reference to Plato—desire, reason, and *thymos* (or "spiritedness"). As Francis Fukuyama puts it, in *The End of History and the Last Man,* xvi–xvii: "Most of human behavior can be explained as a combination of the first two parts: desire and reason. Desire induces men to seek things outside themselves, while reason or calculation shows them the best way to get them. But human beings seek recognition of their own worth, or of the people, things or principles that they invest with worth."
5. On these aspects of Adam Smith's deliberations, see Muller, *Adam Smith in His Time and Ours: Designing the Decent Society.*
6. On the traditional understanding of the concept of civilization, see Coomaraswamy, *What Is Civilisation and Other Essays.*
7. Barber, *Jihad,* 193.
8. See, for example, Carter, *The Culture of Disbelief: How American Law and Politics Trivialize Religious Devotion.*
9. Communism proclaimed its image of humanity, society, and the world to be a universal truth. Anything contrary to it, therefore, was mere falsehood, and must cease to be. The self is defined solely by that ideological truth, and must be subordinate to it as a malleable substance without any inner sanctity. If it opposes the interpretations and demands of the "pure center," its subjugation to a reconstruction assumed to be able and required to encompass the totality of its presumed changeability becomes desirable and justified. This shuts the self off from its transcendental roots. In the harshness of its use of the forcible reconstruction of selfhood, Yugoslavia's break with that "universal communist community" in 1948 demonstrated the true nature of communism in its understanding and "development" of society. Goli Otok, a concentration camp for the reconstruction of communists who were insubordinate to the "pure center," was the entire expression of this ideological image of the world and the political movement of which it was the foundation. It is only in the relationship between the antagonistic advocates of one and the same ideology that its true nature can be seen, along with the distortions of human thought and conduct that derive from it. See Banac, *With Stalin against Tito: Cominformist Splits in Yugoslav Communism,* 243–54.

Chapter 5: Pride and Humility

1. Imam Zayn al'Abidin, *Sahifa: Al-Sahifat al-Kamilat al-Sajjadiyya* (*The Psalms of Islam*), 40.
2. This is explicitly indicated by the Qur'anic verse 5:48: "To every one of you We have appointed a right way and an open road. If God had willed, He would have made you one nation; but that He may try you in what has come to you. So be you forward in good works; unto God shall you return, all together; and He will tell you of that whereon you were at variance."
3. Arendt, "Thinking and Moral Consideration," 420–21.
4. Qur'an 7:146.
5. Qur'an 57:16.
6. Qur'an 1:5–7. Although the phrase "the straight path" is commonly used in English translations of the Qur'an, in his Bosnian original, the author opts for the word whose nearest English equivalent is "upright" instead of "straight," denoting the vertical relationship between humanity and God.
7. Weber, "Science as a Vocation," 139.
8. Smith, *Forgotten Truth*, 16.

Chapter 6: The Dispute over Names

1. This is the well-known stance of the Divine Revelation in the Semitic languages, which admit of no compromise as regards Divine Unity and Unicity, and are opposed to associating Him in any way with anything else: "I am the first, and I am the last; and beside me there is no God"(Isaiah 44:6); "To whom then will ye liken me, or shall I be equal?" (Isaiah 40:25); "Ye cannot serve God and mammon" (Matthew 6:24). These biblical pronouncements resonate also in the Qur'anic revelations: "God, there is no god but He" (Qur'an 2:255); "He is the First and the Last, the Outward and the Inward; He has knowledge of everything" (Qur'an 57:3); "Like Him there is naught" (Qur'an 42:11); "and equal to Him is not any one" (Qur'an 112:4).
2. "Associationism" is used here to designate the Islamic concept of *shirk*, a word that derives from the triliteral Arabic root meaning "to associate," "to become a partner of," "to participate in." The one unforgivable sin in Islam, *shirk* means "polytheism" or "idolatry" in the narrow sense usually attributed to it, but, in the broader sense, it means "to absolutize anything"—including an opinion or interpretation—"other than God, the One Absolute," "to associate anyone or anything with God."
3. Qur'an 113:1–5.
4. Imam 'Ali, *Nahjul-Balagha: Sermons, Letters and Sayings*, 492.
5. Qur'an 95:4–5 and 96:1–2.
6. See, for example, Qur'an 2:117: "and when He decrees a thing, He but says to it 'Be,' and it is"—a direct command, as distinct from the biblical "Let there be."
7. Qur'an 7:180.
8. Qur'an 35:14.
9. Qur'an 2:62.
10. Qur'an 7:159.
11. Qur'an 45:16–17.
12. See Qur'an 41:12.

13. Qur'an 41:53; see Qur'an 41:21.
14. Qur'an 7:40 and 7:182.
15. Dahrendorf, "Homo sociologicus," in *Essays on the Theory of Society,* 77–78.
16. Qur'an 89:1–4.
17. The phrase "sacred tradition" (hadith al-qudsi) here refers to a saying of the Prophet Muhammad regarded as being directly inspired by God. Bukhari, *Sahih,* 9:482.
18. Qur'an 36:35.
19. Qur'an 57:3.
20. Qur'an 2:31 and 2:32.
21. Qur'an 22:18.
22. See Qur'an 59:19: "Be not as those who forgot God, and so He caused them to forget their souls."
23. Qur'an 95:4–5.
24. Qur'an 41:34.
25. Bodin, *Colloquium of the Seven about Secrets of the Sublime* (*Colloquium Heptaplomeres de Rerum Sublimium Arcanis Abditis*), 337.

Chapter 7: The Word Held in Common

1. See Hamidullah, *Le Prophète de l'Islam: Sa vie et son oeuvre,* 1:572–763; and see esp. Ibn Ishaq, *Sirat Rasul Allah* (*The Life of Muhammad*), 270–77.
2. Jesus said: "'No man can serve two masters: for either he will hate the one, and love the other; or else he will hold to the one, and despite the other" (Matthew 6:24).
3. Qur'an 4:48.
4. See Qur'an 2:97 and 26:192–94.
5. Qur'an 6:152.
6. Qur'an 3:55.
7. Hamidullah, *Prophète,* 1:574. The year 10 A.H. (*anno hegirae*) corresponds to 630 A.D.
8. See Qur'an 48:10; "the Word held in common": the words *kalimatu sawaim* in the Arabic original mean "common/shared/joint word" or speech. This may be the correlate of the *Ursprache,* the one and only original language that lies behind the present discord and fierce altercations between conflicting languages ever since the fall of the Tower of Babel. George Steiner, referring to Walter Benjamin on the *Ursprache,* explains: "This 'pure language'— . . . Logos which makes speech meaningful but which is contained in no single spoken idiom—is like a hidden spring seeking to force its way through the silted channels of our differing tongues. . . . A translation from language A into language B will make tangible the implication of a third, active presence. It will show the lineaments of that 'pure speech' which precedes and underlies both languages." Steiner, *After Babel: Aspects of Language and Translation,* 67.
9. Qur'an 17:110.
10. See Qur'an 41:21 and 30:22.
11. Qur'an 30:30.

12. Qur'an 2:152.
13. Qur'an 3:83.
14. Lings, *The Heralds and Other Poems*, 26.
15. Steiner, *After Babel*, 47.
16. Qur'an 3:133–34.
17. The equivalent of *hearing* in Hebrew is *shama'*.
18. Proverbs 7:3.

CHAPTER 8: WEALTH IN POVERTY

1. Qur'an 7:180.
2. Imam Muslim, *Sahih Muslim*, 1:53.
3. One of the ninety-nine beautiful names of God is "Peace" (*al-salam;* Qur'an 59:23).
4. Qur'an 45:23; see also Qur'an 2:165 and 2:200.
5. See Qur'an 6:152. It should be noted here that the human individual's supreme potential lies in its relation with God as the All-faithful. This derives from the fact that trust is the essence of their covenant. As such, this relationship confirms the truth that human beings are powerless but free, and that God is the All-powerful, but Self-restrained from coercing the human individual, as powerless, into belief in Him as the All-powerful. It is from human powerlessness that the absolute mercy of God derives, and His only due: that all returns to Him as the Merciful. This is the conundrum of the debt of the powerful sultan to the powerless friar. The friar's rights derived from the friar's powerlessness, and the sultan's indebtedness, from the sultan's power.
6. Qur'an 47:38.
7. Voegelin, "Science, Politics," 309.
8. Qur'an 3:159.
9. A further factor here is the underhand operation of reason, which prevents the attainment of the equality that would result from comparison alone. Conversely, recognition of this fact would mean the acceptance that reason derives from the higher, which is the same as the acceptance of ontological poverty. But the starting point for modernity is the affirmation of reason as the ultimate and supreme potential in the progress of humankind toward perfection, where reason is both meaning and purpose.
10. To these two forms of human brutishness as distortions in the experience of reality (illusory gain and cruel cunning), a third should be added: criminal stupidity, which manifests itself in a society that has collapsed into disorder. Stupidity then rises to the surface and becomes socially influential. Given that stupidity then represents a threat to others, in such social circumstances it must be classed as criminal. Even if stupidity is not criminal in itself, it becomes so in certain social circumstances. See Musil, "On Stupidity," in *Precision and Soul: Essays and Addresses*, 268–86; and Luft, *Robert Musil and the Crisis of European Culture 1880–1942*, 282–86.
11. Qur'an 102:1–8.
12. Smith, *Forgotten Truth*, 129.
13. Mark 10:18. The expression "there is none good but one" means, inter alia, that there is no self but the Self (Qur'an 20:14), and that there is none other than Him (Qur'an 6:164), but also that His Self and Bounty, His First-

ness and Otherness to all else is with Him. They are the beginning and the end, the inner and the outer, the arbiter of all things, as the Prophet says in Qur'an 8:29: "O believers, if you fear God, He will assign you a salvation, and acquit you of your evil deeds, and forgive you; and God is of bounty abounding." This "fear" and the assignment of a "salvation" points to the full Word of the Self and His Bounty. For if good and evil are not equal (Qur'an 41:34), this means that "fear" is but the state of the contingent self, its sentiments, its image, in which the illusion of duality is proffered as a reality in which there are two principles—evil and good. But inherent in "salvation," or discernment, is the testimony that there is no god but God, and that only He is good. It begins and ends in the relationship between Unicity and Infinity, and its expression is the openness of the measurable to both Unicity and Infinity as essentially inseparable. The Self thereby manifests itself in the self in tension through the First Intellect, where discernment does not also mean the potential for two principles. That same Unicity and Infinity, however, are not inherent in science, in the modern sense of the word. For science, the dependability of its principles, universally applicable to the world as its object of study in the construction of a "scientific" picture, is derived from this, and is accompanied by the disregard for or refutation of the inherence of the self in the Self, and thereby in each of Its manifestations. For more on the universality of modern scientific methods, see Whitehead and Russell, *Principia Mathematica,* vols. 1–3. The prerequisites of modern science are that it be closed to and disregard the self, on the one hand, and the world as an object for which universal scientific principles hold good, on the other. But every sacred tradition has as its starting point the opposing postulate, of openness to and inherence in Unicity and Infinity. For more on these postulates in mathematical language, see, for example, Guénon, *Les principes du calcul infinitésimal.*

14. Muslim, *Sahih,* 1:113.

15. Dolan, *Unity and Reform: Selected Writings of Nicholas of Cusa,* 8–9.

16. Sometimes equated with science and philosophy, the word *wisdom* (*hikma*) in its ancient use is present in the Greek word *sophia*, which designates equilibrium and harmony as a state of maturity. Being knowledge of the supreme spiritual truths, connected with the original human purity as the elemental content of every individual, wisdom is thus a fundamental concept of the tradition. In it, knowledge and being are oriented toward their original Unicity. Those who have wisdom live according to that wisdom. This is not knowledge that allows the self to remain without being set in motion toward it and without change. In other words, only in wisdom do phenomena in the world become the signs of God. Science may be without inquiry on this, when it is preoccupied solely with the lower levels of being and not with their higher source and confluence, where quantity and comparison must end. Only with wisdom in the human self is the way to Perfection opened.

17. Job 28:12–28.

Chapter 9: Other Gods but Him

1. Muslim, *Sahih,* 4:3. See also Chittick, *The Sufi Path of Knowledge: Ibn al-'Arabi's Metaphysics of Imagination,* 292 n.33, and Graham, *The Divine Word and Prophetic Word in Early Islam,* 178–80.

2. Qur'an 11:53.
3. Qur'an 37:36.
4. Qur'an 36:73.
5. Qur'an 36:23.
6. Qur'an 16:51.
7. Nietzsche, *The Will to Power,* 451.
8. The world that has been stripped of the nature of a sign, or where this nature has been forgotten, becomes a delusion and a falsehood. To repudiate it is to reject falsehood. This may explain the persistency with which the most prominent adherents to and interpreters of the tradition draw attention to the ephemerality and illusoriness of the world. There are many such examples in the words of 'Ali ibn Abi Talib (see 'Ali, *Nahjul-Balagha*, in particular, sayings 28, 52, 62, 63, 81, 82, 98, 102, 110, 112, 128, 132, 144, 160, 187, 202, and 224). The reduction of the totality of being to "this world," accompanied by the exclusion of the "other" as first principle, is the result of an inversion of outlook from the Absolute to its manifestation as sole and self-sufficient being ordered by quantifiable relations. This is the repeated content of the explanation for humanity's downfall: "No indeed; but you love the hasty world, and leave be the Hereafter" (Qur'an 75:20–21), or "Surely these men love the hasty world, and leave be behind them a heavy day" (Qur'an 76:27). The terms the "other world" and the "heavy day" signify the higher expression of the Absolute, without which all phenomena of lower order in the totality of being are without purpose or meaning. The world that presents itself as direct to us, as part of that world, is always in relation to "otherness"; and only that "otherness" can be its first principle because "otherness," itself, is not. Inherent to every tradition is the steadfast inversion of the illusions in which that which is close becomes distant, in which creation or manifestation has the semblance of independence from the first principle. The formula used in this inversion is "there is no god but God," which is applicable to every expression: "there is no life other than Life," "no world other than the World," "no proximity other than the Proximity," "no truth other than the Truth," "no beauty other than Beauty," and so on. Many of Jesus the Messiah's sayings use this perennial formula, among them: "For whosoever will save his life shall lose it; but whosoever shall lose his life for my sake and the gospel's, the same shall save it. For what shall it profit a man, if he shall gain the whole world, and lose his soul" (Mark 8:35–36); "He that loveth his life shall lose it; and he that hateth his life in this world shall keep it unto life eternal" (John 12:25); "For what is a man advantaged, if he gain the whole world, and lose himself, or be cast away?" (Luke 9:25).

9. Qur'an 31:30; see also Qur'an 7:171. The conceptual basis of the Arabic word *haqq* (truth, reality, justice) can be seen in the triliteral root *hqq*, which *haqq* shares with words meaning "incision," "carving in stone" or "inscription" on stable material, and "prescription" determined by decree, law, or order. The Hebrew word for the truth, *'emeth*, is linked to the verb *'aman* (endorse, establish), the noun *'emuna* (stability, fidelity), and the adverb *'amen* (truly, in truth). The Arabic word *iman* (faith) is of the same origin, deriving from the verbal root *'mn*, with the associated meanings of "being certain," "having confidence in," "orientation toward." The first letter of the Hebrew form of the word *'emeth* symbolizes reality. Without this

initial letter, the word means "death." See Scholem, *On the Kabbalah and Its Symbolism,* 159.

10. Qur'an 2:200.

11. See Qur'an 12:53.

12. See Qur'an 75:2.

13. The literal equivalent of "the potential of returning to Unicity" is *universalism* as used in many Protestant Christian modern age sects, a theological doctrine according to which every soul will ultimately find redemption in God.

14. Qur'an 89:27–30.

15. Bukhari, *Sahih,* 9:398.

16. Schuon, *Castes and Races,* 79.

17. These reflections could be extended to include the name "Musa/ Moses," Hebrew *"Moeh,"* Egyptian *"Msy,"* meaning "to be born" or "son." Narratives link the name to the Hebrew word *maa,* meaning "taken out of," in the case of Moses, out of the water. That Moses was taken out of the water can be interpreted as a restoration of the primal link with God or the receiving of the revelation in the midst of the world of multiplicity and motion, by means of which the prevailing view of the past and the present was altered from the Pharaonic to the penitential.

18. See, for example, Bodin, *Colloquium,* 269–70.

19. In Hinduism, infinity is *nir-aguna* (without attribute); in Buddhism, it is *nir-vana* (non-drawing, as when a fire ceases to draw when all combustible matter has burned up in it); and *sunyata* (void, nothingness); in Taoism it is the Tao that cannot be spoken; in Judaism, *'n-sof* (non-ending).

20. The word *merciful* in Arabic is *rahmun,* from the verbal root *r-h-m,* from which also derive the Divine names *"ar-rahman"* (the Merciful) and *"ar-rahim"* (the Most Merciful).

21. Psalms 69:34.

22. Psalms 42:5.

CHAPTER 10: TWO HISTORIES

1. The term "reason" could also be used here, with the proviso that it be defined as the presence and manifestation of Intellect in the individual human nature.

2. The correlate of domination of the present is "knowledge of the Hour," the return of being to a "now" that is indivisible from the first principle: "The people will question thee concerning the Hour. Say: 'The knowledge of it is only with God; what shall make thee know? Haply the Hour is nigh.'" (Qur'an 33:63). From the fact that "knowledge of the Hour is only with God," it follows that dominance of the presence is impossible without an acceptance of the vertical portion of Intellect and Spirit in every human "now." The entirety of time is with the reality of the Hour: "'Heavy is it in the heavens and the earth; it will not come on you but—suddenly!'" (Qur'an 7:187). The coming of the Hour that is everywhere and always designates the opening of the self to the Word; and with this opening the illusion of the durability and opacity of the world falls away and is dispersed: "The Hour has drawn nigh: the moon is split" (Qur'an 54:1).

3. For more on Guénon's view of this alienation, a view of the world, which explains the departure from principles and reinforces the obsession with quantity as "development," see Guénon, *The Crisis of the Modern World.*

4. Voegelin, "The New Science of Politics: An Introduction," 141–42.

5. Huntington, *The Clash of Civilizations and the Remaking of World Order,* and Barber, *Jihad vs. McWorld,* examine, albeit in different ways and with different degrees of convincingness, the relationship between the two approaches to world events.

6. Confucius, as quoted in Smith, *Forgotten Truth,* 150. See also Yutang, *The Wisdom of Confucius,* 140.

7. See Oldmeadow, *Traditionalism: Religion in the Light of the Perennial Philosophy.*

CHAPTER 11: THE IDEOLOGY OF NATION

1. Matthew 4:8–10.
2. Bukhari, *Sahih,* 5:157.
3. Muslim, *Sahih,* 1:2.
4. There are various interpretive models of nationalism. Tom Nairn sees nationalism and the dialectic of imperialism as inseparable from the very trends of economic globalization that they initiate. See Nairn, *The Break-Up of Britain,* esp. "The Modern Janus," 329–63. To Ernest Gellner, nationalisms are the product of a complex course of social negotiation, which implies the initiation of action of social and cultural mutualities, and of emotional roles among potential members of the national community, as well as the existence of a strategy to implement interests and acquire power, both individual and collective. See Gellner, *Nations and Nationalism.* The roots of nationalism, as Benedict Anderson sees it, lie in the decline of the religious "imagined communities" in the early modern period in Europe, in the gradual silencing of Latin as a spoken language following the revolutionary discovery of printing methods, in the secularization that followed in the wake of the Enlightenment, and in the weakening of the great dynastic states. See Anderson, *Imagined Communities: Reflections on the Origin and Spread of Nationalism.* For an instructive overview and reexamination of these views, see Taylor, "Nationalism and Modernity."

5. Seligman, *Modernity's Wager: Authority, the Self and Transcendence,* 42–43.

6. The Arabic noun *'alem* (world) derives from the verbal root *'lm* (to know).

7. Qur'an 67:3–4.

CHAPTER 12: THE CHASM OF THE FUTURE

1. Ibn Maja, *Kitab al-Sunan,* 2:908. Here "my community" means the uniform world in which every individual and the whole have meaning in the differentiation into those who praise, the praise itself, and the one who is praised. Praise is the inner and outer essence of the firstness and lastness of the Truth. Praising the Truth as ever present in the relationship of the I-self to

the you-self, whether the you-self be the world, another individual, or the totality of humanity, opens the praiser to the discovery and manifestation of the praiser's primal perfection.

2. Qur'an 6:163–64.

3. In the Qur'anic narration, this duality is defined as *akhir* (the ultimate, the end) and *dunya* (the world, derived from the verbal root *dana*, "to be close"). The ultimate is also the first, and the first principle of all that is quantifiable. The first and ultimate is reality, and all else, regardless of how close or distant, is contingent and determined by the first.

4. On this model of how evil comes into the world through the rift in the self, see Coomaraswamy, "Who Is 'Satan' and Where Is 'Hell'?" 23–33. It is worth noting that contemporary humans recognize that their deeds have led to appalling disfigurement and pollution of the earth and its atmosphere. In the growing awareness of environmental issues, and the movements it has given rise to, attempts are being made to stop and eliminate this pollution. It is seldom recognized, however, that the current state of the earth and its atmosphere is the consequence of corruption in the human self, and that the proper sequence would be first to redeem the human self and then the outer world. In the modern view, neither humankind nor nature is perfect, but each is perfectible through the action of that elementally incomplete "creator." But rectifications of this kind give rise to corruption "in the land and sea": "Corruption has appeared in the land and sea, for that men's own hands have earned, that He may let them taste some part of that which they have done, that haply so they may return" (Qur'an 30:41). For modern humans, nature is the raw material with which they themselves allocate meaning and restructuring by destruction, disassembly, and rearrangement. In this view, the purpose of nature to which it bears witness and speaks of the Ineffable has no place. Speech of the Supreme Being, which realizes itself through nature and the Revelation, vanishes from absolutized reason and the dis-enchanted world. Human speech becomes "supreme." There is nothing above humankind, and all that is not human is beneath it. The signs in the outer horizons are transformed into somber matter, "susceptible to rectification."

5. Weber, "Science," 155–56.

6. Voegelin, "New Science," 91.

7. Barber, *Jihad,* 156.

8. Dizdar, *Kameni,* 78.

Bibliography

Abidin, Imam Zayn al', 'Ali ibn al-Husayn. *Sahifa: Al-Sahifat al-Kamilat al-Sajjadiyya (The Psalms of Islam)*. Translated by William C. Chittick. Qum, Iran: Ansariyan, 1987.

———. *Sahifa: Potpuna knjiga Sedžadova: Moljenja i šaptanja imama 'Ali ibn el-Husejna Zejnul Abidina*. Translated into Bosnian by Rusmir Mahmutćehajić and Mehmedalija Hadžić, Sarajevo: DID, 1997.

Abu Bakr, Sirâj ad-Dîn, *The Book of Certainty: The Sufi Doctrine of Faith, Visions and Gnosis*. Cambridge: The Islamic Texts Society, 1992.

'Ali, Imam. *Nahjul-Balagha: Sermons, Letters and Sayings*. Translated by Syed Ali Raza. Qum, Iran: Ansariyan, 1989.

Anderson, Benedict. *Imagined Communities: Reflections on the Origin and Spread of Nationalism*. London: Verso, 1983.

Andrić, Ivo. *Deca*. Sarajevo: Svjetlost, 1981.

Arendt, Hannah. "Thinking and Moral Consideration." *Social Research* 38 (1971): 417–46.

Asad, Muhammad. *The Message of the Qur'an*. Gibraltar, Spain: Dar al-Andalus, 1980.

Balić, Smail. "Zur Geschichte der Muslime in Österreich." In *Islam zwischen Selbstbild und Klischee*, edited by Susanne Heine, 23–35. Cologne: Bölau, 1995.

Banac, Ivo. *With Stalin against Tito: Cominformist Splits in Yugoslav Communism*. Ithaca, N.Y.: Cornell University Press, 1988.

Barber, Benjamin R. *Jihad vs. McWorld*. New York: Ballantine Books, 1996.

Benhabib, Seyla. *Situating the Self: Gender, Community and Postmodernism in Contemporary Ethics*. Cambridge: Polity Press, 1992.

Bodin, Jean. *Colloquium of the Seven about Secrets of the Sublime (Colloquium Heptaplomeres de Rerum Sublimium Arcanis Abditis)*. Translated by Marion Leathers D. Kuntz. Princeton, N.J.: Princeton University Press, 1975.

Buber, Martin. *I and Thou*. Translated and with prologue by Walter Kaufman. New York: Scribner's, 1970.

Bukhari, Imam al-. *Sahih al-Bukhari*. Translated by Muhammad Muhsin Khan. Beirut: Dar al Arabia, 1980.

Carter, Stephen. *The Culture of Disbelief: How American Law and Politics Trivialize Religious Devotion*. New York: Basic Books, 1993.

Chittick, William C. *The Sufi Path of Knowledge: Ibn al-'Arabi's Metaphysics of Imagination*. Albany: State University of New York Press, 1989.

Cohen, Hermann. *The Religion of Reason: Out of the Sources of Judaism*. Atlanta: Scholars Press, 1995.

Coomaraswamy, Ananda K. *The Bugbear of Literacy*. Bedfont, England: Perennial Books, 1979.

―――. *What Is Civilisation and Other Essays*. Ipswich, England: Golgonooza Press, 1989.

―――. "Who Is 'Satan' and Where Is 'Hell'?" In *Coomaraswamy: Selected Papers, Metaphysics*, edited by Roger Lipsey, 23–33. Princeton, N.J.: Princeton University Press, 1977.

Dahrendorf, Ralf. *Essays on the Theory of Society*. Stanford, Calif.: Stanford University Press, 1968.

Dizdar, Mak. *Kameni spavač/Stone Sleeper*. Translated by Francis R. Jones. Afterword by Rusmir Mahmutćehajić. Sarajevo: DID, 1999.

―――. *Stari bosanski tekstovi*, Sarajevo: Svjetlost, 1971.

Dobrača, Kasim. "*Tuhfetul-musallin ve zubdetul haši'in* od Abdul-Vehaba Žepćevije—Ilhamije." *Anali Gazi Husrev-begove biblioteke* 2–3 (Sarajevo, 1974): 41–69.

Dolan, John P., ed. *Unity and Reform: Selected Writings of Nicholas of Cusa*. Notre Dame, Ind.: University of Notre Dame Press, 1962.

Durkheim, Emile. "Individualism and the Intellectuals." In *Emile Durkheim on Morality and Society*, edited by Robert Bellah, 43–57. Chicago: University of Chicago Press, 1973.

Eisenstadt, Schmuel N. "Heterodoxies and Dynamics of Civilizations." *Proceedings of the American Philosophical Society* 128, no. 2 (1984): 104–13.

Fukuyama, Francis. *The End of History and the Last Man*. New York: Free Press, 1992.

Gellner, Ernest. *Nations and Nationalism*. Oxford: Blackwell, 1983.

Graham, William A. *The Divine Word and Prophetic Word in Early Islam*. The Hague: Mouton, 1977.

Guénon, René. *The Crisis of the Modern World*. Translated by Marco Pallis and Richard Nicholson. London: Luzac, 1975.

―――. *Les principes du calcul infinitésimal*. Paris: Gallimard, 1946.

―――. *Le règne de la quantité et les signes des temps*. Paris: Gallimard, 1972.

Hamidullah, Muhammad. *Muhammad a.s.: Život (Life of Muhammad)*. Translated into Bosnian by Nerkez Smajlagić. Sarajevo: Supreme Council of the Islamic Community of Bosnia and Herzegovina, 1983.

―――. *Le Prophète de l'Islam: Sa vie et son oeuvre*. Vol. 1. Paris: El-Najah, 1988.

Huntington, Samuel P. *The Clash of Civilizations and the Remaking of World Order*. New York: Simon and Schuster, 1996.

Ibn Ishaq. *Sirat Rasul Allah (The Life of Muhammad)*. Translated by Alfred Guillaume. Karachi, Pakistan: Oxford University Press, 1980.

Ibn Maja. *Kitab al-Sunan*, Cairo: Dar al-Hadis, 1994.

Jambrek, Stanko. *Hrvatski protestantski pokret XVI i XVII stoljeća*. Zaprešić, Croatia: Matica hrvatska, 1999.

Jaspers, Karl. *Reason and Existenz*. New York: Noonday Press, 1955.

Keiji, Nishitani. *The Self-Overcoming of Nihilism*. Translated by Graham Parkes and Setsuko Aihara. New York: State University of New York Press, 1990.

The Koran Interpreted. Translated by A. J. Arberry. London: George Allen and Unwin, 1981.

Kovač, Nikola. *Bosnie: Le prix de la paix*. Paris: Éditions Michalon, 1995.

Kuna, Herta. *Srednjovjekovna bosanska književnost*. Sarajevo: Svjetlost, 1992.

Lin Yutang, ed. *The Wisdom of Confucius*. New York: Random House, 1938.

Lings, Martin [Abu Bakr Siraj ad Din]. *The Book of Certainty: The Sufi Doctrine of Faith, Vision and Gnosis*. Cambridge: Islamic Texts Society, 1992.

———. *The Heralds and Other Poems*. London: Perennial Books, 1973.

———. *Muhammad: His Life Based on the Earliest Sources*. London: George Allen and Unwin, 1983.

Lossky, Vladimir. *Théologie négative et connaissance de Dieu chez Maître Eckhart*. Paris: Vrin, 1998.

Lovrenović, Ivan. *Bosnien und Herzegowina: Eine Kulturgeschichte*. Translated from Bosnian by Klaus Detlef Olof. Vienna: Volio, 1998.

Luft, David S. *Robert Musil and the Crisis of European Culture, 1880–1942*. Berkeley: University of California Press, 1980.

Mahmutćehajić, Rusmir. *Bosanski odgovor: O modernosti i tradiciji*. Zagreb: Durieux, 2001.

———. *Bosnia the Good: Tolerance and Tradition*. Translated by Marina Browder. Budapest: Central European University Press, 2000.

———. *The Denial of Bosnia*. University Park: Pennsylvania State University Press, 2000.

———. *Prozori: Riječi i slike*. Sarajevo: DID, 2000.

———. *Une réponse bosniaque: Modernité et tradition*. Translated by Paul Ballanfat. Zagreb/Frankfurt: Durieux/Textor, forthcoming.

———. *Una risposta bosniaca: Modernità e tradizione*. Translated by Diletta Bovino. Genoa/Milan: Marietti, forthcoming.

———. *Sarajevo Essays: Politics, Ideology, and Tradition*. Albany: State University of New York Press, 2003.

———. *Sarajevski eseji: Politika, ideologija, tradicija*. Zagreb: Durieux, 2000.

———. *Windows: Words and Images*. Translated by Francis R. Jones and Milena Marić. Sarajevo: DID, forthcoming.

Malcolm, Noel. *Bosnia: A Short History*. London: Papermac, 1996.

Marx, Karl, *Der historische Materialismus: Die Frühschriften*. Edited by S. Landshut and J. P. Mayer. Leipzig: Alfred Kroner, 1932.

McCarthy, Justin. *Death and Exile: The Ethnic Cleansing of Ottoman Muslims, 1821–1922*. Princeton, N.J.: Darwin Press, 1999.

Muller, Jerry Z. *Adam Smith in His Time and Ours: Designing the Decent Society*. New York: Free Press, 1992.

Musil, Robert. *Precision and the Soul: Essays and Addresses*. Translated and edited by Burton Pike and David S. Luft. Chicago: University of Chicago Press, 1990.

Muslim, Imam. *Sahih Muslim.* Translated by 'Abdul Hamid Siddiqi. 4 vols. Riyadh: International Islamic, n.d.

Nairn, Tom. *The Break-Up of Britain.* London: New Left Books, 1977.

Nametak, Alija. *Rukopisni tursko-hrvatskosrpski riječnici,* Zagreb: Jugoslavenska akademija znanosti i umjetnosti, 1968.

Nasr, Seyyed Hossein. *Knowledge and the Sacred.* Albany: State University of New York Press, 1989.

Nietzsche, Friedrich. *The Will to Power.* Edited by Walter Kaufmann. Translated by Walter Kaufmann and R. J. Hollingdale. New York: Vintage Books, 1968.

Oldmeadow, Kenneth. *Traditionalism: Religion in the Light of the Perennial Philosophy.* Colombo: Sri Lanka Institute of Traditional Studies, 2000.

Perry, Whitall N. *A Treasury of Traditional Wisdom.* Cambridge: Quinta Essentia, 1991.

Qur'an, The Holy. Translated by Abdullah Yusuf 'Ali. Lahore, Pakistan: Ashraf Press, 1975.

Rycaut, Paul, *The Present State of the Ottoman Empire, Containing the Maxims of the Turkish Politie, the Most Material Points of the Mahometan Religion, Their Sects and Heresies, Their Convents and Religious Votaries. Their Military Discipline, with an Exact Computation of Their Forces Both by Land and Sea. Illustrated with Diverse Pieces of Sculpture, Representing the Variety of Habits among the Turks.* 3 vols. 3rd ed. London: John Starkey and Henry Brome, 1670.

Schluchter, Wolfgang. *The Rise of Western Rationalism.* Berkeley: University of California Press, 1981.

Scholem, Gershom. *On the Kabbalah and Its Symbolism.* Translated by Ralph Manheim. New York: Schocken Books, 1996.

Schuon, Frithjof. *Castes and Races.* Translated by Marco Pallis and Macleod Matheson. Bedfont, England: Perennial Books, 1982.

———. *Language of the Self.* Translated by Marco Pallis and Macleod Matheson. Madras, India: Ganesh, 1959.

———. *Logic and Transcendence.* Translated by Peter N. Townsend. London: Perennial Books, 1984.

Seligman, Adam B., *The Problem of Trust.* Princeton, N.J.: Princeton University Press, 1997.

———. *Modernity's Wager: Authority, the Self and Transcendence,* Princeton, N.J.: Princeton University Press, 2000.

Šabanović, Hazim. "Turski dokumenti u Bosni i Hercegovini iz druge polovine XV stoljeća." *Istorisko-pravni zbornik,* 2:177–222. Sarajevo, 1949.

Šanjek, Franjo. *Bosansko-humski krstjani i katarsko-dualistički pokret u Srednjem vijeku.* Zagreb: Kršćanska sadašnjost, 1975.

Smith, Huston. *Forgotten Truth: The Common Vision of the World's Religions.* San Francisco: HarperCollins, 1992.

Steiner, George. *After Babel: Aspects of Language and Translation.* Oxford: University Press, 1998.

Tawney, R. H. *Commonplace Book.* Edited with introduction by J. Winter and D. Joslin. Cambridge: Cambridge University Press, 1972.

Taylor, Charles. "Nationalism and Modernity." In *Utvara nacije/Spectre of Nation,* edited by Obrad Savić, 11–33. Belgrade: Belgrade Circle, 1997.

———. *Sources of the Self: The Making of Modern Identity.* Cambridge, Mass.: Harvard University Press, 1989.
Trouillard, Jean. "Erigène et la Théophanie créatrice." In *The Mind of Erigena*, edited by John J. O'Meara and Ludwig Bieler, 98–113. Dublin: Irish University Press, 1973.
Vinaver, Vuk. *Prve ustaničke borbe protiv Turaka.* Belgrade: Prosveta, 1953.
Voegelin, Eric, *Hitler and the Germans.* Edited by Detler Clemens and Brendan Purcell. Columbia: University of Missouri Press, 1999.
———. *Modernity on Endless Trial.* Columbia: University of Missouri, 2000.
———. "The New Science of Politics: An Introduction." In *Modernity without Restraint: The Political Religions, the New Science of Politics, and Science, Politics and Gnosticism,* edited by Manfred Henningsen, 75–241. Columbia: University of Missouri Press, 2000.
———. "Science, Politics and Gnosticism: Two Essays." In *Modernity without Restraint: The Political Religions, the New Science of Politics, and Science, Politics and Gnosticism,* edited by Manfred Henningsen, 243–313. Columbia: University of Missouri Press, 2000.
Weber, Max. "Science as a Vocation." In *From Max Weber: Essays in Sociology,* translated and edited by H. H. Gerth and C. Wright Mills, 129–56. London: Routledge, 1991.
Whitehead, Alfred North, and Bertrand Russell. *Principia Mathematica.* Vols. 1–3. Cambridge: Cambridge University Press, 1927.

Other Works by Rusmir Mahmutćehajić

Krhkost. Sarajevo: Veselin Masleša, 1977.
Krv i tinta. Sarajevo: Veselin Masleša, 1983.
Zemlja i more. Sarajevo: Svjetlost, 1986.
Živa Bosna: politički eseji i intervjui. 1st ed. Ljubljana: Oslobođenje International, 1994.
Živa Bosna: politički eseji i intervjui. 2nd ed. Ljubljana: Oslobođenje International, 1995.
Living Bosnia: Political Essays and Interviews. Translated by Spomenka Beus and Francis R. Jones. Ljubljana: Oslobodenje International, 1996.
O nauku znaka. Sarajevo: DID, 1996.
Četrdeset kaligrafskih listova Ćaima Hadžimejlića. Sarajevo: DID, 1997.
Dobra Bosna. Zagreb: Durieux, 1997.
Kriva politika: Čitanje historije i povjerenje u Bosni. Tuzla, Bosnia: Radio Kameleon, 1998.
Riječi kao boje zdjela: Odrazi vječne mudrosti u sonetima Skendera Kulenoviča. Sarajevo: DID, 2000.
Words like Wells of Colour: Traditional Wisdom Reflected by the Sonnets of Skender Kulenovič. Translated by Francis R. Jones, Milena Marić, and Saba Risaluddin. Sarajevo/London: DID/Bosnian Institute, 2001.
Subotnji zapisi: S političkih razmeđa. Sarajevo: Buybook, 2002.
Benim Güzel Bosnam. Translated by Zeynep Ozbek. Istanbul: Gelenek Yayinlari, 2004.
Mesdžid: Srce smirenosti. Sarajevo: Buybook, 2004.
O ljubavi. Sarajevo. Buybook, 2004.
Une politique erronée: Lecture de l'histoire foi en la Bosnie. Translated by Mauricette Begić and Nicole Dizdarević. Zagreb/Frankfurt: Durieux/Textor, forthcoming.
Bosanski odgovor: O modernosti i tradiciji (2nd ed.). Zagreb: Durieux, 2005.

Index

Abel, 75
Abraham, Patriarch, xx
Absolute, xxiv, xxvii
Abstention, 63, 66
Affluence, 137
Aim, xvi, xxvii, 28, 42, 54, 85, 91
Allah. *See* Good
Alterity, 10, 27, 47, 60, 91, 114, 127
Andrić, Ivo, 13, 130, 131
Angel, xvii, 42, 74, 99
Anva, xiv, xx
Arendt, Hannah, 62
Aristotle, 37
Arrogance, xx, 49, 85, 110, 130, 135, 137, 139
Art, xviii, 13, 56, 125, 142n6
Ascent, 25, 133
Attributing, 7, 66, 112
Auschwitz, 106
Austria-Hungary, xxi, 20, 27, 142n1
Authority, xxiv, 2, 6, 20, 23, 38, 41, 59, 60, 62, 64, 90, 91, 108, 114, 118, 121, 128, 132, 133, 154n5
Awareness, xxv, 2, 12, 18, 28, 40, 41, 65, 70, 95, 96, 100, 106, 123, 133, 144n21, 155n4

Bacon, Roger, 34
Barber, Benjamin R., 7, 16, 51, 132
Beauty, xxiv, 24, 26, 27, 37, 80, 81, 83, 86, 98, 101, 113, 124, 139, 152n8

Becoming, 12, 33, 58, 66, 76, 83, 105
Belief, xi, xiii, xxvii, 13, 21, 28, 29, 40, 41, 65, 68, 71, 75, 133, 138, 145n2, 150n5
Benjamin, Walter, 149n8
Book, the Divine, 29, 32, 75, 78 121
Bosnia, xii, xiv–xvi, xxi–xxv, xxvii–xxix, 1, 5, 6, 8–15, 17–20, 24, 27, 37, 67, 106, 113, 114, 126, 131, 133, 135, 136, 138, 141n1, 142n1, 143nn10, 12, 3, 4, 5, 146n14
Bosnia and Herzegovina. *See* Bosnia
Bosniacs, 67
Bosnian Church, 20, 142n4
Boundary, 7, 19, 20, 29, 30, 49, 65, 66, 85, 92, 127, 128
Buber, Martin, xvii, xix, xx
Buddhism, 21, 153n19

Casamaris, Johannis de, 5
Christ. *See* Jesus Christ
Christianity, xxi, 13, 21, 27, 63, 67, 68, 80, 137, 144n21
Christians, 67, 71, 75, 76, 78, 84, 142n3
Christology, xxiv, 19, 142n4
Church, xxii, xxiv, 6, 19, 20, 35, 129, 130, 131, 145n11

Civilization, xi, xii, xiv, xviii, xxi, 50, 51, 72, 117, 118, 121, 127, 143*n*6, 147*n*6, 154*n*5
Clemency, xiv, xx, 13, 53, 80, 83, 88, 119, 135
Coercion, xix, 13, 69
Cohen, Hermann, xvii, xix, xx
Communism, xi, xiv, 53, 54, 111, 147*n*9
Community, xxi, xvi, xxii, 6, 44, 45, 61, 67, 89, 121, 125, 128, 129, 146*n*3, 147*n*9, 154*n*1
Comparison, 52, 91, 95, 96, 98, 150*n*9, 151*n*16
Confidence, 9, 12, 13, 17, 19, 28, 29, 40, 41, 44, 45, 48, 52, 59, 65, 82, 88, 92, 117, 119, 132, 146*nn*7, 9, 10, 152*n*9
Confucianism, xiv
Consciousness, xviii, xxii, 9, 20, 25, 27, 28, 33, 47, 50, 51, 58, 115
Contingency, 34, 68, 98, 107, 122, 124, 127, 129
Coomaraswamy, Ananda K., 2
Country, xxii, xxvi, 5, 6, 8, 9, 11, 13, 14, 18, 114, 135, 142*n*1, 143*n*5
Covenant, 6, 40, 79, 89, 132, 150*n*5
Creation, xxv, xxvi, 23, 24, 41, 47, 68, 75, 79, 87, 95, 96, 98, 104, 117, 123, 124, 135, 136, 152*n*8
Croatia, xiv, xxii, 11
Croats, 8, 67, 143*n*4

Dahrendorf, Ralf, 73
Darkness, iv, 65, 68, 69, 73, 74, 98, 127, 128, 130, 136
Darwin, Charles R., 90
Dawn, 14, 73, 83
Daybreak, 68, 69, 73, 74, 127
Dayton, xv, xvi, 11
Debt, 36, 94, 127, 150*n*5
Death, xxvi, 2, 23, 28, 33, 37, 43, 47, 52, 53, 62, 69, 81, 85, 93, 95, 96, 97, 106, 115, 127, 128, 134, 143*n*12, 153*n*9
Democracy, 11, 59, 105, 109, 110
Denial, xxi, 10, 14, 19, 22, 28, 35, 40, 68, 70, 76, 77, 86, 88, 102, 106, 119, 120, 131, 141*n*6, 145*n*22, 146*n*14

Denmark, 109
Descartes, René, 2
Descent, xxiv, 25, 96, 97, 129
Desire, xiv, xvii–xix, 28, 30, 32, 38, 41, 45, 46, 65, 66, 80, 84, 91, 108, 110, 112, 115, 117, 147*n*4
Development, xxii, 12, 19, 20, 22, 23, 28, 50, 52, 62, 90, 105–107, 109–11, 116, 120, 132, 133, 147*n*9, 154*n*3
Dialogue, xii, xiv, xv, xviii–xx, xxii, 8, 10, 52, 58, 116
Dignity, xx, xxvi, xxviii, 36, 105, 110
Din. *See* debt
Direction, 47, 64, 117, 138, 139
Disease, iv, 23, 28
Diversity, xxiv, xxv, 6–11, 14, 17, 18, 20, 21, 23, 29, 30, 34, 35, 37, 43, 52, 58, 63, 66, 67, 78, 79, 83, 92, 111, 114, 117–19, 139, 142*n*6
Divine, xvi, 18, 20, 22, 25–28, 36, 56, 63, 68, 70–72, 75–77, 95, 105, 106, 109, 122, 144*n*19, 148*n*1, 151*n*1, 153*n*20
Dizdar, Mak, iv, 134
Doctrine, xvi, 17–20, 25, 30–32, 40, 44, 46, 48, 50, 51, 77, 97, 109, 115, 121, 146*n*3, 153*n*13
Durkheim, Emile, 20, 121

Earth, 23, 24, 32, 35, 40, 42, 56, 60, 63, 66, 73, 80, 83, 87, 90, 93, 103, 106, 112, 122, 131, 144*n*19, 153*n*2, 155*n*4
Eckhart, Meister, 33, 145*n*21
Ego, 11, 57, 90
Eisenstadt, Shmuel N., 19
Elite, xi, 20, 21, 38, 46, 53, 120, 131, 132
Enlightenment, 10, 12, 54, 55, 57, 58, 77, 111, 118, 119, 132, 133, 154*n*4
Environment, 18, 58, 98, 108
Envy, 69, 100, 127
Essence, xxv, 2, 22–24, 29, 30, 40–42, 50, 54, 66, 69, 80, 81, 85, 87, 91, 97, 98, 101, 108, 115, 119, 126, 150*n*5, 154*n*1

Eternity, 11, 22, 24, 28, 36, 37, 44, 47, 48, 52, 60, 74, 81, 95, 99, 106, 107, 121, 122
Ethics, xvii, xix, 146*n*3
Ethnic cleansing, xii, 143*n*12
Ethnonationalism, xxii
Europe, xii, xxi, xxii, 11, 29, 143*n*12, 154*n*4
Evil, 2, 7, 14, 23, 29, 37, 38, 42, 49, 52, 53, 57, 59, 68, 73, 74, 93, 98, 105, 112, 113, 116, 119, 127, 130, 131, 144*n*13, 146*n*8, 147*n*4, 151*n*13, 155*n*4

Face, xiii, xiv, xvii–xxii, xxviii, 7, 21, 39, 40, 42, 63, 73, 79, 91, 106, 111, 136, 146*n*11
Faith, xxvii, 5, 8, 9, 26, 29, 31, 41, 50, 81, 146*n*7, 152*n*9
Falsehood, 42, 52, 59, 77, 78, 96, 97, 123, 147*n*9, 152*n*8
Fantasy, 87
Fascism, xi
Fear, xviii, 6, 13, 14, 23, 31, 32, 34, 68, 71, 81, 87–89, 91, 92, 93, 118, 119, 128, 133
Forbidden, xvii, 9, 10, 36, 78, 144*n*13
Force, xiii, xv, 20, 34, 35, 42, 43, 49, 65, 69, 100
Forebears, 97, 111
Form, iii, xi, xiv, xvii, xxii, xxv, 8–139 passim, 142*n*3, 150*n*10, 152*n*9
Fragility, 46, 51, 63, 69, 81, 85, 107
Franz Ferdinand, Archduke of Austria, xi
Freedom, iii, xii, 9, 10, 12, 24, 33, 35–40, 45, 47–49, 58, 59, 64, 65, 73, 78, 81, 90, 91, 105, 110, 111, 114, 115, 122, 137, 138, 146*n*15
Freud, Sigmund, 90
Friendship, xiv, 28, 29
Fundamentalism, xvi, 53, 54, 111, 119, 120, 129

Gabriel, angel, 81, 146*n*7
Gadamer, Hans-Georg, xxi
Generation, 51, 71
Generosity, xxvii, 53, 68, 80, 85
Gnosticism, xi, 144*n*12, 150*n*7
God, association with, xiii, 7, 47, 68, 69, 76–78, 80, 86, 87, 98, 112, 127, 148*n*2
Goldzhier, Ignaz, xx
Good, xx, 2, 7, 9, 24, 32, 37, 46, 47, 49, 52, 57, 68, 70, 71, 73, 74, 77, 78, 83, 86, 89, 90, 98, 99, 101, 105, 110, 112, 119, 130, 131, 139
Gospel, 47, 142*n*4, 152*n*8
Government, xiv, xv, 46, 47, 61, 110
Groningen, xiii
Guénon, René, 106

Hatred, 8, 12–14, 23, 34, 76, 92, 101, 118, 119, 132, 138, 143*n*5
Heart, 10, 23,–25, 31, 42, 48, 63, 64, 71, 76, 77, 84, 88, 99, 111, 113, 117
Heaven, 14, 23, 24, 32, 34, 35, 40, 42, 48, 56, 60, 66, 72, 80, 83, 87, 90, 93, 98, 101, 103, 111, 118, 122, 144*n*19, 153*n*2
Hegel, Georg W. F., 22
Heidegger, Martin, 22
Hell, 42, 89, 98, 99, 155*n*4
Hereafter, 152*n*8
Heritage, xiv, xxiv, 7, 21, 46, 115, 142*n*6
Hilm. See clemency
History, xi, xxii, xxiv, xxvii, 5, 6, 13, 17, 19, 20, 24, 25, 34, 41, 44, 46, 51, 62, 97, 104–106, 108, 114, 115, 116, 125, 132, 133, 142*n*1, 143*nn*5, 12, 146*n*14, 147*n*4
Hobbes, Thomas, 34
Holocaust, 1, 126
Holy Writ, 42, 126
Hour, 13, 14, 18, 24, 117, 134, 153*n*2
Human being, 43, 79, 82, 88, 90, 124, 143*n*13, 147*n*14, 150*n*15
Hume, David, xviii
Humility, xiv, xvi, xvii, xix, xx, xxvi, 13, 18, 35, 43, 53, 58, 60, 63, 68, 69, 71, 76, 78, 80, 83, 85–88, 91, 94, 97, 128, 135, 143*n*2
Huston, Smith, 34, 65
Hypocrisy, 68, 71, 76, 119

Ibn Arabi, Muhyiddin, 81
Identity, xii, xv, xvi, 9–11, 19, 28, 46, 51, 57, 58, 61, 67, 82, 120, 127, 142n6, 146n3
Ideology, iii, xv, xxii, xxvii, 1, 12, 20, 21, 24, 29, 38, 45–47, 51, 55, 57, 67, 77, 86, 98, 105, 110, 111, 114, 115, 117, 119, 120, 123, 125, 131, 146n14, 147n9
Idolatry, 112, 148n2
Ilhamija, Abdul-Vehab Žepčevija, 8, 143n9
Illusion, xxvi, 45, 56, 57, 63, 70, 76, 81, 82, 85, 87, 95–97, 101, 107, 115, 117, 128, 151n13, 152n13, 153n8
Image, xix, xxiv, xxv, 20, 24, 26, 33–35, 41, 45, 47, 52, 60, 66, 69, 77, 79, 80, 85, 88, 98, 103–106, 111, 112, 116, 117, 121, 130–32, 135, 142n3, 147n9, 151n13
Image of God, 45, 80, 105, 121
Iman. *See* faith
Immeasurability, 96
Ineffable, 2, 35, 49, 53, 63, 65, 66, 68, 70, 71, 74, 75, 82, 92, 102, 105, 107, 126, 155n4
Infinity, xxvi, 22, 28, 32, 36, 37, 44, 47, 48, 60, 61, 74, 81, 90, 98, 99, 106, 122, 123, 128, 151n13, 153n19
Inheritance, 136
Intellect, xxv, xxvi, 24–26, 33, 35, 37, 42, 49, 55, 56, 60, 65, 77, 82–84, 87, 89, 92, 105, 122, 126, 129, 145n21, 151n13, 153nn1, 2
Intolerance, 8, 67, 108
Isaac, prophet, 75
Islam, xii, xx–xxii, 6, 13, 20, 21, 63, 67, 68, 80, 86, 137, 146n7, 148n1, 2, 151n1
Izetbegović, Alija, xiv
Izutsu, Toshihiko, xx

Jacob, prophet, 75
Jaspers, Karl, xiii, xv–xvii, xix, xx, xxii
Jesus Christ, 90, 101, 116, 142n4, 149n2, 152n8

Jews, 6, 11, 14, 67, 71, 76, 78, 84
Job, prophet, 75, 91, 92, 151n17
Johnson, Samuel, xii
Jones, Francis R., xxviii
Judaism, xxi, 6, 13, 21, 63, 67, 68, 80, 137, 141n8, 153n19
Justice, xix, 13, 14, 70, 71, 75, 135, 152n9

Kant, Immanuel, 72, 121
Killing, 1, 37, 38, 51, 58, 86, 91, 100, 107, 114, 123, 131, 133, 138
Kin, 7, 8, 74
Kulin, ban, 5

Land, xxi, 6, 8, 92, 155n4
Learning, 81, 91
Levenfeld, Maks, 13, 130, 131
Levinas, Emmanuel, xvii, xix, xx
Liberalism, xxi, 49, 52, 109–11, 133, 141n14
Light, 13, 15, 20, 25, 30, 37, 43, 56, 62, 68, 73, 82, 84, 91, 97, 98, 112, 126, 132, 154n7
Lineage, 8, 98
Lings, Martin, 80
Logos, 23, 56, 63, 70, 82, 96, 102, 126, 129, 149n8
Love, 13, 25, 26, 31, 32, 42, 80, 81, 83, 86, 87, 104, 119, 144n18, 149n2, 152n8
Lucifer, 145n22

Macrocosm, 2, 44, 68, 90, 56, 102, 142n1
Mahmutćehajić, Rusmir, xiv
Mandeville, Bernard de, xviii
Margin, xii, xxi, xxii, 21
Marx, Karl, 90
Marxism, 129
McWorld, 47, 49–51, 132, 147n16, 154n5
Measuring, 89, 108
Mecca, 76
Mehmed el-Fatih, Sultan, 6
Memory, 81, 82, 86, 97
Merciful, 8, 65, 72, 79, 95, 99, 103, 123, 124, 150n5, 153n20

Messenger, 26, 32, 33, 71, 75, 79, 84, 102
Metaphysics, 2, 62, 151*n*1, 155*n*4
Method, xi, 100, 112, 130, 131, 151*n*13, 154*n*13
Microcosm, 2, 44, 68, 90, 96, 102, 141*n*1
Mind, 64, 75, 83, 84, 98, 101, 107, 108, 111, 114, 115, 132, 135, 140
Modesty, xii, xx, xxvi, xxvii, 63, 123, 128, 130, 139
Moon, 35, 56, 122, 153*n*2
Moses, 71, 153*n*17
Mosque, xii, xvi, xxii, xxiv, 6, 14, 19, 35, 143*n*2, 145*n*11
Most Merciful, 65, 99, 124, 153*n*20
Mrkonjić-Grad, 143*n*10
Muhammad, prophet, xx, xxi, 55, 64, 75, 79, 87, 88, 91, 99, 102, 115, 116, 125, 142*n*3,4,5 146*n*7, 147*n*4, 149*nn*17, 1
Musa, prophet, 153*n*17
Mystery, xxvi, 24, 48, 64, 75, 82, 101, 104, 105, 138

Najran, 79
Name, 18, 30, 35, 47, 51, 67, 69–75, 79, 86, 92, 94, 95, 98, 99, 102, 103, 105, 115, 131, 135, 142*n*1, 145*n*22, 150*n*3
Names of God, 35, 70, 72, 144*n*18, 145*n*11
Narcissism, xiv
Nation xv, 11, 20, 21, 23, 27, 32, 41, 45, 51, 57, 71, 86, 110, 113, 114, 115, 120, 123, 131, 132, 139, 154*n*4, 148*n*2
Nationalism, 54, 111, 115, 119, 120, 131, 132, 154*n*4
Nation state, xv, 11, 20, 21, 27, 45
Nazism, xi
Newton, Isaac, 34
Nietzsche, Friedrich, 22, 62, 97
Nihilism, 58, 62, 63, 146*n*3
Noah, prophet, 75

Oneness, 24, 30, 43, 55, 64, 72, 79, 83, 120, 126, 144*n*19
Ontology, xvii

Openness, xv, xxiv–xxvii, 2, 9, 10, 15, 22, 23, 28, 32, 36, 37, 44, 57, 59–61, 64, 73, 76, 79, 81, 82, 85, 112, 118, 121, 123, 125–30, 138, 151*n*13
Opinion, 148*n*2
Orientation, 7, 18, 27, 41, 60, 70, 73, 75, 77, 86, 88, 89, 113, 114, 117, 120, 123, 127, 131, 133, 136, 152*n*9
Origin, xix, 6, 7, 24, 25, 55, 60, 77, 79, 90, 105, 121, 126, 152*n*9, 154*n*4
Orthodox Church, 13
Orthodoxy, 6
Other, xvi, xvii, xxviii, 5–10, 12, 17, 19, 27–29, 35, 40, 45, 58, 59, 66, 74, 92, 94, 131, 147*n*6, 150*n*14
Otherness, 13, 18, 106, 108, 110, 119, 123, 127–29, 151*n*13, 152*n*8
Ottoman, xxi, 6, 20, 142*n*5, 143*n*12
Outer horizons, 30, 37, 43, 60, 66, 82, 88, 90, 94, 96, 101, 122, 123, 125–27, 130, 138, 155*n*4
Outer world, xxvi, 2, 31, 32, 35, 42, 44, 47, 60, 63, 65, 66, 69–71, 92, 100, 102, 122, 125, 137, 138, 141*n*1, 155*n*4

Paradise, 98, 99, 129, 131
Parents, 77, 78, 86, 97, 98
Particularity, xiii, 12, 52, 59, 70
Patience (Ar. *sabr*), 32
Peace, xv, xvi, 2, 5, 11, 39, 42, 44, 49, 51, 66, 68, 71, 86–88, 91, 98, 106, 108, 113, 115–17, 135, 136, 139, 147*n*4, 150*n*3
Perpetrator, 10
Philosophy, xx, xxvi, 105, 121, 151*n*16, 154*n*7
Phosphoros, 145*n*22
Picture, 13, 47, 88, 91, 106, 108, 151*n*13
Plurality, xii–xiv, xxii, 2, 18, 19, 21, 24, 31, 32, 48, 50, 52, 62, 65, 78, 79, 91, 97, 118, 132
Politics, xi, xviii, xxvi, xxviii, 59, 111, 144*n*12, 147*n*8, 150*n*7, 154*n*4

Polytheism, 148*n*2
Poverty, 78, 85–90, 94, 95, 97, 103, 128, 150*n*9
Praise, 2, 35, 36, 43, 71, 72, 75, 84, 88, 101, 102, 103, 104, 121, 125, 126, 144*n*18, 154*n*1
Prayer, 8, 13, 14, 19, 43, 59, 63, 64, 65, 68, 70, 84, 90, 126, 143*n*2
Progress, xi, 10, 54, 55, 76, 105, 115, 120, 133, 150*n*9
Promise, 1, 2, 9, 14, 32, 91, 111, 113, 119, 129–31, 133, 137, 138
Prophet, xxvi, xxvii, 75, 84, 87, 99, 103, 121, 125, 130
Prostration, 18, 83, 143*n*2
Protestantism, 81
Purification, 49, 68, 83

Qur'an, 7, 47, 71, 76

Ratio, 13, 33, 55, 122
Rationalism, 21, 91, 131, 143n 10
Reading, 34, 51, 88, 115, 121, 126, 127, 142*n*4, 146*n*14
Real, 25, 42–44, 52, 62, 65, 68, 69, 85, 87, 89, 96–98, 107, 120
Recognition, xiv, xv, xviii, xix, 19, 28, 35, 42, 45, 50–53, 59, 68, 71, 75, 80, 91, 92, 95, 103, 127, 142*n*1, 147*n*4, 150*n*9
Relativism, xiii, xiv, xviii, 58, 63
Relativity, xiii
Remembrance, 13, 14, 18, 36, 47, 63, 64, 79, 85, 86, 90, 97, 136, 137, 144*n*18
Revelation, xxv, xxvii, 23, 25, 26, 34, 39, 40, 64, 68, 75, 78, 82, 84, 86, 89, 95, 104, 107, 117, 121–23, 137, 144*n*19, 148*n*1, 153*n*17, 155*n*4
Revolution, 90, 111
Rite, 13, 48, 61, 97, 98
Roman Church, 5
Rumi, Jalaluddin, 81

Sabaeans, 71
Sacred, xvi, xvii, xxv, 6–9, 17, 18, 20, 24, 25, 28, 29, 32–34, 36, 44, 45, 51, 56, 72, 73, 77, 81, 84, 97, 105, 121, 131, 144*nn*13, 21, 145*nn*21, 11, 151*n*13
Salam. See peace
Salvation, xi, 28, 40, 54, 130, 151*n*13
Sanctity, xxiv, xxvi, 6, 10, 26, 27, 29, 54, 121, 147*n*9
Sarajevo, xi, xiv–xvi, xxviii, 13, 131, 146*n*14
Satan, 74, 116, 145*n*22, 155*n*4
Science, xi, 1, 2, 22, 34, 48, 54, 65, 73, 100, 111, 129–32, 144*n*12, 148*n*7, 150*n*7, 151*nn*13, 16, 154*n*4, 155*nn*5, 6
Scientism, xv, 129
Scripture, xxvi, 7, 102, 145*n*3
Secular, xi, xiv, xxi, 10, 12, 28, 45, 52–54, 116
Secularism, 51, 118
Seir, 130
Seligman, Adam B., xi, xxviii, 121
Serbia, 11
Serbs, xv, 8, 67, 143*n*4
Shirk. *See* association with God
Slaughter, xxv, 3, 9, 14, 133, 143*n*12
Smith, Adam, xviii, 50, 147*n*5
Sociology, 73
Solidarity, xii
Soul, 10, 20, 33, 36, 42, 51, 55, 56, 59, 60–62, 64, 98, 107, 108, 128, 129, 145*n*21, 147*n*4, 149*n*22, 150*n*10, 152*n*8, 153*n*8
Sovereignty, 59, 119, 120, 132
Space, xv, xxv, 18, 24, 25, 42, 45, 47, 61, 66, 116
Speech, 7, 26, 28, 35, 36, 42, 43, 45, 47–49, 55, 56
Spirit, xxvi, 25, 38, 42, 56, 66, 77, 92, 105, 122, 153*n*2
Stoicism, xiii
Stolac, xiv, 135
Stranger, xvii, xix, 74, 94
Strength, 13, 29, 59, 81, 101
Sublimity, 18, 143*n*2
Submission, iii, xx, 25, 35–40, 42, 47, 49, 68, 69, 71, 74, 76–85, 88, 90, 116, 126, 137, 146*n*7
Symbol, xvi, 10, 13–15, 18, 21, 23, 34, 43–47, 50, 51, 53, 61–63, 66,

67, 70–72, 76, 77, 80, 90, 112, 127, 128, 135, 138
Symbolism, 153n9

Teachings, 6, 17, 18, 24, 31, 34, 55, 62, 76, 137, 142n3, 146n7
Technology, 22, 54, 55, 132
Temple, xxii, xxiv–xxvi, 34–37, 137
Testimony, 1, 10, 29, 33, 75, 86, 88, 99, 102, 104, 138
This world, 38, 43, 49, 60, 114, 116, 152n8
Thought, xi, xiv, xviii, xx, xxii, 2, 10, 21, 31, 69, 100, 111, 126, 137, 138, 145n21, 147n9
Tito, Josip Broz, xiv, 147n9
Tocqueville, Alexis de, 39
Tolerance, xii–xv, xviii, xix, xx, 6–10, 20, 21, 28, 29, 45, 57, 58, 60, 62, 63, 66, 67, 71, 78, 79, 143n3
Transcendence, xii, xiii, xv, xvii–xix, xxii, 22, 23, 27, 29, 36, 37, 57, 72, 82, 91, 99, 107, 108, 118, 128, 129, 145n2, 154n5
Translation, xv, xix, xx, xxviii, 7, 18, 34, 35, 43, 53, 66, 75, 92, 118, 128, 138, 139, 141n1, 142nn5, 7, 146nn8, 9, 11, 149n8
Trust, 9, 12, 17, 28, 40, 41, 45, 46, 48, 52, 59, 88, 97, 119, 120, 132, 143nn11, 14, 146nn7, 9, 10, 150n5

Unity, xvi, xxvii, 5, 6, 8, 11, 19, 21, 23, 24, 29, 31, 42, 44, 49, 52, 63, 64, 72, 83, 114, 139, 148n1, 151n15
Uskufi, Muhammed Hevaji, 8

Violence, xxiv, xxvii, 1, 12, 40, 41, 45, 49, 51, 58, 59, 77, 86, 87, 100, 108, 119, 133, 135, 136, 138
Virtue, xiv, xviii, xxvii, 2, 13, 36, 45, 72, 80, 83, 100, 112, 121, 130
Vision, xxi, 43, 53–55, 97, 145n8, 146n3
Visočica, 18
Voegelin, Eric, xi, xix–xxi, 38, 87
Volition, 24

Wealth, 50, 79, 85, 86, 89, 94, 97, 103, 138
Weber, Max, 62, 65, 73, 129–31
Will, 6, 20, 25, 26, 31, 32, 36, 40, 42, 76, 85, 87, 97, 105, 106, 111, 119, 120, 123, 133, 136, 137, 152n7
Wisdom, xxv, 2, 8, 31, 53, 62, 72, 83, 91–94, 107, 111–13, 138, 143n10, 144n18, 145n3, 151n16, 154n6
Witnessing, 43, 68, 69
World War I, xi, 14, 130
Writ, 42, 126
Writing, xv, xxi, xxiii, 34, 126, 127, 151n15

Yugoslavia, 142n1, 147n9

Zarathustra, 62
Zvizdović, brother Anđeo, 6